Contents

Introduction

J. Grimley Evans

The Carnegie Inquiry into the Third Age was launched by the Carnegie UK Trust in 1990. Its aim was to examine issues affecting the life, work and livelihood of people who have finished their main job or career and completed the raising of their families but have twenty or more years of healthy active life ahead of them. The stimulus to the inquiry was the recognition that although this section of the population is now of considerable size it has been largely ignored in social policy and organisation. This is chiefly because the demographic and economic processes that have produced the phenomenon of the third age are historically recent. Provided there is no unforeseen cataclysm, however, the third age is destined to be a permanent feature of economically developed societies and it is timely to consider accommodations to the needs and aspirations of people in a vulnerable but potentially rewarding phase of life.

The third age is defined in terms of social function, and people enter and leave it at a range of different ages, but for statistical purposes the inquiry took the ages 50 to 74 as representative. In the first eight of its series of reports it addressed employment, income, learning, leisure, homes and travel, caring, volunteering and citizenship. The report on health, published by the Carnegie United Kingdom Trust (Carnegie Inquiry into the Third Age, 1992), came ninth and last for administrative reasons but has implications for all the other issues. It was produced by summarising and abridging a series of papers presented and discussed at a seminar held in the summer of 1992 under the chairmanship of Sir Donald Acheson. Preparation of the papers, which are collected here, and the costs of the seminar, were underwritten by a grant from the Nuffield Provincial Hospitals Trust.

Although the initial commission was to examine health we recognised early in the enterprise that health is important for the individual through its effects on function, and function is valued as a means to happiness. We therefore stepped beyond the bounds of a traditional concern with the treatment and control of disease to examine aspects of physical and psychological function. Here we found that the general public perception of age-associated change in function is inaccurate in a number of important ways that distort public policy and inhibit individual wellbeing. Chapter 2 therefore presents an introductory outline of the origins of differences between younger and older people with an emphasis on how a misunderstanding of the processes involved can lead to inappropriately pessimistic views about ageing.

We were also conscious of the overlap between health and social wellbeing. Loneliness, poverty and lack of occupation are miserable things even before they produce effects on physical or mental health. While we address the common problem of depression as defined in medical terms, more unhappiness in middle age (as at all ages) may arise from problems of adjustment than from mental disease. Women experience the menopause which in some instances is associated with distressing physical changes and spontaneous mood changes but may also carry psychosocial implications in self-perception and change of role. Although there are some minor changes in sex hormone secretion in middle life there is in men no physiological discontinuity corresponding to the menopause. Paradoxically, however, the psychological stress associated with the transition from second to third age may be greater in men. There are many reasons for this. In modern western society the role of the older man is not as well defined nor as biologically useful as that of the older woman in her functions as grandmother or aunt which involve her practically in the present and psychologically in the future. The social function of a man is more focused on his roles as doer and provider, neither of which may outlive his employment. The discharge of these roles during working life may leave no time for the development of other interests that can provide reasons for living in retirement years.

In times of social change both men and women may come to feel alienated from a world in which they seem to have no place, in which the ideals they have lived for are despised, and the labours of their early lives undervalued. The stresses induced by such disjointing of the personal world contribute not only to the well-recognised phenomenon of the 'midlife crisis' but also to a more chronic *Weltschmerz* or 'existential neurosis' that precludes contentment and corrodes social relationships. It is not a new phenomenon, but a culture preoccupied with achievement, money and youth may provide a particularly uncongenial setting for the compulsorily retired and pensioned older citizen. Doctors should recognise this condition of alienation and may have to address it in the counselling of individual patients for whom it is increasing the burden of more specifically medical problems. As a widespread source of unhappiness in the third age it merits more systematic attention. Its prevention and control lie in the re-ordering of social values and structures that the Carnegie Inquiry hopes to initiate. Men and women in the third age need to have access to a sense of personal worth that transcends work, wealth and family.

Anxieties and uncertainties about sexual activity may affect both men and women in the third age. There is great individual variation, as at all ages, but in the absence of illness, sexual interest and activity may continue into old age for both men and women. Moreover, in this liberated era the middle aged should no longer fear the disapproval of the young for indulging in licit amatory pleasures. The hazards of promiscuity will be the same at any age but medical science has not so far identified any general benefit of celibacy for the healthy adult.

The papers we present vary in range and format. Where topics are familiar, for some diseases for example, we have restricted ourselves to summary outlines of current knowledge and identification of main issues. Where the material is less familiar we have provided more of a critical review.

We are grateful to the Nuffield Provincial Hospitals Trust for the generous financial support for this enterprise. We are grateful also to the participants at the Health Seminar whose contributions to the discussion of the first drafts of these papers led to valuable emendations and additions. We would like to express especial thanks to Dr Hugh Markowe of the Department of Health Central Monitoring Unit who provided data on the burden of disease which identified the specific conditions that impose the most important limitations on life in the third age.

Reference

Carnegie Inquiry into the Third Age. Research Paper No. 9. *Health: abilities and wellbeing in the third age.* Carnegie United Kingdom Trust, Dunfermline, 1992.

Human ageing and the differences between young and old

J. Grimley Evans

Ageing in the sense of senescence is characterised by a loss of adaptability of an individual organism as time passes. A fundamental feature of living organisms is a range of physiological and behavioural responses that enable them to react adaptively to life-threatening challenges from the external or internal environment. At a physiological level these adaptive responses include the so-called homoeostatic mechanisms, feed-back loops that detect any potentially hazardous variation in some important physiological condition—such as body temperature or blood sugar level—and activate a series of corrective changes. As we grow older these homoeostatic mechanisms become on average less sensitive, slower, less accurate and less well sustained. At a behavioural level our ability to recognise dangerous situations and to deal with or escape from them may also become impaired. Sooner or later we succumb to some challenge from the internal or external environment and die. A rise with age in mortality rates therefore is the basic indicator of the rate and form of ageing at an organismic level. As the data presented in Chapter 3 show, ageing first becomes apparent in the human around the age of 13 and is a continuous and broadly exponential process thereafter. There is no biological basis for the separation of people aged over 65 or 75 from the rest of the adult human race as 'the elderly'. If we are post-pubertal we are senescent.

The continuous and exponential rise in death rates represents ageing of the organism as a whole; that is to say it reflects the probability of failure of at least one of the many vital body systems in the face of day to day challenge. It does not imply that any particular single body system will show the same continuous and exponential pattern of ageing. One starting point for identifying the ageing pattern of specific body systems and their functions is to compare those functions in people of different ages. This is the so-called 'cross-sectional' method. The alternative, 'longitudinal' approach is to carry out repeated measurements of function on particular individuals as they grow older. For obvious reasons long-term studies of this kind are rarely practicable in the human and most popular ideas about ageing are based on cross-sectional data. Unfortunately these can be misleading because in addition to ageing several other processes contribute to differences observed between young and old people (Table 2.1).

Selective survival

People who reach later life are the survivors from those who were born at the same time and will differ in various ways from those who died in middle life and earlier. Those who survive are the products, as it were, of a lifetime of natural selection. It is easiest to identify genetic differences contributing to survival in this way; examples

Table 2.1

Differences between young and old		
Non-ageing	Selective survival	
	Differential challenge	
	Cohort effects	
True ageing	Primary	Intrinsic
		Extrinsic
	Secondary	

include inherited lipoprotein patterns and histocompatibility genes linked to risk of various diseases, but lifestyle and psychological factors will also contribute.

Differential challenge

If ageing is defined in terms of adaptability it can only be measured accurately if we apply the same challenge to people of different ages and assess the response. In many ways we present older people with more severe challenges than face the young and we are too ready to interpret their poorer response as due to ageing rather than inequity. In the past, poorer and colder housing was probably as important a contributor to death from hypothermia among the older population as was age-associated deterioration in physiological ability to maintain body temperature. The most obvious form of differential challenge currently offered is in poor health care provided for older people. This has been documented in the management of cancer in the USA (Greenfield *et al.*, 1987), in the provisions for renal dialysis (Wing, 1984; Winearls *et al.*, 1992) and for cardiac investigation and surgery in Britain (Elder *et al.*, 1991). Most recently evidence has been published showing that 20% of coronary care units in Britain have upper age limits for admission and 40% have upper age limits for life-saving thrombolytic therapy (Dudley and Burns, 1992). This is illogical since thrombolytic therapy probably saves more lives if given to older people following heart attacks than if given to younger patients and is clearly cost-effective (Krumholz *et al.*, 1992). A Working Group of the Royal College of Physicians (1991) has stated authoritatively that there are no clinical grounds for excluding patients from cardiological investigation and intervention on the ground of age alone but clearly it happens. In many health districts medical patients referred to hospital as emergencies are sent to geriatric rather than medical departments if they are over an arbitrary age, and geriatric departments tend to be less well staffed and equipped than the parallel medical services. Fiscal pressures arising from the new arrangements for Trust Hospitals and fund-holding general practitioners in the National Health Service could intensify such ageist discrimination if older patients and their families do not insist on a proper standard of care and if casemix and audit arrangements are not put in place to enforce it.

Cohort effects

In rapidly developing societies older people were born and educated into a very different society from that of younger people. Older people may never have had the opportunity to acquire skills, such as use of electronic computers, that are common-place among the young, and some skills that they do have, for example with irregular Latin verbs, are no longer regarded as useful or relevant to modern conditions. Cross-sectional estimates of psychological function in particular will confound age-associated changes with these cultural differences between generations. Some important aspects of this distortion of ageing patterns are discussed in Chapter 17. Longitudinal studies, in which individuals are compared with their own former selves rather than with other people younger than they are, show in general smaller and later declines in psychological function than appear in cross-sectional studies.

Secondary ageing

Secondary ageing comprises changes in function or structure that are adaptations to primary age-associated changes. An example may be the functional restriction in visual fields as a means of restricting the amount of visual information that needs to be processed through a central sensory channel of reduced capacity. Mildly obsessional behaviour is a means of coping with reduced memory. At a genetic level the female menopause is probably an evolved response to the age-associated reduction in the efficiency of reproduction. When our species developed a cumulative culture based on speech and began to evolve a longer lifespan there would have come a time in a woman's life when, in terms of getting her genes into succeeding generations (the fundamental basis of evolution), it would have been better for her to give up increasingly unsuccessful (and dangerous) attempts to produce children of her own, even though each would contain 50% of her genes, and instead to contribute to the survival of her grandchildren, each of whom would contain 25% of her genes. (For the male with so much less biological investment in unsuccessful pregnancies the optimal evolutionary strategy would be to remain fertile as long as possible and to take a series of younger mates throughout his life.)

True ageing

True ageing, changes which come about to an individual as he or she grows older is due to an interaction between intrinsic (genetic) and extrinsic (environmental and lifestyle) factors. Much evidence has accumulated over recent years that much of what was once thought to be intrinsic in ageing is under powerful environmental influence. The rise of blood pressure with age that brings so much in the way of vascular disease in middle and later life seems to be due in part to the susceptibility of some people to environmental factors including diet. Variation in the incidence of age-associated diseases such as coronary heart disease, stroke, osteoporotic fractures and cancers between different places and times indicate that these are not diseases entirely due to intrinsic ageing as was once thought. Probably at least half of the ubiquitous loss of high-tone hearing which can be so socially disabling is due to the ambient level of noise to which the modern town-dweller is continuously subjected (Goycoolea et al., 1986).

The genes which determine intrinsic ageing at a cellular level will probably turn out to be concerned with systems for repairing damage arising from unavoidable agencies such as heat, cosmic radiation and cellular chemical reactions (Kirkwood, 1981). There is no immediate prospect of our being able to modify the action of these genes and the desirability of so doing would need to be debated. Some other intrinsic features of human ageing arise from the conditions under which our species evolved. The rather curious statistic of the ratio of testicular to body size indicates that we are descended from an ape species that had a harem type of social organisation (Harcourt et al., 1980). One consequence of this is the greater longevity of females than males since the latter have more opportunities for reproduction and therefore come under less selective pressure for survival. Another consequence is the larger size of males who in order to reproduce had to compete for control of a harem and attract females who would preferentially consort with males able to defend them and their offspring against marauders. Because of their smaller size, women start adult life with less muscle bulk and strength than men on average, and as both sexes lose muscle during life women are more likely than men to become disabled in old age simply from not having enough strength to get up and about. The scope for overcoming this intrinsic disadvantage by extrinsic factors such as exercise patterns is emphasised in Chapter 15.

There are good grounds for using what we know about extrinsic factors to modify present patterns of human ageing. As discussed in Chapter 4 life expectancy is increasing but part of this life extension is being achieved by medical and surgical interventions prolonging the survival of people with significant disabilities. The alternative strategy is to attack the extrinsic factors in the environment and lifestyle that produce the age-associated diseases and disabilities that necessitate the interventions. This approach should be a good investment for society as well as for individuals since the evidence suggests that the longer one postpones the onset of disability, the shorter the period of disability one can expect to endure and society to pay for (Working Party of the Royal College of Physicians, 1991). This follows from the very nature of ageing which implies that because of loss of adaptability the later the onset of a disease such as stroke the more likely one is to die from it rather than linger in a disabled state.

While modification of ageing through extrinsic factors in environment and lifestyle will have its greatest effect if started and continued from early in life, it is now clear that benefits in function and wellbeing can be obtained by adopting a healthy lifestyle at any age. Various Chapters that follow emphasise that it is never too late to gain something from an improved environment and lifestyle. This fact needs to evoke appropriate responses from individuals and in social policy.

References

Dudley NJ, Burns E. The influence of age on policies for admission and thrombolysis in coronary care units in the United Kingdom. *Age Ageing*, 1992; 21: 95–98.

Elder AT, Shaw TRD, Turnbull CM, Starkey IR. Elderly and younger patients selected to undergo coronary angiography. *Brit Med J*, 1991; 303: 950–953.

Goycoolea MV, Goycoolea HG, Rodriguez LG, Martinez GC, Vidal R. Effect of life in industrialized societies on hearing in natives of Easter Island. *Laryngoscope*, 1986; 96: 1391–1396.

Greenfield S, Blanco DM, Elashoff RM, Ganz PA. Patterns of care related to age of breast cancer patients. *J Am Med Assoc*, 1987; 257: 2766–2770.

Harcourt AH, Harvey PH, Larson SG, Short RV. Testis weight, body weight and breeding system in primates. *Nature*, 1980; 293: 55–57.

Kirkwood TBL. Evolution of repair: survival versus reproduction. In Townsend CR, Calow P (ed.), *Physiological ecology: an evolutionary approach to resource use*. Blackwell Scientific, Oxford, 1981.

Krumholz HM, Pasternak RC, Weinstein MC, Friesinger GC, Ridker PM, Tosteson ANA, Goldman L. Cost effectiveness of thrombolytic therapy with streptokinase in elderly patients with suspected acute myocardial infarction. *New Engl J Med*, 1992; 327: 7–13.

Winearls CG, Oliver DO, Auer J. Age and dialysis. *Lancet*, 1992; 339: 432.

Wing AJ. Why don't the British treat more patients with kidney failure? *Brit Med J*, 1984; 287: 1157–1158.

Working Group of the Royal College of Physicians. Cardiological intervention in elderly patients. *J Roy Coll Phys Lond*, 1991; 25: 197–205.

Working Party of the Royal College of Physicians. Preventive medicine p. 171. Royal College of Physicians, London, 1991.

Disease in the third age: a profile from routine statistics

3

M.J. Goldacre

Introduction

The World Health Organisation has defined health as a state of 'complete physical, mental and social wellbeing and not merely the absence of disease and infirmity'. This definition emphasises that attitudes to health should be positive ones but, for practical purposes, heavy reliance is placed on negative indices—death, disease and disability—in measuring health status in populations.

In this paper, a statistical profile of ill health in the third age is presented. Most information about patterns of ill health in large, representative populations derives from routinely collected vital and health-care statistics (e.g. death certificates and statistical abstracts of records of hospital care). This is particularly so for information about trends in ill health over long periods of time and for information used for geographical comparisons. Mortality statistics, which have been collected and analysed routinely in the United Kingdom for 150 years, occupy a special place in the measurement of disease because of their ready availability for historical and geographical comparison. Detailed information can be obtained from them about patterns of mortality by time period, place, age, sex and specific diseases (Office of Population Censuses and Surveys[c]).

Most routinely available information on morbidity in the population comes from statistics about the contact of people with health services. Hospital inpatient statistics have been collected nationally on a one-in-ten sample basis since the 1950s (Office of Population Censuses and Surveys[b]); and they have been collected as a complete enumeration of hospital inpatient admissions in most parts of the United Kingdom since the late 1960s. Among other data, they include information on each patient's age, sex, diagnostic reason for admission and any operation performed. A partial limitation of routine hospital inpatient statistics is that each admission is enumerated separately when a person has more than one admission and it is not generally possible to distinguish between numbers of admissions and numbers of people in receipt of care.

The only routinely available information on the use of hospital outpatient care is that on total counts of outpatients who attend clinics. In particular, there is no routine information collected by the health service on the demographic or clinical characteristics of the use of outpatient services. A certain amount of information is available on the self-reported use of outpatient care from rotating sample surveys of the population undertaken in the General Household Survey (Office of Population Censuses and Surveys[a]), which covers many topics in addition to health.

Hospital patients constitute a small proportion of all doctor–patient contacts. Well over 90% of all episodes of illness which result in medical consultation are managed wholly within general practice. There are no routine data, universally collected, about the use of general practitioner care. However, data have been collected, pooled and published periodically from a few dozen general practices across England and Wales (data have been published for the years 1960–62, 1970–72 and 1980–82) (Royal College of General Practitioners and OPCS, 1986).

Routine data on illnesses and disabilities which do not result in contact with health care are sparse in the United Kingdom but some information on self-reported ill health is available from the General Household Survey (OPCS[a]). In addition, sample surveys are undertaken from time to time by researchers and by departments of government to determine the occurrence of particular diseases or disabilities in the community. There are also some diseases which are recorded in systems of disease notification and registration: in particular, new cases of cancers are registered in regional and national cancer registries and cancer statistics are published regularly (see Chapter 10, Table 10.1).

Much of the clinical data described below are classified and coded in the various data collection systems according to the World Health Organisation's International Classification of Diseases (World Health Organisation, 1977) or the Office of Population Censuses and Surveys' classification of operations (OPCS, 1975). In general, the codes and terminology in these classifications are used in this paper. Most data are shown as age- and sex-specific rates, i.e. the numerator is the number of affected people in each age–sex group and the denominator is the total number of people in the population in the age–sex group. Where it has been straightforward to do so, the data on the third age are presented in age groups which span 50–74 years of age. Sometimes, when data on these age groups are not readily accessible, the age range 45–74 years has been used. In illustrating profiles of disease by age group, some of the data are also shown across a wider age range so that the reader can see how the pattern of disease changes before, during and after the third age.

Mortality in the third age

Mortality rates rise with age from early adult life (Figure 3.1). In all age groups in adult life, including the third age, age-specific male mortality rates are about double those of females. Figure 3.1 shows absolute age- and sex-specific rates in quinquennial age groups; and it shows that mortality rates rise exponentially with age in both males and females. In Figure 3.2 the same data are plotted on a logarithmic scale: in effect, this shows the rate of increase in mortality rates in each successive age group. This indicates that within the third age the rate of increase, in each quinquennial age group compared with the previous one, is approximately constant with advancing age. It also shows that the rate of increase with age is similar in males and females although the absolute levels of mortality are considerably higher in males than females.

Tables 3.1 and 3.2 show the most common causes of death in males and females aged 45–54, 55–64 and 65–74 years (expressed as rates per million population in each age–sex group). In males the commonest causes of death in each age group are, in order of frequency, myocardial infarction (heart attacks) and other ischaemic heart disease, lung cancer and cerebrovascular disease (strokes). Together, these causes account for just over half of all deaths in males in this age group. Other common

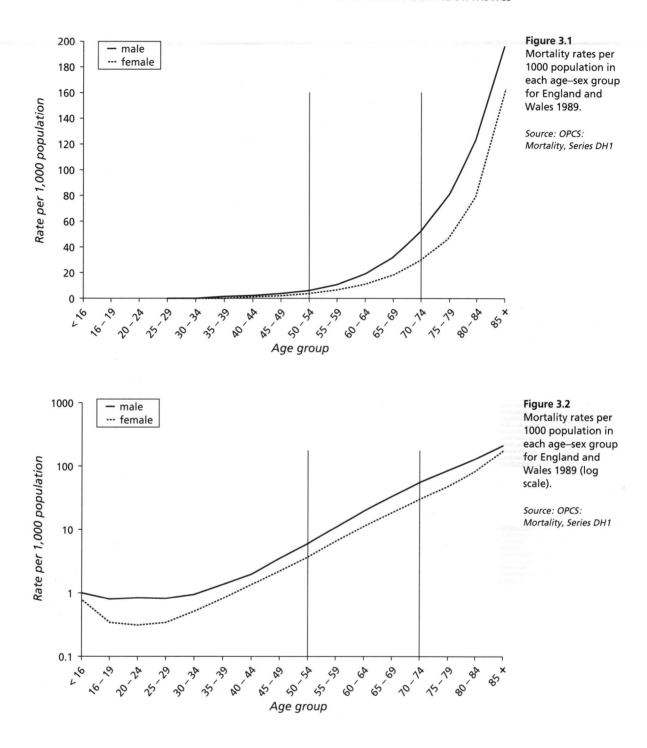

Figure 3.1
Mortality rates per 1000 population in each age–sex group for England and Wales 1989.

Source: OPCS: Mortality, Series DH1

Figure 3.2
Mortality rates per 1000 population in each age–sex group for England and Wales 1989 (log scale).

Source: OPCS: Mortality, Series DH1

causes of death in males in the two older age groups include chronic obstructive airways disease (notably chronic bronchitis); cancer of the stomach, large bowel, pancreas, prostate and bladder; leukaemias and lymphomas; and diabetes mellitus. The most common causes of death in females vary a little more across the age groups than they do in males. The most common causes of death include cancer of the breast, cancer of the lung, acute myocardial infarction and other ischaemic heart disease, and cerebrovascular disease. Together, these causes account for just over half of all deaths in females in this age group. Other common causes of death in females include cancer of the ovary and, in the two older age groups, cancers of the stomach and large bowel, chronic obstructive airways disease and diabetes mellitus.

Table 3.1

Principal causes of death in males aged 45–54, 55–64 and 65–74 years: rates per million population in each age–sex group (England and Wales 1989, first five causes in each age group ranked in parentheses)

	Males		
Cause of death and ICD number	*45–54*	*55–64*	*65–74*
Malignant neoplasm of stomach (151)	96	366 (5)	953
Malignant neoplasm of colon (153)	114	340	876
Malignant neoplasm of rectum, rectosigmoid junction and anus (154)	73	233	543
Malignant neoplasm of pancreas (157)	66	230	537
Malignant neoplasm of trachea, bronchus and lung (162)	392 (2)	1844 (2)	4620 (2)
Malignant neoplasm of prostate (185)	19	226	1177 (5)
Malignant neoplasm of bladder (188)	33	167	492
Malignant neoplasm of lymphatic and haematopoietic tissue (200–208)	147 (4)	335	742
Diabetes mellitus (250)	43	167	446
Senile and pre-senile organic psychotic conditions (290)	3	26	214
Parkinson's disease (332)	2	22	212
Acute myocardial infarction (410)	1038 (1)	3483 (1)	8442 (1)
Cerebrovascular disease (430–438)	209 (3)	812 (3)	3123 (3)
Pneumonia (480–486)	61	162	667
Chronic obstructive airways disease (490–493, 496)	96	688 (4)	2919 (4)
Ulcer of stomach and duodenum (531–533)	27	91	297
Chronic liver disease and cirrhosis (571)	121 (5)	167	200
Motor vehicle traffic accidents (E810–E819)	91	102	133
Accidental falls (E880–E888)	39	60	118
Suicide and self-inflicted injury (E950–E959)	141	130	133

Source: OPCS: Mortality, Series DH2.

The increase in mortality rates with age, comparing males and females, is illustrated for myocardial infarction and other manifestations of ischaemic heart disease (Figure 3.3), cerebrovascular disease (Figure 3.4), malignant neoplasms as a combined group (Figure 3.5), malignant neoplasms of lung separately (Figure 3.6), and malignant neoplasms of the female breast separately (Figure 3.7). Most of these causes of death rise strikingly with advancing age. Death rates ascribed to accidental falls are shown in Figure 3.8: they rise strikingly with age, more so after the age of about 75 years. Deaths from motor vehicle accidents (Figure 3.9) and deaths recorded as suicide (Figure 3.10) show a more variable pattern in relation to age in the third age.

Table 3.2

Principal causes of death in females aged 45–54, 55–64 and 65–74 years: rates per million population in each age–sex group (England and Wales 1989, first five causes in each age group ranked in parentheses)

Cause of death and ICD number	Females		
	45–54	*55–64*	*65–74*
Malignant neoplasm of stomach (151)	36	126	343
Malignant neoplasm of colon (153)	90	285	639
Malignant neoplasm of rectum, rectosigmoid junction and anus (154)	39	113	256
Malignant neoplasm of pancreas (157)	48	169	364
Malignant neoplasm of trachea, bronchus and lung (162)	193	833 (3)	1602 (3)
Malignant neoplasm of female breast (174)	617 (1)	1012 (2)	1345 (4)
Malignant neoplasm of uterus (179–182)	111 (5)	205	351
Malignant neoplasm of cervix uteri (180)	81	118	186
Malignant neoplasm of ovary and other uterine adnexa (183)	166 (3)	353	488
Malignant neoplasm of bladder (188)	11	58	150
Malignant neoplasm of lymphatic and haematopoietic tissue (200–208)	91	237	497
Diabetes mellitus (250)	32	122	394
Senile and pre-senile organic psychotic conditions (290)	2	23	202
Parkinson's disease (332)	1	10	109
Acute myocardial infarction (410)	187 (2)	1113 (1)	3933 (1)
Cerebrovascular disease (430–438)	165 (4)	601 (4)	2431 (2)
Pneumonia (480–486)	32	102	483
Chronic obstructive airways disease (490–493, 496)	97	459 (5)	1241 (5)
Ulcer of stomach and duodenum (531–533)	15	56	168
Chronic liver disease and cirrhosis (571)	72	122	150
Motor vehicle traffic accidents (E810–E819)	32	49	73
Accidental falls (E880–E888)	11	25	98
Suicide and self-inflicted injury (E950–E959)	58	60	55

Source: OPCS: Mortality, Series DH2.

Age-specific mortality rates are higher in Wales, and considerably higher in Scotland and Northern Ireland, than those in England (Table 3.3).

Age-specific mortality rates in the third age have declined over time, as they have in other age groups, since the beginning of the present century (Figures 3.11, 3.12). Whilst the decline in the older quinquennial age groups may seem more dramatic than that at younger ages (Figures 3.11, 3.12), mortality rates have declined from a

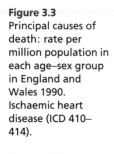

Figure 3.3
Principal causes of
death: rate per
million population in
each age–sex group
in England and
Wales 1990.
Ischaemic heart
disease (ICD 410–
414).

*Source: OPCS:
Mortality, Series DH2*

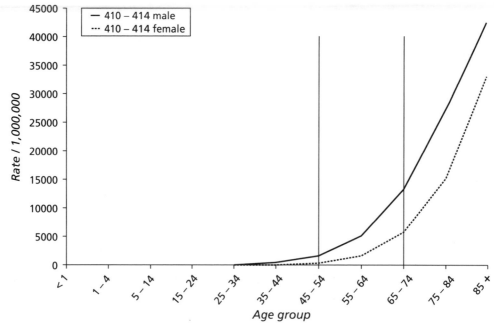

Figure 3.4
Principal causes of
death: rate per
million population in
each age–sex group
in England and
Wales 1990.
Cerebrovascular
disease (ICD 430–
438).

*Source: OPCS:
Mortality, Series DH2*

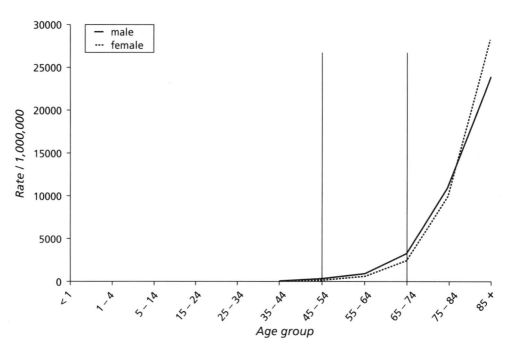

higher absolute level in the older age groups than the young. Age-specific mortality rates are plotted on a logarithmic scale in Figures 3.13 and 3.14. The transformed data indicate that the decline over time has been broadly similar in each group.

The major component of the decline in mortality in the first half of the century was a reduction in deaths from infectious diseases. Considering individual age groups within the third age, the declines have nonetheless not been entirely smooth over time when considered in detail. For example, in people aged 70–74 years there was a steady decline in death rates for both males and females from the turn of the century until the 1930s. Male death rates then levelled off over time (Figure 3.11) whilst female death rates continued to decline (Figure 3.12). Whilst death rates from infectious diseases in both sexes in these age groups continued to fall, the levelling

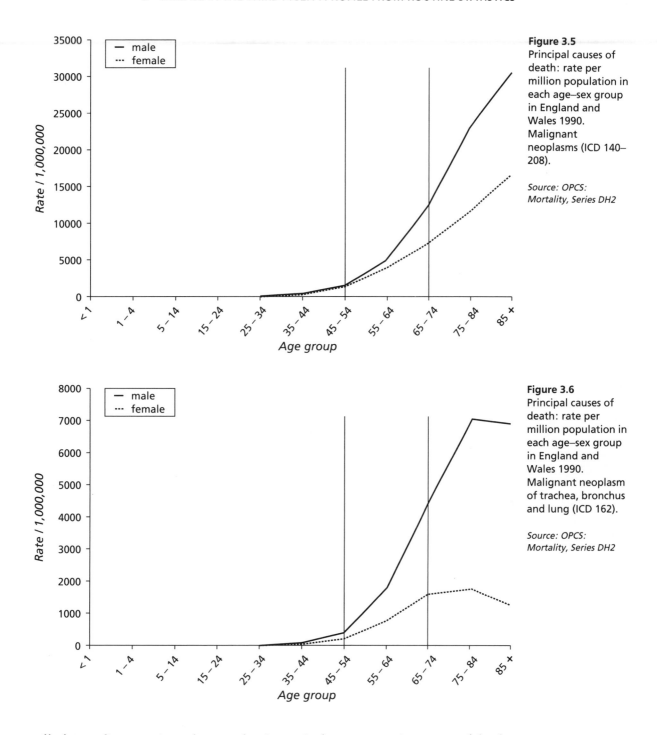

Figure 3.5
Principal causes of death: rate per million population in each age–sex group in England and Wales 1990. Malignant neoplasms (ICD 140–208).

Source: OPCS: Mortality, Series DH2

Figure 3.6
Principal causes of death: rate per million population in each age–sex group in England and Wales 1990. Malignant neoplasm of trachea, bronchus and lung (ICD 162).

Source: OPCS: Mortality, Series DH2

off of mortality rates in males was due in particular to two major causes of death, lung cancer and ischaemic heart disease, which increased during this period and which were considerably more common in males than females. In recent years the mortality rates in males and females have shown further declines. As another illustration of inconsistency in the detail of the declines, Figure 3.15 shows mortality rates in people aged 50–54 years: there was a steady decline in mortality in this age group until the late 1950s, levelling off for some time thereafter, and then further declines in the most recent years.

Table 3.4 shows age-specific mortality rates over the last two decades in greater detail. Data on people in the quinquennial age groups from 30–49 years are also included in this table to show data about people in age groups as they approach the

Figure 3.7
Principal causes of death: rate per million population in each age–sex group in England and Wales 1990. Malignant neoplasm of female breast (ICD 174).

Source: OPCS: Mortality, Series DH2

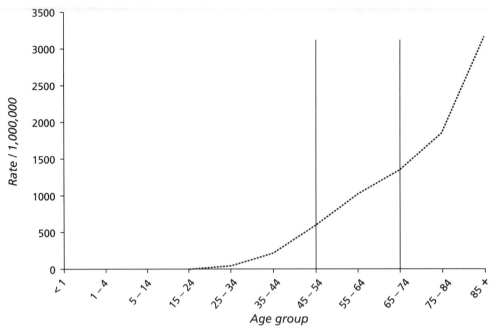

Figure 3.8
Principal causes of death: rate per million population in each age–sex group in England and Wales 1990. Accidental falls (ICD E880–E888).

Source: OPCS: Mortality, Series DH2

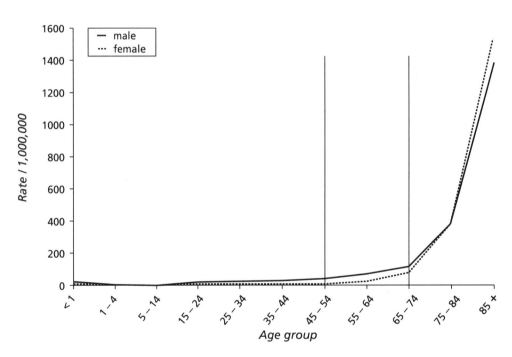

third age. An interesting and potentially important question concerns the extent to which declines in mortality at a given age and at a given time period reflect (a) the influence of the time period (i.e. result from improvements in health attributable to the period in which people of that age lived), and/or reflect (b) the effect of birth cohort (i.e. represent a generation of healthier people now reaching the relevant age group). In practice, calendar time period and birth-cohort effects are substantially intertwined. It is difficult to separate them out; and it is also difficult to predict with precision what future mortality rates may be. The declines in the past in some age- and sex-specific mortality rates, followed by levelling off, followed by further declines indicate the difficulty of simple extrapolation. However, it seems safe to predict, in general terms, that mortality rates will continue to decline; and will

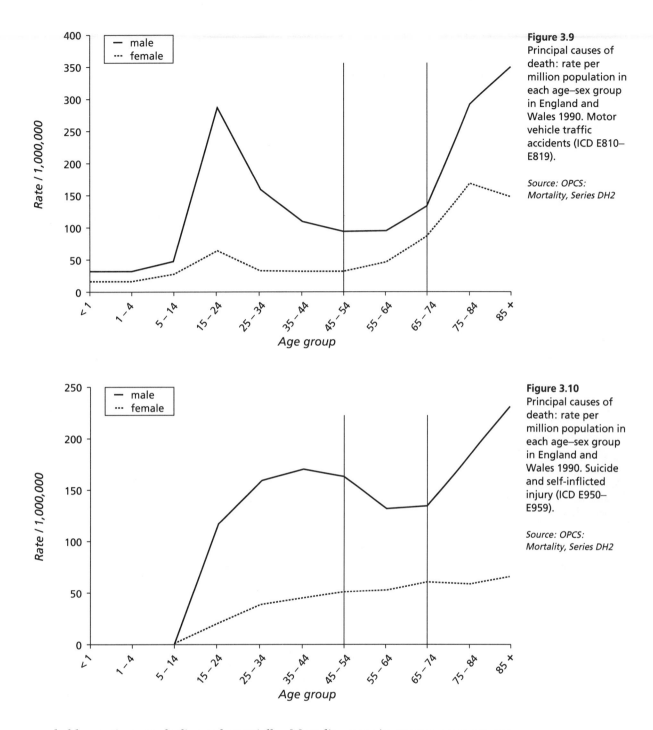

Figure 3.9
Principal causes of death: rate per million population in each age–sex group in England and Wales 1990. Motor vehicle traffic accidents (ICD E810–E819).

Source: OPCS: Mortality, Series DH2

Figure 3.10
Principal causes of death: rate per million population in each age–sex group in England and Wales 1990. Suicide and self-inflicted injury (ICD E950–E959).

Source: OPCS: Mortality, Series DH2

probably continue to decline substantially. Mortality rates in younger age groups for recent birth cohorts, prior to their reaching the third age, have shown striking declines (Table 3.4) and presumably the experience of these 'healthier' cohorts will continue into their third age. The mortality experience of successive birth cohorts, shown by calendar year of birth and age at death, are illustrated in Figures 3.16 and 3.17.

Age-specific mortality rates over the past two decades are shown in quinquennial age groups for some of the most common causes of death (Tables 3.5–3.8). The tables include data on mortality in the age groups 30–49 years, i.e. in the quinquennia prior to moving into the third age. From the end of the 1970s death rates from ischaemic heart disease in males started to decline; and the decline has been increasingly

19

Table 3.3

Mortality rates per 10,000 people in each age–sex group, comparing England, Wales, Scotland and Northern Ireland

	Males (Age group years)			Females (Age group years)		
Causes	45–54	55–64	65–74	45–54	55–64	65–74
All causes						
England	46.7	146.6	391.3	29.5	87.1	224.2
Wales	49.0	159.7	430.9	31.0	91.2	243.7
Scotland	61.3	192.3	484.3	39.2	114.9	284.0
Northern Ireland	54.4	172.4	465.8	33.1	95.9	246.7
Ischaemic heart disease						
England	16.3	53.7	131.1	2.9	16.9	59.2
Wales	17.1	61.0	153.9	3.7	18.8	68.2
Scotland	21.1	74.6	171.7	5.4	25.3	85.9
Northern Ireland	18.4	69.3	179.2	4.1	23.1	77.5
Lung cancer						
England	3.9	18.4	46.1	2.0	8.3	16.0
Wales	4.2	18.5	47.0	1.1	7.8	16.8
Scotland	5.6	24.7	58.7	3.2	11.1	22.9
Northern Ireland	5.0	20.9	46.3	0.9	7.8	11.5

Figure 3.11
Age-specific mortality rates in England and Wales for males aged 50–74 years.

Source: OPCS: Mortality, Series DH1

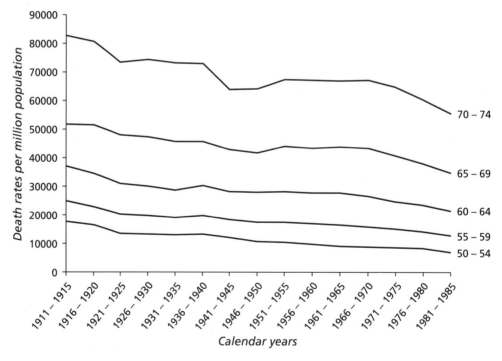

striking in successively younger generations (Table 3.5). A similar decline, from a much lower baseline, has been seen in mortality rates for ischaemic heart disease in females (Table 3.5). Table 3.6 shows that death rates for lung cancer in males have declined in the past two decades, strikingly so in men under the age of about 65 years. The table shows that mortality rates for lung cancer in women over the age of 60 years have increased in the past two decades. The contrasting trends in men

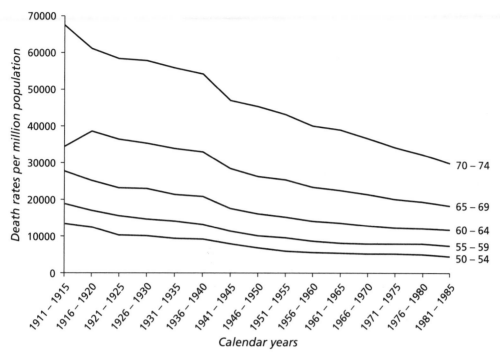

Figure 3.12
Age-specific mortality rates in England and Wales for females aged 50–74 years.

Source: OPCS: Mortality, Series DH1

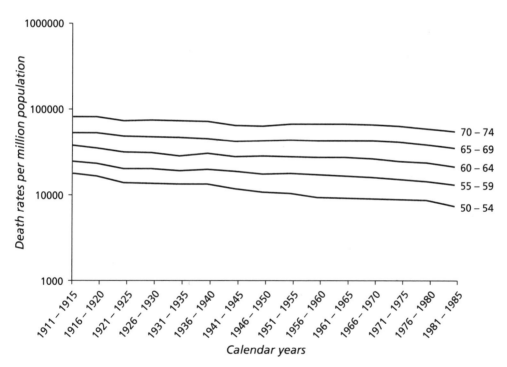

Figure 3.13
Age-specific mortality rates in England and Wales for males aged 50–74 years (log scale).

Source: OPCS: Mortality, Series DH1

and women undoubtedly reflect changes in the prevalence of cigarette smoking. Table 3.7 shows that mortality rates for breast cancer in women over 55 years have increased markedly in the past two decades. Table 3.8 shows the decline in death rates for chronic bronchitis in men and in young (but not in older) women.

Summary statistics on the expectation of life, expressed as average numbers of years of life from each age, are shown in Tables 3.9 and 3.10. Table 3.9 shows the increase in expectation of life over recent calendar years for people aged 45 and 65 years. Table 3.10 shows the expectation of life from different ages, calculated at 1987–89.

Figure 3.14
Age-specific
mortality rates in
England and Wales
for females aged 50–
74 years (log scale).

*Source: OPCS:
Mortality, Series DH1*

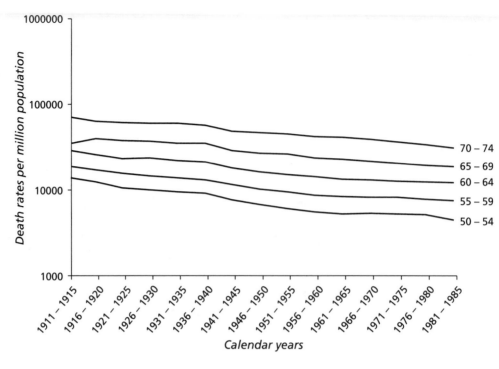

Figure 3.15
Age-specific
mortality rates in
England and Wales
for people aged 50–
54 years.

*Source: OPCS:
Mortality, Series DH1*

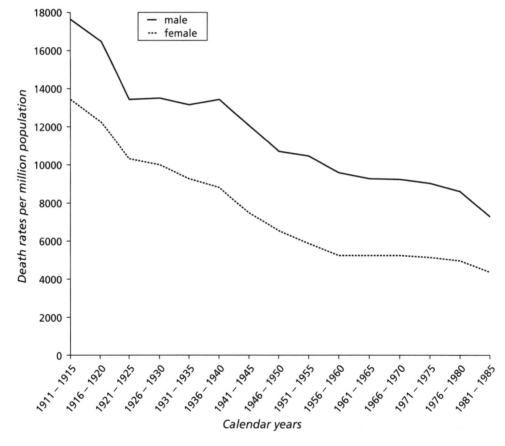

Morbidity in the third age—use of health services

Hospital inpatient care

The most comprehensive information available about morbidity is that obtainable from statistics on hospital inpatient admissions. Figures 3.18–3.31 depict admission

Table 3.4

Age-specific mortality rates per 10,000 people in each age–sex group, England 1968–90

All causes, males

Age group (years)	1968–73	1974–78	1979–84	1985–90
30–34	10.8	10.0	9.6	9.7
35–39	16.3	15.2	13.4	13.3
40–44	29.7	26.4	23.4	20.6
45–49	53.7	49.5	42.7	36.6
50–54	91.9	89.6	77.7	64.0
55–59	156.7	146.0	137.6	114.7
60–64	260.7	243.5	223.8	201.8
65–69	429.2	395.6	363.4	324.2
70–74	671.6	633.8	577.7	527.8

All causes, females

Age group (years)	1968–73	1974–78	1979–84	1985–90
30–34	7.2	6.5	6.0	5.6
35–39	11.7	10.8	9.3	8.7
40–44	20.7	18.6	15.7	13.9
45–49	34.6	32.2	27.6	23.7
50–54	53.1	52.0	46.8	39.0
55–59	80.4	78.3	75.6	66.9
60–64	125.8	122.4	118.1	114.0
65–69	206.4	195.3	186.4	177.3
70–74	354.9	327.8	304.7	289.6

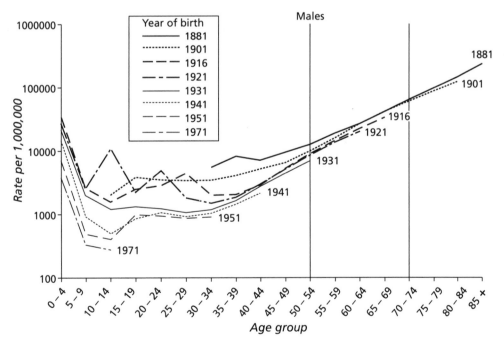

Figure 3.16
Mortality rates: comparison of age-specific mortality rates in different birth cohorts: males.

Calculated from OPCS: Mortality, Series DH1

rates for hospital inpatient care by age group and sex. The data used come from two main sources. The first is the Hospital Inpatient Enquiry (HIPE) for England and the second is the Oxford Record Linkage Study. As mentioned above, HIPE and most other routine statistics on hospital inpatient care are episode-based: that is, each hospital admission is counted separately and it is not possible to distinguish

Figure 3.17
Mortality rates:
comparison of age-
specific mortality
rates in different
birth cohorts:
females.

*Calculated from OPCS:
Mortality, Series DH1*

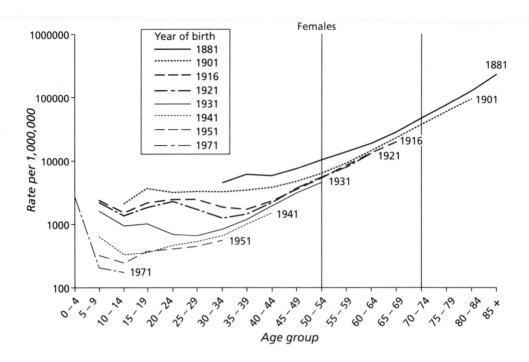

Table 3.5

Age-specific mortality rates per 10,000 people in each age–sex group, England 1968–90

Ischaemic heart disease (ICD codes 410–414), males

Age group (years)	1968–73	1974–78	1979–84	1985–90
30–34	1.1	0.9	0.9	0.7
35–39	3.4	3.3	2.7	2.2
40–44	9.4	9.0	7.3	5.5
45–49	19.9	19.4	16.8	12.7
50–54	34.6	36.4	32.4	24.9
55–59	55.6	57.0	55.1	44.7
60–64	87.2	88.6	85.5	75.5
65–69	137.0	136.3	129.6	116.1
70–74	198.2	201.7	191.2	177.3

Ischaemic heart disease (ICD codes 410–414), females

Age group (years)	1968–73	1974–78	1979–84	1985–90
30–34	0.2	0.2	0.2	0.1
35–39	0.5	0.6	0.4	0.4
40–44	1.5	1.5	1.2	0.8
45–49	3.0	3.3	2.7	2.0
50–54	6.3	6.8	6.4	4.9
55–59	12.4	13.6	13.7	11.6
60–64	26.3	27.0	26.6	25.2
65–69	50.9	50.7	48.6	45.7
70–74	91.7	90.8	85.6	82.0

between numbers of admissions and numbers of individual people admitted to hospital. To supplement these data with information relating to numbers of individual people admitted to hospital, linked data from the Oxford Record Linkage Study are also shown (these have been used to count each individual once only in the average annual admission rates shown in each figure). Figure 3.18 shows hospital admission

Table 3.6

Age-specific mortality rates per 10,000 people in each age–sex group, England 1968–90

Lung cancer (ICD code 162), males

Age group (years)	1968–73	1974–78	1979–84	1985–90
30–34	0.2	0.2	0.1	0.1
35–39	0.6	0.6	0.4	0.4
40–44	2.0	1.5	1.2	1.0
45–49	5.2	4.4	3.3	2.7
50–54	11.0	10.5	8.2	5.9
55–59	21.3	19.3	17.6	13.5
60–64	36.2	33.7	30.5	26.8
65–69	52.2	50.2	46.3	40.9
70–74	66.3	66.9	63.9	58.0

Lung cancer (ICD code 162), females

Age group (years)	1968–73	1974–78	1979–84	1985–90
30–34	0.1	0.1	0.1	0.1
35–39	0.3	0.2	0.2	0.2
40–44	0.7	0.7	0.6	0.6
45–49	1.7	1.7	1.4	1.4
50–54	3.0	3.5	3.3	2.6
55–59	4.4	5.4	6.2	5.6
60–64	5.9	7.7	9.3	10.9
65–69	7.2	9.2	11.9	14.3
70–74	8.1	9.9	13.1	16.8

Table 3.7

Age-specific mortality rates per 10,000 people in each age–sex group, England 1968–90

Breast cancer (ICD code 174), females

Age group (years)	1968–73	1974–78	1979–84	1985–90
30–34	0.6	0.6	0.6	0.6
35–39	1.5	1.6	1.5	1.5
40–44	3.2	3.2	3.0	2.9
45–49	5.3	5.5	5.4	5.1
50–54	7.0	7.6	7.7	7.4
55–59	8.8	9.0	9.4	9.4
60–64	9.8	10.1	10.6	11.2
65–69	10.9	11.3	11.9	12.6
70–74	11.9	12.5	13.3	14.5

rates overall, to all specialties combined, expressed as age- and sex-specific admission rates for episodes of care (the data for England) and for individuals in receipt of care (the data for the Oxford Regional Health Authority). The broad patterns of usage are similar in both sets of data. Comparisons between episode-based and person-based admission rates show slightly higher rates in the former than the latter (as expected), more so with increasing age because multiple admissions per person are, in general, more common in the elderly than in the young. The data show that hospital admission rates in early adult life are broadly similar across age groups up to the age of about 50 years; and that admission rates for females are higher than

Table 3.8

Age-specific mortality rates per 10,000 people in each age–sex group, England 1968–90

Chronic bronchitis (ICD codes 490–492 (8TH), 490–492, 496 (9TH)), males

Age group (years)	1968–73	1974–78	1979–84	1985–90
30–34	0.1	0.0	0.0	0.0
35–39	0.2	0.1	0.1	0.0
40–44	0.5	0.3	0.2	0.1
45–49	1.7	1.0	0.6	0.3
50–54	4.2	2.7	1.8	1.1
55–59	9.7	6.1	5.1	3.6
60–64	20.8	13.8	10.8	9.9
65–69	39.4	26.0	21.9	20.0
70–74	65.1	48.0	40.6	39.3

Chronic bronchitis (ICD codes 490–492 (8TH), 490–492, 496 (9TH)), females

Age group (years)	1968–73	1974–78	1979–84	1985–90
30–34	0.0	0.0	0.0	0.0
35–39	0.1	0.1	0.0	0.0
40–44	0.3	0.2	0.1	0.1
45–49	0.8	0.6	0.3	0.2
50–54	1.4	1.2	0.1	0.8
55–59	2.4	2.0	2.3	2.2
60–64	3.9	3.4	3.9	5.0
65–69	6.6	4.9	5.9	8.2
70–74	10.6	7.6	8.2	11.8

Table 3.9

Expectation of life from age 45 and age 65 years, England and Wales: average years of life from each age

	Age 45		Age 65	
Year	Males	Females	Males	Females
1950–52	26.5	30.8	11.7	14.3
1960–62	27.1	32.1	12.0	15.3
1970–72	27.4	32.9	12.2	16.1
1980–82	28.7	34.0	13.0	17.0

Source: OPCS: Series DH1 No. 23, Table 14.

Table 3.10

Expectation of life from various ages, England and Wales, 1987–89: average years of life from each age

Age (years)	Males	Females
50	25.6	30.3
55	21.3	25.8
60	17.4	21.6
65	13.9	17.7
70	10.9	14.1
75	8.3	10.9

Source: OPCS: Series DH1 No. 23, Table 15.

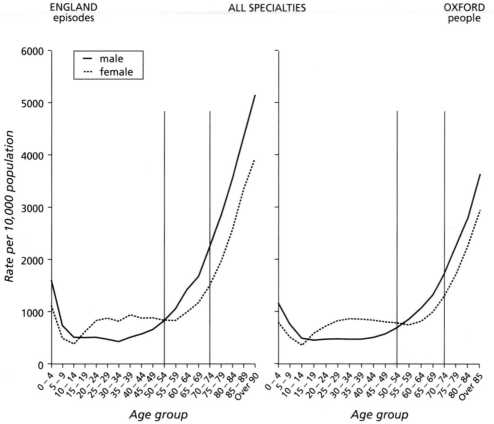

Figure 3.18
Hospital admission rates per 10,000 people in each age–sex group: episode-based hospital admission rates in England and person-based admission rates in the Oxford region. All specialties.

Source: Hospital Inpatient Enquiry (England) and Oxford Record Linkage Study

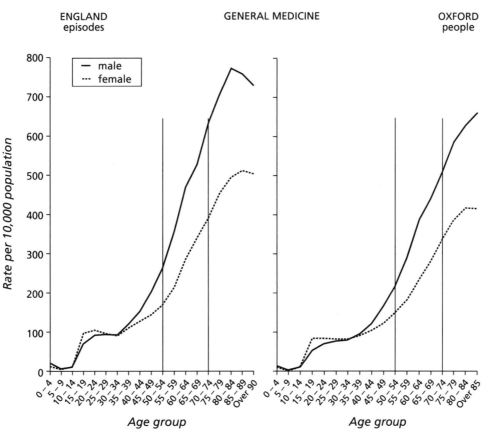

Figure 3.19
Hospital admission rates per 10,000 people in each age–sex group: episode-based hospital admission rates in England and person-based admission rates in the Oxford region. General medicine.

Source: Hospital Inpatient Enquiry (England) and Oxford Record Linkage Study

Figure 3.20
Hospital admission rates per 10,000 people in each age–sex group: episode-based hospital admission rates in England and person-based admission rates in the Oxford region. Geriatrics.

Source: Hospital Inpatient Enquiry (England) and Oxford Record Linkage Study

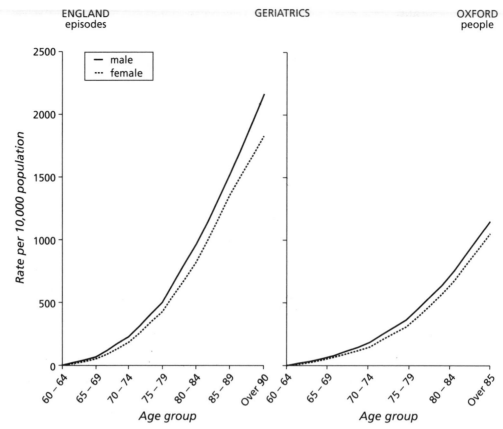

Figure 3.21
Hospital admission rates per 10,000 people in each age–sex group: episode-based hospital admission rates in England and person-based admission rates in the Oxford region. General surgery.

Source: Hospital Inpatient Enquiry (England) and Oxford Record Linkage Study

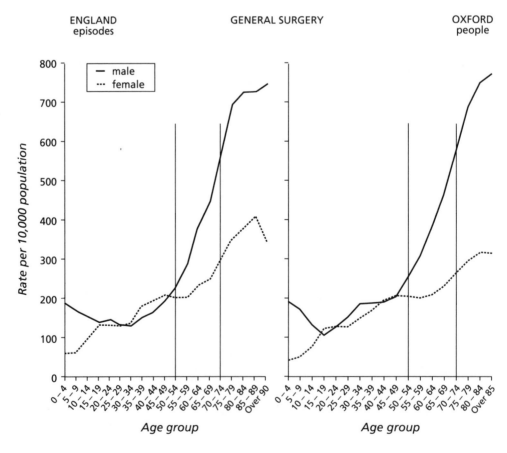

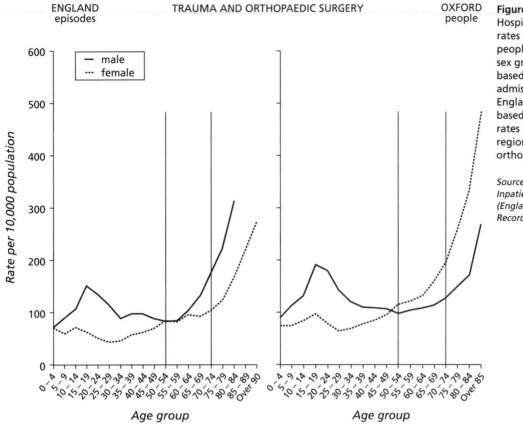

ENGLAND
episodes

TRAUMA AND ORTHOPAEDIC SURGERY

OXFORD
people

Figure 3.22
Hospital admission rates per 10,000 people in each age–sex group: episode-based hospital admission rates in England and person-based admission rates in the Oxford region. Trauma and orthopaedic surgery.

Source: Hospital Inpatient Enquiry (England) and Oxford Record Linkage Study

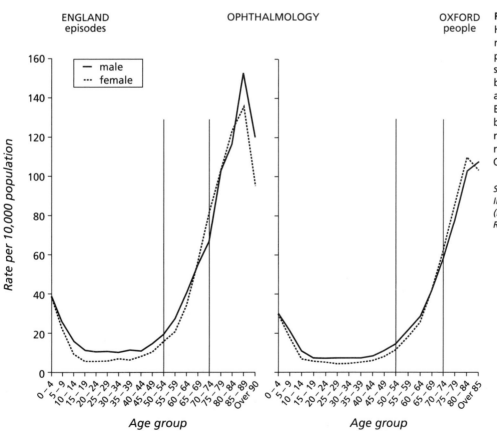

ENGLAND
episodes

OPHTHALMOLOGY

OXFORD
people

Figure 3.23
Hospital admission rates per 10,000 people in each age–sex group: episode-based hospital admission rates in England and person-based admission rates in the Oxford region. Ophthalmology.

Source: Hospital Inpatient Enquiry (England) and Oxford Record Linkage Study

29

Figure 3.24
Hospital admission rates per 10,000 people in each age–sex group: episode-based hospital admission rates in England and person-based admission rates in the Oxford region. Gynaecology.

Source: Hospital Inpatient Enquiry (England) and Oxford Record Linkage Study

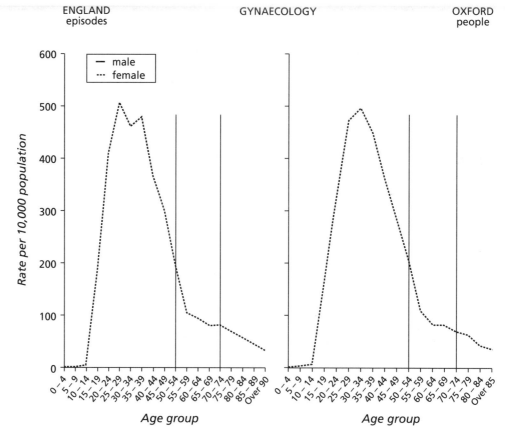

Figure 3.25
Hospital admission rates per 10,000 people in each age–sex group: episode-based hospital admission rates in England and person-based admission rates in the Oxford region. Ear, nose and throat surgery.

Source: Hospital Inpatient Enquiry (England) and Oxford Record Linkage Study

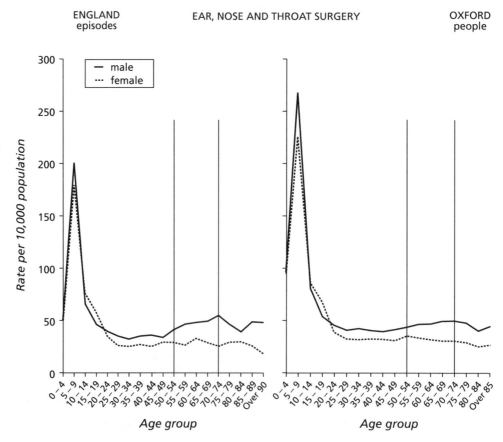

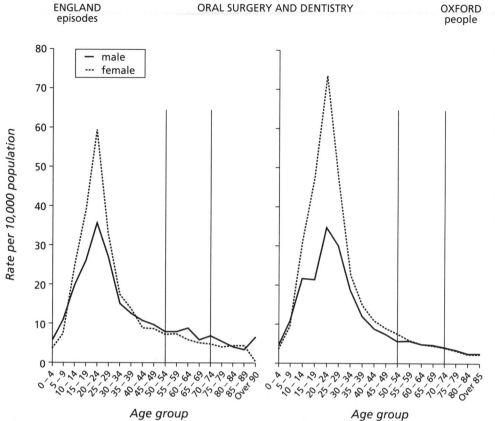

ORAL SURGERY AND DENTISTRY

Figure 3.26
Hospital admission rates per 10,000 people in each age–sex group: episode-based hospital admission rates in England and person-based admission rates in the Oxford region. Oral surgery and Dentistry.

Source: Hospital Inpatient Enquiry (England) and Oxford Record Linkage Study

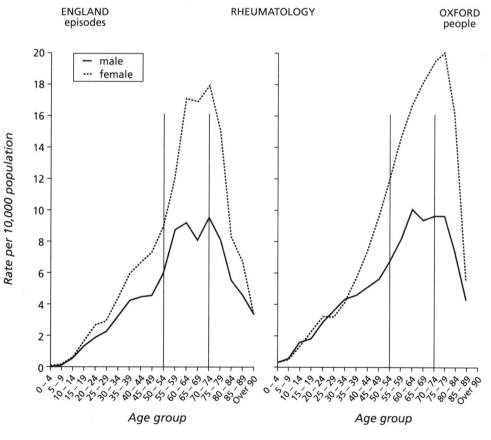

RHEUMATOLOGY

Figure 3.27
Hospital admission rates per 10,000 people in each age–sex group: episode-based hospital admission rates in England and person-based admission rates in the Oxford region. Rheumatology.

Source: Hospital Inpatient Enquiry (England) and Oxford Record Linkage Study

Figure 3.28
Hospital admission rates per 10,000 people in each age–sex group: episode-based hospital admission rates in England and person-based admission rates in the Oxford region. Radiotherapy.

Source: Hospital Inpatient Enquiry (England) and Oxford Record Linkage Study

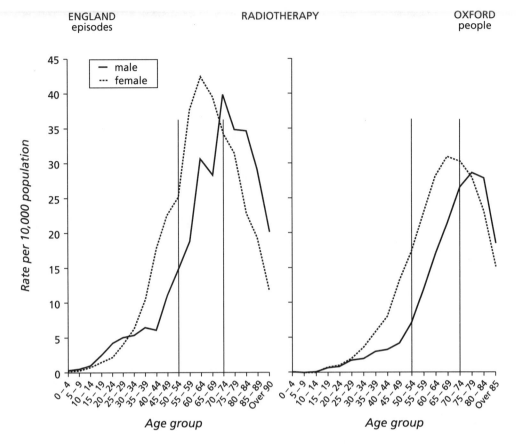

Figure 3.29
Age-specific hospital admission rates per 100,000 population in each age–sex group: first admissions to mental illness hospitals in England in 1976 and 1985.

Source: Mental Health Enquiry (England)

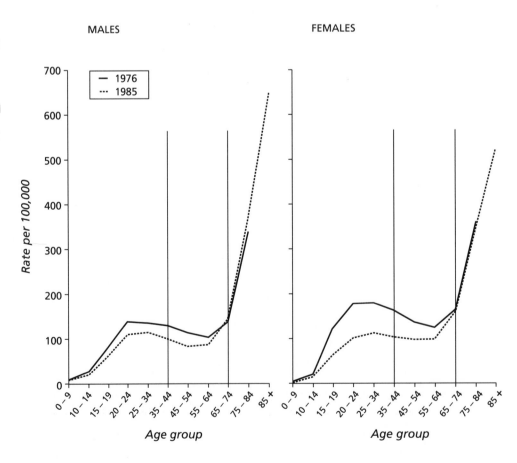

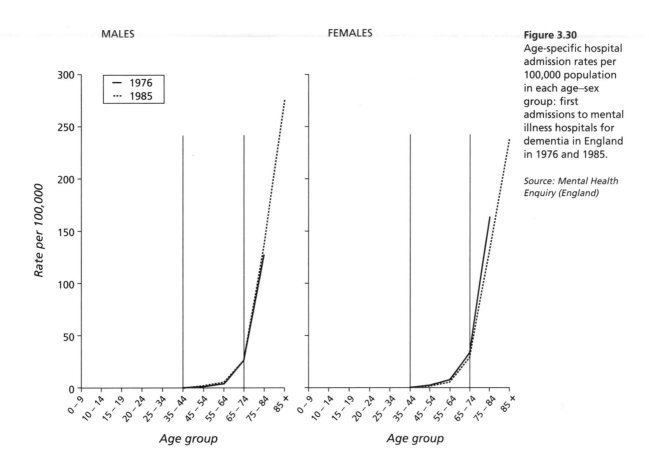

MALES   FEMALES

Figure 3.30
Age-specific hospital admission rates per 100,000 population in each age–sex group: first admissions to mental illness hospitals for dementia in England in 1976 and 1985.

Source: Mental Health Enquiry (England)

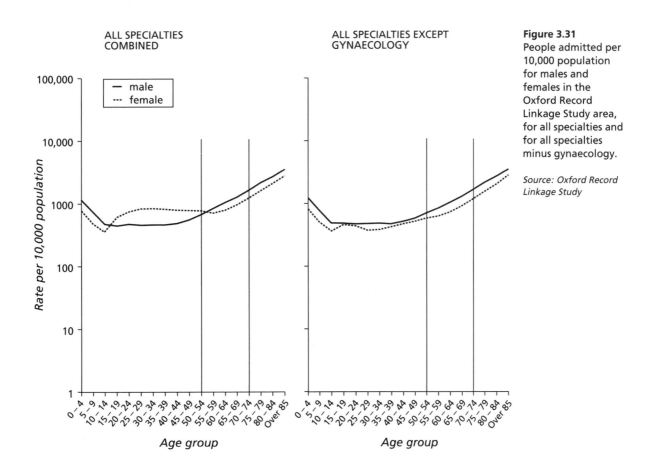

ALL SPECIALTIES COMBINED

ALL SPECIALTIES EXCEPT GYNAECOLOGY

Figure 3.31
People admitted per 10,000 population for males and females in the Oxford Record Linkage Study area, for all specialties and for all specialties minus gynaecology.

Source: Oxford Record Linkage Study

those for males. Thereafter, admission rates start to rise with increasing age, more so in males than in females, from the age of about 50 years in males and about 60 years in females.

A striking increase in admission rates with advancing age through the third age is seen in the specialties of general medicine (Figure 3.19), geriatrics (Figure 3.20), general surgery (Figure 3.21), trauma and orthopaedic surgery (Figure 3.22) and ophthalmology (Figure 3.23). Admissions in gynaecology decline through the third age (Figure 3.24); and there are no striking trends through the third age in admissions to the specialties of ear, nose and throat surgery (Figure 3.25), or dentistry and oral surgery (Figure 3.26). Admission rates rise and fall across the third age in rheumatology (Figure 3.27) and radiotherapy (Figure 3.28). First-ever admission rates to mental illness hospitals are shown in Figure 3.29, and first-ever admission rates to mental illness hospitals for pre-senile and senile dementia are shown in Figure 3.30. There is a small increase with age in admission rates for the latter but the data are otherwise unremarkable in their age distribution across the third age.

The data for hospital admission rates to all specialties, shown as rates in Figure 3.18, are plotted on a logarithmic scale in Figure 3.31. In effect, these depict the rate of increase in admission rates from each quinquennial age group to the next. The logarithmic transformation of the data shows that the rate of increase in admission rates after the age of about 50 years in males and 60 years in females is broadly constant from one quinquennial age group to the next. The second graph on Figure 3.31 also shows data for all specialties combined except that admissions to the specialty of gynaecology are excluded. This shows that the higher admission rates in females than males in adult life under the age of 50 years are wholly attributable to gynaecological admissions: when these are excluded, male admission rates tend to be a little higher than those in females throughout adult life. From the age of 50 years, the rate of increase in admission rates in males and females is similar.

The most common reasons for hospital admission in males and females aged 45–64 and 65–74 years are shown in Tables 3.11–3.14. Common reasons for hospital admission in males aged 45–64 years include repair of inguinal hernia, myocardial infarction and other ischaemic heart disease, prostatectomy, head injury, lung cancer, varicose veins, stroke and diabetes mellitus. The most common reasons for hospital admission in males aged 65–74 years include prostatectomy, myocardial infarction and other ischaemic heart disease, inguinal hernia, lung cancer, stroke, heart failure, bladder tumours and operations for cataract. The most common reasons for hospital admission in females aged 45–64 years include uterine dilatation and curettage, hysterectomy, operations on the breast, gallbladder disease, varicose veins and disorders of the back. The most common reasons for hospital admission in females aged 65–74 years include stroke, myocardial infarction and other ischaemic heart disease, breast cancer, hip arthroplasty, operations for cataract, heart failure, diabetes mellitus, hysterectomy, gallbladder disease and fractured neck of femur.

Patients' length of stay in hospital tends to increase with advancing age. The pattern of inpatient bed utilisation—conventionally expressed as the average number of beds occupied daily per million people—looks broadly similar in terms of age distribution to the patterns seen in episode-based and person-based admission rates except that the increase in utilisation rates with advancing age is more marked. Age-

Table 3.11

Males aged 45–64 years: some common reasons for hospital admission

Diagnosis/operation	ICD/OPCS code	Rate per 10,000 people
Inguinal hernia	D.550	42.7
Myocardial infarction	D.410	37.9
Other ischaemic heart disease	D.411–414	20.7
Prostatectomy	O.630–634	15.6
Intracranial injury	D.850–854	13.1
Lung cancer	D.162	12.2
Varicose veins	O.893–894	12.1
Stroke	D.431–434, 436	10.5
Diabetes mellitus	D.250	9.7
Haemorrhoids	D.455	8.9
Cholecystectomy	O.522	8.7
Bladder cancer	D.188	8.6
Duodenal ulcer	D.532	8.3
Disorders of urethra and urinary tract	D.599	7.8

Source: ORLS.

Table 3.12

Males aged 65–74 years: some common reasons for hospital admission

Diagnosis/operation	ICD/OPCS code	Rate per 10,000 people
Prostatectomy	O.630–634	83.1
Myocardial infarction	D.410	69.0
Inguinal hernia	D.550	63.1
Lung cancer	D.162	44.8
Stroke	D.431–434, 436	44.2
Heart failure	D.428	33.6
Bladder tumours	D.188	32.4
Operations on lens	O.170–179	27.4
Other ischaemic heart disease	D.411–414	26.4
Chronic airways obstruction	D.496	21.1
Hip arthroplasty	O.810	22.0
Diabetes mellitus	D.250	19.9
Chronic bronchitis	D.491	17.1
Disorders of urethra and urinary tract	D.599	16.8
Bronchopneumonia	D.485	16.1
Peripheral vascular disease	D.443	15.1
Intracranial injury	D.850–854	14.2
Cardiac dysrhythmias	D.427	14.1
Cholecystectomy	O.522	12.2

Source: ORLS.

and sex-specific bed utilisation rates are illustrated for all specialties combined and for the specialties of general medicine and general surgery in Figures 3.32–3.34.

Hospital admission rates have risen for many years in most age groups in most specialties. Data on the rise in admission rates in general medicine and general surgery in the third age are illustrated in Figure 3.35.

Table 3.13

Females aged 45–64 years: some common reasons for hospital admission

Diagnosis/operation	ICD/OPCS code	Rate per 10,000 people
Dilatation and curettage	O.703–704	72.1
Hysterectomy	O.690–696	41.8
Operations on breast	O.380–385	28.5
Gallbladder disease	D.574–575	17.8
Varicose veins	D.454	17.5
Disorders of back	D.724	11.2
Carpal tunnel syndrome	D.354	10.5
Rheumatoid arthritis	D.714	10.2
Colporrhaphy	O.710–713	10.6
Myocardial infarction	D.410	8.6
Diabetes mellitus	D.250	8.0
Hip arthroplasty	O.810	8.5

Source: ORLS.

Table 3.14

Females aged 65–74 years: some common reasons for hospital admission

Diagnosis/operation	ICD/OPCS code	Rate per 10,000 people
Stroke	D.431–434, 436	32.7
Myocardial infarction	D.410	30.7
Breast cancer	D.174	29.4
Hip arthroplasty	O.810	31.4
Operations on lens	O.170–179	30.2
Heart failure	D.428	20.8
Diabetes mellitus	D.250	20.1
Gallbladder disease	D.574–575	19.5
Hysterectomy	O.690–696	20.2
Fractured neck of femur	D.820	18.2
Dilatation and curettage	O.703–704	18.1
Other ischaemic heart disease	D.411–414	15.4
Rheumatoid arthritis	D.714	15.3
Social admissions	D.V60	14.7
Lung cancer	D.162	12.6

Source: ORLS.

Hospital outpatient care

There is an increasing gradient with age for attendances at hospital outpatient clinics and casualty departments (Table 3.15). However, the increase with age, before during and after the third age, is not as striking as that seen in either mortality rates or in hospital inpatient admission rates. There has been a gradual increase in outpatient attendance rates over time (Table 3.15). The increase is seen in the third age and, as with the increase in inpatient admission rates, in other age groups too.

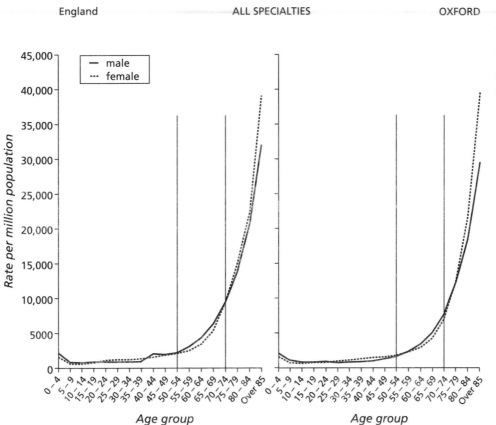

England ALL SPECIALTIES OXFORD

Figure 3.32
Average number of hospital beds used daily per million people in each age–sex group. All specialties.

Source: Hospital Inpatient Enquiry (England) and Oxford Record Linkage Study

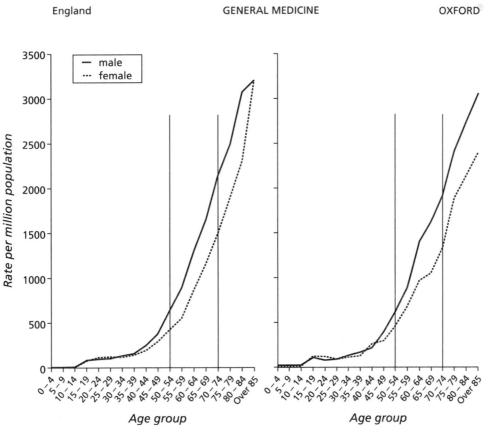

England GENERAL MEDICINE OXFORD

Figure 3.33
Average number of hospital beds used daily per million people in each age–sex group. General medicine.

Source: Hospital Inpatient Enquiry (England) and Oxford Record Linkage Study

Figure 3.34
Average number of hospital beds used daily per million people in each age–sex group. General surgery.

Source: Hospital Inpatient Enquiry (England) and Oxford Record Linkage Study

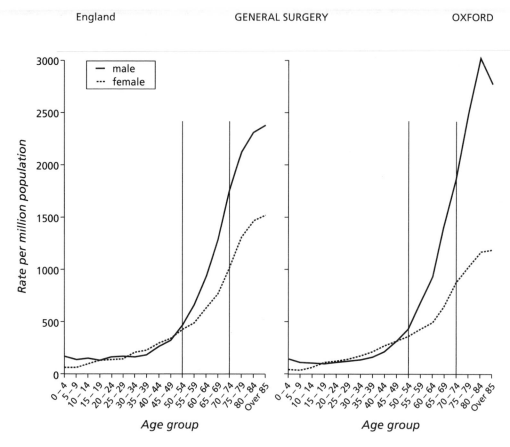

England GENERAL SURGERY OXFORD

Figure 3.35
Admission rates per 10,000 people by age group for general medicine and general surgery in six districts of the Oxford Region 1976–1986.

Source: Oxford Record Linkage Study

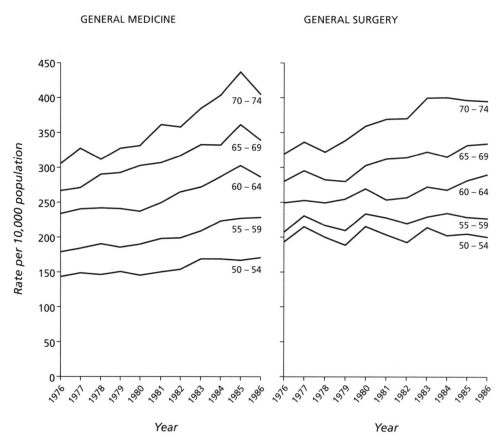

GENERAL MEDICINE GENERAL SURGERY

Table 3.15

Percentage of the population who reported attending an outpatient or casualty department in a 3 month period prior to interview in Great Britain, 1972–1989

	1972*	*1976*	*1979*	*1981*	*1983*	*1985*	*1987*	*1988*	*1989*
Males									
16–44	11	9	11	11	12	12	13	12	12
45–64	11	10	13	12	13	16	16	14	15
65–74	10	11	15	14	15	16	17	18	18
75 or over	10	11	13	14	19	15	21	21	16
Females									
16–44	9	8	12	11	11	12	13	12	13
45–64	11	11	13	13	15	15	16	16	17
65–74	12	11	16	16	18	17	18	17	19
75 or over	13	10	16	16	16	17	20	20	20

*1972 figures relate to England and Wales.

Source: General Household Survey, 1989.

General practice consultations

There is an increasing gradient with age for consultation rates with general practitioners (Figures 3.36, 3.37). As with outpatient attendances, the increase with age is not as striking as that seen in either mortality rates or hospital admission rates. The data on general practitioner consultation rates are subdivided into illnesses scored as trivial, intermediate and serious (Royal College of General Practitioners and OPCS, 1986). Serious illnesses are defined in morbidity statistics from general practice as 'those which at the time are invariably serious; those which invariably

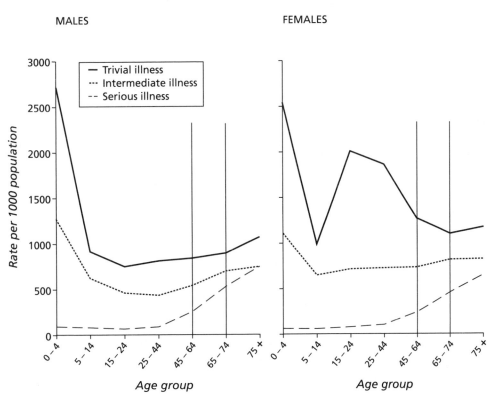

Figure 3.36
Episodes of illness resulting in general practitioner consultation expressed as age-specific rates per 1000 population in each age–sex group: England and Wales.

Source: Morbidity statistics from general practice: Third National Study 1981/82

Figure 3.37
Episodes of illness
resulting in general
practitioner
consultation
expressed as age-
specific rates per
1000 population in
each age–sex group:
England and Wales
comparing rates in
1971/72 with those in
1981/82.

*Source: Morbidity
statistics from general
practice: Second
National Study 1971/72;
Third National Study
1981/82*

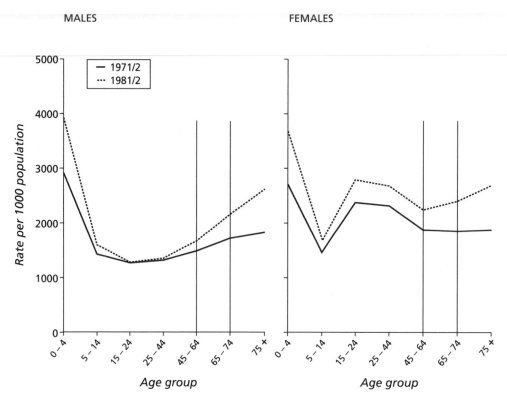

require surgical intervention; and those which carry a high probability of serious complications or significant recurring disability'. Intermediate diseases include 'those which, though often not serious, are usually brought to the attention of the general practitioner' and conditions which 'though sometimes potentially serious . . . span a wide range of severity'. Trivial diseases include 'illnesses commonly treated without recourse to medical advice and minor self-limiting illnesses which require no specific treatment'. The profile of consultations for serious illness looks broadly similar, in respect of age, to that seen in mortality and hospital inpatient admission statistics. General practitioner consultation rates for 'intermediate illnesses' show a very gradual rise with increasing age through the third age. Consultation rates for 'trivial illnesses' through the age range of the third age show a slight increase with increasing age in males and a decrease in females (although it is a decrease in females from a much higher baseline at younger ages than that in males). General practitioner consultation rates increased in most age–sex groups between the Second National Study in 1971/72 and the Third National Study in 1981/82 (Figure 3.37).

Self-reported illness

Information on self-reported ill health, recorded in the General Household Survey (OPCS[a]), defines chronic sickness in two ways. The first is long-standing illness, disability or infirmity; and the second is long-standing illness giving rise to limitation of activity.

The percentages of people who reported long-standing illness, and who reported limiting long-standing illness, are shown by age group and sex in Figures 3.38 and 3.39. The data show a gradual increase throughout adult life, and through the third

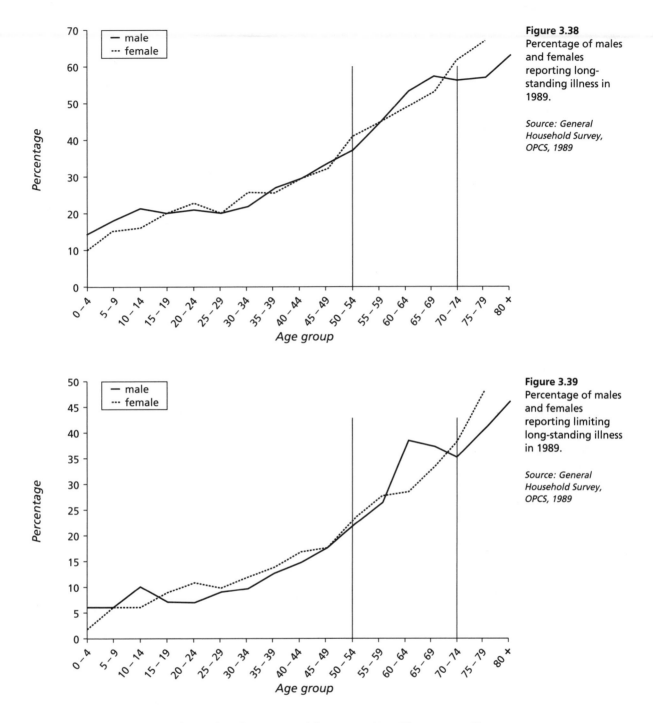

Figure 3.38
Percentage of males
and females
reporting long-
standing illness in
1989.

*Source: General
Household Survey,
OPCS, 1989*

Figure 3.39
Percentage of males
and females
reporting limiting
long-standing illness
in 1989.

*Source: General
Household Survey,
OPCS, 1989*

age, in the percentage of people who reported long-standing illness according to both definitions. As expected, the percentage of people who reported limiting long-standing illness was lower than those who reported long-standing illness without limitation of activity; but, in general, the overall patterns and trends with age were similar for both measures.

There has been a slight increase over time in the percentage of people reporting long-standing illness in most but not all age–sex groups (Figures 3.40, 3.41; Table 3.16).

The most common conditions which account for self-reported long-standing illnesses are tabulated in broad diagnostic groups in the General Household Survey (Table 3.17). In the third age the most common conditions are those relating to the

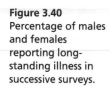

Figure 3.40
Percentage of males
and females
reporting long-
standing illness in
successive surveys.

*Source: General
Household Survey,
Great Britain*

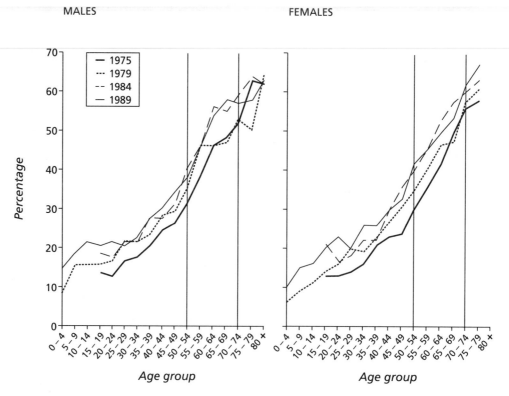

Figure 3.41
Percentage of males
and females
reporting limiting
long-standing illness
in successive surveys.

*Source: General
Household Survey,
Great Britain*

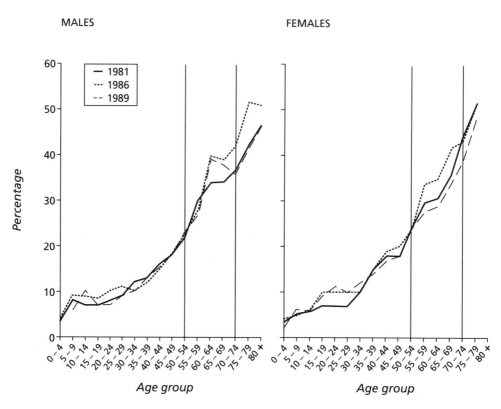

musculoskeletal system and the circulatory system, followed by respiratory, digestive and neurological conditions, and by visual and hearing problems.

The percentage of people who described their health as being less than 'reasonably healthy', ascertained in surveys in the Oxford region, is shown in Table 3.18. The data for the under 65s come from the Oxford Regional Health Authority's healthy

Table 3.16

Percentage of people in Great Britain who reported long-standing illness

	Percentage who reported								
	1972	*1976*	*1979*	*1981*	*1983*	*1985*	*1987*	*1988*	*1989*
Males									
16–44	14	17	21	22	23	21	25	25	24
45–64	29	37	39	40	44	42	45	44	42
65–74	48	52	50	51	58	55	60	59	58
75 or over	54	63	56	60	67	58	69	61	61
Females									
16–44	13	17	20	21	23	22	25	24	24
45–64	31	35	38	41	45	43	46	44	43
65–74	48	54	52	58	63	56	63	61	57
75 or over	65	68	64	70	70	65	73	71	70

Source: General Household Survey, 1989.

Table 3.17

Chronic sickness: people who reported long-standing illness by grouped condition, per 1000 people in each age–sex group

	Males		*Females*	
Conditions	*45–64*	*65–74*	*45–64*	*65–74*
XIII Musculoskeletal system	166	205	189	270
VII Heart and circulatory system	133	259	115	220
VIII Respiratory system	59	100	52	72
IX Digestive system	47	54	47	65
VI Nervous system	29	26	32	32
VI Eye complaints	20	49	16	50
VI Ear complaints	26	58	21	35

Source: General Household Survey.

Table 3.18

General health: percentage of people who described their health as less than 'reasonably healthy'

Years*	*% of each age group*
18–24	10
25–34	8
35–44	10
45–54	14
55–64	18

Years**	*% of each age group*
65–69	20
70–74	26
75–79	31
80–84	38
85+	49

* Source: ORHA, Healthy Lifestyle Survey.

** Source: ORHA, Health Survey of Elderly People.

Table 3.19

Walking about freely: percentages of people who reported that they remained 'fully active' in response to the question, 'Are you able to get about freely or do you have problems walking and moving about?'

Age	%
65–69	73
70–74	60
75–79	50
80–84	35
85+	20

Source: ORHA, Health Survey of Elderly People.

Table 3.20

Pain when walking: percentage of people who answered 'yes' to the question, 'Are you in pain when you walk about?'

Age	%
65–69	20
70–74	29
75–79	30
80–84	36
85+	44

Source: ORHA, Health Survey of Elderly People.

Table 3.21

Hearing: percentage of people who reported difficulty with hearing

Age	%
65–69	24
70–74	27
75–79	36
80–84	44
85+	58

Source: General Household Survey, 1985.

lifestyle survey; and those for people aged 65 years and over are from the region's health survey of elderly people. The percentage of people who described their health as less than 'reasonably healthy' increased from 10% of people aged 35–44 years, to 20% of people aged 65–69 years, to 31% of people aged 75–79 years.

The percentage of people who reported that they are able to walk about freely and unaided declined from 73% at age 65–69 years to 50% at age 75–79 years (Table 3.19). Those who reported that they experienced pain when walking increased from 20% at age 65–69 to 30% at age 75–79 years (Table 3.20). The percentage who reported difficulty with hearing rose from 24% at age 65–69 years to 36% at age 75–79 years (Table 3.21); and the percentage who reported difficulty with eyesight rose from 17% at age 65–69 years to 26% at 75–79 years (Table 3.22).

Table 3.22

Eyesight: percentage of people who reported difficulty with eyesight when asked 'whether they had difficulty reading with or without glasses'

Age	%
65–69	17
70–74	22
75–79	26
80–84	36
85+	52

Source: General Household Survey, 1985.

Trends in mortality and morbidity: synopsis and interpretation

Mortality rates have declined over time within each quinquennial age group for both sexes. In detail, there has been some inconstancy in the declines which make specific projections difficult. However, in general terms it is safe to predict that mortality rates in the third age will continue to decline. The favourable age-specific mortality rates in recent generations which have not yet reached the third age suggest that, when they do reach this age, their mortality experience will be lower than that of present and preceding generations.

The decline in age-specific mortality has not been accompanied by a decline in health-care utilisation rates. Indeed, these have increased. The use of health services depends not only on levels of ill health but also on levels of provision of services, advances in treatment and care, expectations of individuals for their own health, individuals' thresholds for self-referral, and professional thresholds for referral and use of specialist care. It is therefore difficult, from morbidity statistics based on health-care utilisation alone, to interpret trends over time in utilisation as a reflection of trends in levels of morbidity. In similar ways, self-reported illness may reflect not only absolute levels of morbidity but also individuals' expectations about their health and about the services which may be available to improve it.

Increases over time have occurred across most age groups in hospital admission rates, outpatient attendance rates, general practitioner consultation rates and (to a lesser extent) in self-reported illness. The generality of the increases across age groups suggests that the increases in the third age are unlikely to be wholly or substantially attributable to an increase in residual morbidity as a result of the decline in mortality in the third age. However, more refined data are required than those available from routine vital and health-care statistics to determine whether there is, in fact, any important such effect in this age group.

References

Office of Population Censuses and Surveys. *Classification of surgical operations*, third revision. Office of Population Censuses and Surveys, London, 1975.

Office of Population Censuses and Surveys[a]. *General houshold survey.* HMSO, London, annual.

Office of Population Censuses and Surveys[b]. *Hospital inpatient enquiry.* HMSO, London, annual until 1985.

Office of Population Censuses and Surveys[c]. Series DH1. *Mortality statistics: general.* HMSO, London, annual.

Royal College of General Practitioners and Office of Population Censuses and Surveys. *Morbidity statistics from general practice 1981–1982: Third National Study.* HMSO, London, 1986.

World Health Organisation. *International Classification of Diseases*, ninth revision. World Health Organisation, Geneva, 1977.

Active life expectancy and disability

Malcolm Hodkinson

Prevalence and causes of disability

The most thorough study of the prevalence and causes of disability in the UK has been the OPCS disability survey (Martin *et al.*, 1988, 1991). They used a complex and sophisticated scheme which graded disability from 1 (least) to 10 (most) and their prevalence rates for these disability levels in the third age are shown in Table 4.1. Determination of causes was difficult because of the nature of their survey and because of the complexity of patterns, but diagnoses which occurred in 5% or more of disabled adults are listed in Table 4.2.

Table 4.1

Estimated prevalence of disability as cumulative rates per thousand by disability grade for the age groups 50–59, 60–69 and 70–79

Disability grade	50–59	60–69	70–79
10	2	4	11
9–10	7	16	32
8–10	14	27	57
7–10	22	42	87
6–10	32	57	125
5–10	48	84	169
4–10	64	112	215
3–10	83	143	267
2–10	101	184	332
1–10	133	240	408

Source: Martin et al., *1988.*

Table 4.2

Main causes of disability in adults (percentage prevalence in those disabled), England and Wales

	Percent
Deafness	32
Arthritis	31
Ischaemic heart disease	8
Chronic bronchitis	6
Back problems	6
Depression	5
Stroke	5
Cataract	5

Source: Martin et al., *1988.*

The relationship between mortality and morbidity

One of the major phenomena of this century has been the marked increase in life expectation seen in almost all countries. Most striking have been the improvements in life expectation at birth but in the last decade there have also been substantial gains in expectations even in the highest age groups in many developed countries. However, though the gains in years of life have been clear, there has been controversy as to whether the extra years would be bought at the cost of prolongation of chronic disease and dependency and that there might, indeed, be no gains in the period of active life. Opposing views have been put forward, for example by Fries (1980), taking a highly optimistic standpoint, and Gruenberg (1977) a very pessimistic one. Fries' arguments have been shown to be seriously flawed (Manton, 1982; Schneider and Brody, 1983) and his prediction that life expectation at higher ages would show no further improvement has certainly proved wrong. The more recent literature has generally taken a more pessimistic view. The evidence from a number of studies which have attempted to determine changes in morbidity is somewhat confused but has tended to support the pessimistic view.

Active life expectancy

This has been the general context for the development of measures of an active life expectancy (ALE) or expectation of life without disability (ELWD). They have the potential to demonstrate whether the optimistic or pessimistic views are correct, allow comparisons across countries as well as across time which allow for differences in age composition of the populations and have the potential to be interpreted for individuals. Clearly they could have a useful role in health care planning and monitoring whilst, if their capacity for individual interpretation could be developed, would be of obvious utility in such areas as personal insurance against disability.

Criteria for transition

However, because of this interest in dependency rather than quality of life, some disabilities, for example visual or hearing impairment, are difficult to take into criteria for ALE studies, though they are clearly of great importance to individuals. Despite their inherent attractions, therefore, it seems unlikely that quality of life measurements will provide the right sort of criteria for ALE studies. Similarly scores based on the aggregate of diagnosed impairments and medical conditions in the individual are inappropriate. The most suitable criteria must therefore be based on functional criteria. Many studies have thus used criteria based on the concept of limiting long-term illness (Bebbington, 1988, 1991; Grundy, 1987; Robine et al., 1986; Wilkins and Adams, 1983), particularly in more recent years. However, we should take particular note of the study by Crimmins et al. (1989) who used two different functional criteria, one of disability-free life and one of bed disability/institutionalisation and found that results for change of health with time were quite different for the two criteria. This serves to warn us that results of ALE studies may be very sensitive to alterations in criteria.

Cut-off points must always be an arbitrary matter and there is thus considerable potential value in methods which attempt to grade the continuum of disability such as the sophisticated study of Martin *et al.* (1988). Unfortunately criteria have often been dictated by the fact that determination of ALE was not the primary aim of studies, rather that the data had to be adapted to this secondary purpose. Better criteria can thus only be expected to emerge in studies specifically designed to investigate ALE and are likely to rely on the activities of daily living (ADL) approach, perhaps with special emphasis on instrumental ADL (i.e. such ability as use of a telephone).

Technical issues

Most studies have had to use cross-sectional data and all too often the institutionalised population has been excluded so that broad assumptions have had to be made about the dependency of these individuals who make up an increasing proportion of the disabled at higher ages. Higher ages have often been inadequately sampled. Age groupings are often too broad and this may distort findings quite seriously in the oldest open-ended group. Myers (1989), in his excellent critique of methodology, points out that appropriate analytical techniques have not always been used in published studies.

Serial cross-sectional studies are confounded by cohort differences and these can be substantial as shown by the Goteborg studies (Mellstrom *et al.*, 1981, 1982; Svanborg, 1988a,b). Their analysis is forced to make two basic assumptions, that disability is irreversible and that mortality is the same in the disabled and the non-disabled; both these assumptions are clearly incorrect. The importance of reversibility is most elegantly demonstrated by Manton (1988) who showed that, even at high levels of impairment, there were significant proportions in the community who appeared to have long-term improvements in function. Indeed it is self-evident that disability is reversible if we consider such examples as successful joint replacement in osteoarthritis of the hip.

Similarly, correlations of disability with mortality have been found in many studies and their magnitude may be such that rates for that disability actually fall at the highest ages, for example the falls in the prevalence of hypertension and of respiratory impairment at higher ages found by Cox *et al.* (1987).

As reported figures for ALE from such studies look at the expectations of all subjects, including those already disabled, they seriously underestimate ALE for those who are disability free, particularly for higher ages where initial prevalence of disability is higher. However, as mortality differences between those with and without disability are not known, attempts to estimate ALE for the non-disabled will lead to overestimation given the higher mortality of the disabled and the possibility that some disabled subjects have moved to the non-disabled category at follow-up. Only longitudinal studies can overcome these problems but such studies of adequate size have yet to be reported.

When major longitudinal studies are undertaken it will be important to avoid excessive loss of individuals at follow-up and the sampling frame must ensure that the institutionalised are fully sampled. Good quality longitudinal studies will clearly be very expensive. It is also desirable that future studies make allowance for reversibility and differential mortality in their analysis, using for example the multistate analysis of ALE advocated by Rogers *et al.* (1989).

Reported values for ALE

Females have life expectancy advantages over males at all ages and this is also true for ALE. However, the proportion of life expectancy which represents active life is greater for males. This may be a consequence of the survival advantage of women. Manton (1988) found no sex differences in the risks of becoming disabled, although other studies have found greater incidence rates of dependency in women in later life (Jagger *et al.*, 1993). Social class differences for ALE appear to be larger than the sex differences. Robine and Ritchie (1991) have shown for pooled international data that if the top and bottom social quintiles are compared, the differences for life expectation and ALE for men are 6.3 and 14.3 years, and for women 2.8 and 7.6 years, respectively.

Table 4.3 shows reported values from a number of studies showing the close similarity of estimates from different developed countries. Table 4.4 shows more detailed findings for Great Britain.

Changes in ALE with time

There have been a number of reports of changes of life expectancy and ALE or prevalences of disability with time (e.g. Bebbington, 1988, 1991; Colvez and Blanchet, 1981; Crimmins *et al.*, 1989; Verbrugge, 1984; Wilkins and Adams, 1983). Of particular interest is whether the findings support the optimistic or pessimistic view as to whether the gain in years is or is not at the price of a relative increase in the proportion of life in the disabled state. The findings have generally been pessimistic. Two examples of results are shown in Table 4.5. The study of Crimmins *et al.* (1989) is unusual in that it reports change for a more severe degree of disability, bed

Table 4.3

International comparisons of years life expectation (EL) and EL without disability (ELWD) at birth and age 65

| | | At birth | | At age 65 | |
		EL	ELWD	EL	ELWD
Quebec 1980	M	70.3	59.0	13.9	7.9
	F	78.2	60.2	18.5	8.5
Canada 1978	M	70.8	59.2	14.4	8.2
	F	78.4	62.8	18.7	9.9
France 1982	M	70.7	61.8	14.3	9.1
	F	78.9	67.1	18.5	9.9
England and Wales 1981	M	71.1	58.5	13.1	7.7
	F	76.1	60.6	16.6	8.1

Source: Bebbington, 1988.

disability or long-term institutionalisation, as opposed to the Bebbington study (1991) which, like a number of others deals with limiting longstanding illness.

Problems of interpretation

Many authors have drawn attention to factors which might complicate interpretation of these changes. The central problem is that studies generally rely on the individual's perceptions of his own health status. Such perceptions can be shown to be very complex as elegantly expounded by Blaxter (1990). These perceptions can be shown to differ materially between various categories. Thus there are clear sex, age and social class differences whilst other lifestyle variables such as education, occupation, unemployed status and prosperity are also relevant. Katz *et al.* (1983) have, for example, shown marked ALE differences between the poor and the well off. Other

Table 4.4

Years of life expectancy at ages 45 and 65 for males and females, England and Wales 1976–1988

		1976	1981	1985	1988
Male 45	EL	28.0	28.7	29.4	29.8
	ELWD	19.2	19.7	19.9	19.8
Female 45	EL	33.4	34.1	34.4	34.8
	ELWD	22.0	21.6	22.3	22.0
Male 65	EL	12.5	13.1	13.4	13.7
	ELWD	7.1	7.9	7.9	7.6
Female 65	EL	16.6	17.1	17.3	17.6
	ELWD	8.6	8.5	9.2	8.8

Source: Bebbington, 1991.

Table 4.5

Changes in years ELWD and expectation of life (EL) at birth and at age 65

Study	Category		1970 ELWD	1970 EL	1980 ELWD	1980 EL	Proportion active of gain in EL
Crimmins *et al.*, 1989	Male	0	65.5	67.0	68.4	70.1	94%
(USA)	Female	0	72.1	74.6	74.6	77.6	83%
(bed disability)	Male	65	12.1	13.0	13.2	14.2	83%
	Female	65	15.1	16.8	16.3	18.4	75%

Study	Category		1976 ELWD	1976 EL	1988 ELWD	1988 EL	Proportion active of gain in EL
Bebbington, 1991	Male	0	58.2	70.0	58.5	72.4	13%
(England and Wales)	Female	0	61.7	76.1	61.2	78.1	−25%
(limiting disability)	Male	65	6.9	12.5	7.6	13.7	58%
	Female	65	8.2	16.6	8.8	17.6	60%

writers such as Verbrugge (1984) have considered the impact of changes over time in such things as sickness and disability benefits and diagnostic practice. Clearly, better benefits might be expected to make individuals more willing to accept that they are sick or disabled rather than healthy, whilst increasing medical diagnosis of such asymptomatic conditions as hypertension and the increasing likelihood that minor long-term illnesses will receive medication means that individuals may be less likely to regard themselves as healthy than they would have been in the past. As Colvez and Blanchet (1981) remarked 'the better informed people are, the more limitations they describe'.

The pessimistic findings seem more likely to be due to such changes in expectations and self-reporting of health status than to any real deterioration in health experience over time. This interpretation is supported by the finding that disability rates appear to have risen across all age groups, whilst according to the postulations of opponents of Fries (1980), deterioration ought to be mainly confined to the older age groups where 'survival of the unfittest' would have the greatest impact. Indeed, as we can see from Table 4.5, there appear to have been quite substantial gains in ALE in high age groups, these gains forming a higher percentage of the increase in total life expectation at 65 than at birth! This strongly suggests that changing perceptions in younger age groups, so that individuals are now more likely to think of themselves as having a limiting disability, are mainly responsible for the disappointing results for ALE at birth. This interpretation gains support from the very different findings in the Crimmins study (Table 4.5) which found similar high percentages of the gained years were non-disabled when the more stringent and perhaps more objective criterion of bed disability was used. Clearly we are not seeing the compression of morbidity which Fries hoped for but neither is there clear evidence that longer life is exacting a high price in terms of increased morbidity.

The balance of evidence would appear to show that most of the years of life gained are without major disability, though there would appear to be a genuine though minor increase in the total expected periods of disability. Gains in the length of the third age thus appear to have been considerably greater than those of the fourth over the last 10 or 15 years in the developed countries and it seems reasonable to anticipate the continuation of these trends.

The future situation in the third age

Expectation of life

Consistent falls in mortality rates in all age groups including the elderly have been reported from many developed countries. In England and Wales for the period 1968–85 (OPCS Mortality Statistics Surveillance, 1991), mortality rates for ages 50–75 fell by an average of 0.9% per year in women and 1.3% per year in men over this period. This underlies the rising expectations of life already shown in Tables 4.3 and 4.4.

It seems reasonable to expect these consistent trends to be maintained at least in the short and medium term. Projection from this OPCS data leads to estimates of survival to age 75 from 50 of 74% for women and 59% for men in the year 2000, representing gains of 10% and 28% respectively on expectations in 1975.

Disability

Trends for disability, as already discussed, are far less clear cut. Many social, attitudinal, environmental and medical changes may influence disability rate favourably or adversely and can be broadly expected to cancel out. Recent estimates of disability rates are therefore the best estimated for the medium term future. The most recent detailed data for England and Wales is the OPCS disability survey [11] which graded disability on a scale 1–10. Estimates taking OPCS data for any disability and combining these with survival data estimated for the year 2000 shown in Table 4.6 lead to the estimates for disability-free survival shown in Table 4.7. The estimate is that a non-disabled man of 50 would have a 39% chance of surviving in the non-disabled state to the age of 75 whilst a woman would have a 49% chance.

Table 4.6

Estimated survival from the age of fifty for females and males in the year 2000

| Age | Percentage survival | |
	Females	Males
55	98.3	97.8
60	94.5	91.7
65	88.6	82.1
70	81.2	70.1
75	72.7	57.2

Table 4.7

Estimated survival without disability from a non-disabled state at the age of fifty for females and males in the year 2000

| Age | Percentage survival without disability | |
	Females	Males
55	95.0	94.6
60	87.0	84.5
65	76.3	70.7
70	63.4	54.8
75	49.0	38.5

References

Bebbington AC. The expectation of life without disability in England and Wales. *Soc Sci Med*, 1988; 27: 321–326.

Bebbington AC. The expectation of life without disability in England and Wales; 1976–88. *Population Trends*, 1991; 66: 26–29.

Blaxter M. *Health and lifestyles*. Tavistock Routledge, London, 1990.

Colvez A, Blanchet M. Disability trends in the United States population 1966–76: analysis of reported causes. *Am J Public Health*, 1981; 71: 464–471.

Colvez A, Blanchet M. Potential gains in life expectancy free of disability: a tool for health planning. *Int J Epidemiol*, 1983; 12: 224–229.

Cox BD, Blaxter M, Buckle ALJ *et al*. *The health and lifestyle survey*. Health Promotion Trust, London, 1987.

Crimmins EM, Saito Y, Ingegneri D. Changes in life expectancy and disability-free life expectancy in the United States. *Population & Development Review*, 1989; 15: 235–267.

Department of Health. *On the state of the public health for the year 1990*. HMSO, London, 1991.

Fries J. Aging, natural death and the compression of morbidity. *New Engl J Med*, 1980; 303: 130–135.

Gruenberg EM. The failures of success. *Millbank Mem Fund Q*, 1977; 55: 3–24.

Grundy E. Future patterns of morbidity in old age. In Caird FI, Evans JG (eds). *Advanced Geriatric Medicine*, 1987; 6: 53–72.

Jagger C, Spiers NA, Clarke M. Factors associated with decline in function, institutionalization and mortality of elderly people. *Age Ageing*, 1993; 22: 190–197.

Katz S, Branch LG, Branson MH *et al.* Active life expectancy. *New Engl J Med*, 1983; 309: 1218–1224.

Manton KG. Changing concepts of morbidity and mortality in the elderly population. *Millbank Mem Fund Q*, 1982; 60: 183–244.

Manton KG. A longitudinal study of functional change and mortality in the United States. *J Gerontol*, 1988; 43: S153–S161.

Martin J, Meltzer H, Elliot D. OPCS surveys of disability in Great Britain, Report 1, *The prevalence of disability among adults*. HMSO, London, 1988.

Martin J, White A, Meltzer, H. OPCS surveys of disability in Great Britain, Report 4, *Disabled adults: services transport and employment*. HMSO, London, 1991.

Mellstrom D, Rundgren A, Jagenburg R, Steen B, Svanborg A. Tobacco smoking, ageing and health among the elderly: a longitudinal study of 70-year-old men and age cohort comparison. *Age Ageing*, 1982; 11: 45–58.

Mellstrom D, Rundgren A, Svanborg A. Previous alcohol consumption and its consequences for ageing, morbidity and mortality in men 70–75. *Age Ageing*, 1981; 10: 277–286.

Myers GC. Mortality and health dynamic at older ages. In Ruzicka L, Wunsch G, Kane P (eds), *Differential mortality—methodological issues and biosocial factors*, pp. 189–214. Clarendon Press, Oxford, 1989.

OPCS. Series DH1 No. 22, *Mortality Statistics Surveillance 1968–1985*. HMSO, London, 1991.

Palmore EB. Trends in the health of the aged. *Gerontologist*, 1986; 26: 298–302.

Robine JM, Colvez A, Bucquet D *et al.* L'espérance de vie sans incapacité en France en 1982. *Population (Paris)*, 1986; 41: 1025–1042.

Robine JM, Ritchie K. Healthy life expectancy: evaluation of global indicator of change in population health. *Br Med J*, 1991; 302: 457–460.

Rogers A, Rogers RG, Branch LG. A multistate analysis of active life expectancy. *Public Health Reports*, 1989; 104: 222–226.

Schneider E, Brody J. Aging, natural death and the compression of morbidity: another view. *New Engl J Med*, 1983; 309: 854–856.

Svanborg A. Cohort differences in the Goteborg studies of Swedish 70-year-olds. In Brody JA, Maddox GL (eds), *Aging—an international perspective*, pp. 27–35. Springer Publishing Co, New York, 1988a.

Svanborg A. The health of the elderly population: results from longitudinal studies with age cohort comparisons. In *Research and the ageing population—Ciba Foundation Symposium 134*, pp. 3–16. Wiley, Chichester, 1988b.

Verbrugge LM. Long life but worsening health? Trends in health and mortality of middle aged and older persons. *Millbank Mem Fund Q*, 1984; 62: 475–519.

Wilkins R, Adams OB. Health expectancy in Canada, late 1970s: demographic, regional and social dimensions. *Am J Public Health*, 1983; 73: 1073–1080.

Ischaemic heart disease

5

Malcolm Hodkinson

Ischaemic heart disease (IHD) is one of the major causes of death and of morbidity in the third age in developed countries. In the UK some 300,000 individuals suffer an acute myocardial infarction each year (Royal College of Physicians, 1992) and some 30% of all male deaths and 22% of female deaths are attributable to IHD (Marmot and Mann, 1987). In England and Wales IHD is the commonest cause of death in men in all age groups beyond 35 and second only to cancer in women. It is estimated to account for almost half of all life years lost by death before 65 in men whilst circulatory disease, to which IHD is the major contributor, accounts for a quarter of days of certified incapacity in men (Royal College of Physicians, 1992). The high prevalence rates for Scotland are reported by Smith *et al.* (1990).

Differences in IHD rates

The whole of the UK has high rates for IHD, worst in Northern Ireland, intermediate in Scotland and best in England and Wales. However these differences are less striking than the differences between overall UK rates and those of other developed countries which are generally lower, strikingly so in some instances such as Japan where they are lower by an order of magnitude (Figure 1).

Not only are there considerable differences between rates for IHD in different countries but rates have shown considerable changes with time. Encouragingly, rates have fallen appreciably in some countries in recent years, for example in the USA, Canada and Australia. The position in the UK has lagged behind these

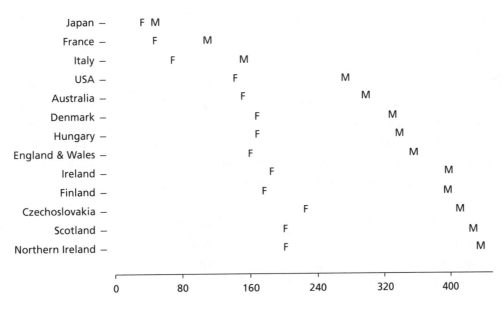

Figure 5.1
IHD mortality rates per 100,000 population all ages 1986 for men and women.

Source: Royal College of Physicians, 1992.

changes but there are strong reasons for optimism that we are now entering a similar phase of improvement. This will be examined in more detail later.

These findings of international and temporal changes in IHD rates support the view that environmental factors play a strong part in the development of IHD. The very detailed epidemiological studies of IHD have allowed these risk factors to be identified. These are reviewed in greater detail by Marmot and Mann (1987) but the important findings for risk factors which can be modified will be summarised here.

Risk factors

Smoking

Certainly in the UK smoking is known to be a major risk factor for IHD. This was powerfully demonstrated by the classical studies of Doll and Peto (1976) and Doll *et al.* (1980) and confirmed by many others. Risk is related to the number of cigarettes smoked and, as is also the case for all potentially reversible risk factors, the relative risks are greatest at younger ages. Thus Doll and Peto (1976) found the relative risk for death from IHD in male doctors smoking 25 or more cigarettes a day as compared with their non-smoking counterparts to be 15 for those under 45, 2.2 for those aged 45–54, 1.6 for those 55–64 and 1.5 for those 65–74. However, in countries such as Japan where other risk factors are favourable and IHD rates are low, smoking appears not to be a risk factor for IHD. Smoking appears to be particularly dangerous when serum cholesterol is high. Risk of IHD falls over subsequent years after cessation of smoking (Doll and Peto, 1976).

Blood pressure

Many studies from a number of countries have shown higher blood pressure to be consistently associated with higher IHD risk (see Marmot and Mann, 1987). There does not appear to be a threshold level for the effect, rather risk appears to rise with blood pressure across the whole range (McMahon *et al.*, 1990). Again the risks associated with blood pressure appear to be influenced by levels of cholesterol, seeming to have little effect on IHD risk in Japan, for example, where levels are low.

Lipids

IHD is uncommon in communities where serum cholesterol levels are low even when risk factors such as smoking or high blood pressure are present. Good correlations between individuals' serum cholesterol values and subsequent IHD mortality have been shown by many studies and more recent work, where fractionation of serum lipids has been performed, shows that the low density lipoprotein fraction (LDL) is associated with bad prognosis whereas high density lipoprotein (HDL) is protective. HDL and LDL levels are influenced by dietary fat intakes. The 'typical western diet' of countries such as the UK which is high in saturated fat and low in polyunsaturated fat is associated with high IHD rates and high cholesterol values. Conversely, countries with high polyunsaturate/saturate ratios in the national diet have low IHD rates and low cholesterol values.

Coagulation factors

Blood levels of the clotting factors fibrinogen and Factor VII have been shown to be predictive of IHD levels, high levels being deleterious (Meade *et al.*, 1980).

Physical exercise

Physical exercise has been shown to have a protective effect against IHD. Moderate exercise levels appear adequate to give full protection, indeed very vigorous exercise may increase risk (Shaper andWannamethee, 1991).

Early life experience and socioeconomic factors

There is an apparent paradox in that, although the rise in IHD in the UK this century has been associated with increasing prosperity, mortality rates are now highest in the least affluent areas. The rates decrease with higher social class and current trends show rates to be falling in upper social classes but to be stationary or rising in the lower ones, contributing to an increasing social class differential in overall mortality (Marmot and McDowall, 1986). These differences can partly be accounted for by the effects of smoking, for there have been bigger falls in the higher classes.

Kaplan and Salonen (1990) have shown that poor socioeconomic state in childhood was associated with IHD in middle life for men in Finland. However, Barker and Osmond (1986) showed that the rates of IHD in the 212 local authority areas in England and Wales correlated with infant mortality rates 50 years earlier. This suggested that poor nutrition in early life might be an important risk factor for IHD. They have explored this hypothesis in a series of further studies which have been recently reviewed (Barker and Martyn, 1992). In a follow-up study of Hertfordshire men born 1911–30 they showed that men with the lowest weights at birth and one year had the highest death rates for IHD, though these weights were independent of social class in the men who died (Barker *et al.*, 1989).

The group have looked for possible mechanisms for such effects. They have found that blood pressure at age four is predicted from measures of foetal growth, namely birth weight, ponderal index at birth and the ratio of head circumference to length at birth (Law *et al.*, 1991). They have been able to correlate the serum risk factors, cholesterol, fibrinogen and Factor VII with measures of early growth and nutrition (Fall *et al.*, 1992; Barker *et al.*, 1992), and also glucose tolerance, diabetes being a known risk factor for IHD (Hales *et al.*, 1991). These risk factor effects appeared to be independent of social class and to remain after allowance for other factors such as smoking. The interpretation of the Barker group is that the relation between retarded growth in early life and adult risk of IHD is due to long-term effects on physiology and metabolism from adverse circumstances at specific critical periods of development (Barker and Martyn, 1992). This hypothesis has provoked challenges but is now supported by an impressive weight of evidence which has largely answered the criticisms (Robinson, 1992). The term 'programming' has been used in this context with the implication that IHD is in some way an inevitable consequence of early life experience. Biologically it is more plausible that the effect of early deprivation is to sensitise the individual to the effects of subsequent affluent lifestyle and thus to define a population group for whom the avoidance of lifestyle risk factors such as smoking and high saturated fat diet is particularly important (Grimley Evans, 1993).

Trends in IHD mortality rates in the UK

This country has seen major changes in IHD mortality rates during this century. Earlier in the century, the disease was associated with higher social class. However as mortality rates rose, the social class association changed so that in more recent years rates are higher in lower social classes (Marmot and McDowall, 1986). Age-specific mortality rates rose progressively but appear to have peaked and now be falling. This effect is well seen in younger age groups as shown for men and women in England and Wales in Figures 2 and 3. Indeed, if all adult age categories are examined, there appears to be a definite cohort effect with improvements in mortality occurring earliest in later cohorts (Osmond and Barker, 1991).

Reasons for changes in mortality rates

The improvements in the UK can certainly be related to changes in cigarette smoking, the differences between social classes being largely explained by differences in smoking, higher groups having reduced their smoking far more than the lower ones. However this is unlikely to be the sole explanation. The findings of the Barker group also seem important, particularly if one accepts their further suggestion that the combination of poor nutrition in childhood coupled with an affluent nutritional pattern in middle life is particularly deleterious. This would fit with the observed changes where IHD appeared first as a disease of the higher social classes but subsequently changed to one of lower social classes and that later cohorts have shown the most striking decreases in IHD mortality.

It is not likely that preventive medical treatment has had any impact so far as this has been on a very small scale, whilst improvements in treatment of existing cases to date are likely to have had only marginal effects, delaying deaths from IHD rather than preventing them.

Possibilities for prevention

Given that a number of risk factors for IHD have been clearly recognised and are potentially modifiable, for example smoking, high cholesterol values, high blood pressure and lack of exercise, the scope for prevention seems clear. However, experience to date has been disappointing where community based programmes of risk factor intervention have been undertaken (see reviews by Marmot and Mann, 1987; Royal College of Physicians, 1992; Oliver, 1992). A number of reasons have been offered for the failure of most of these planned intervention trials to demonstrate benefits despite the strong circumstantial evidence, for example of Doll and Peto (1976) as to the benefits of cessation of smoking.

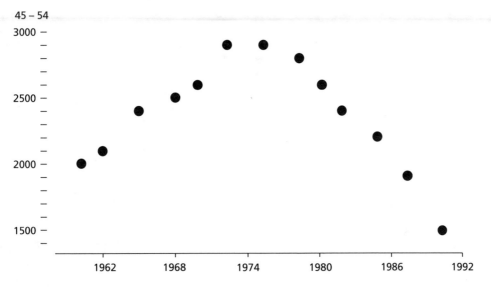

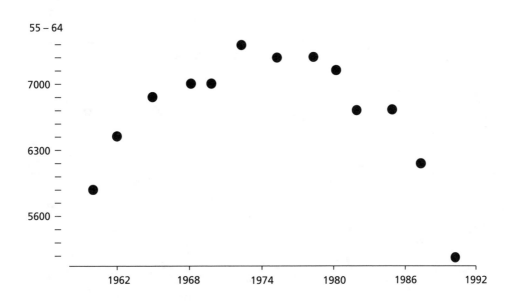

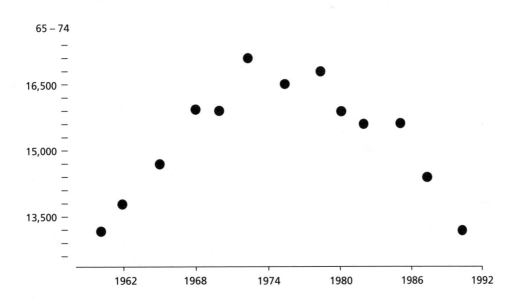

Figure 5.2
Mortality rates per million for IHD for males, England and Wales.
Age groups 45–54, 55–64 and 65–74.

Sources: Registrar General's Statistical Reports; OPCS, 1991.

Figure 5.3
Mortality rates per
million for IHD for
females, England
and Wales.
Age groups 45–54,
55–64 and 65–74.

*Sources: Registrar
General's Statistical
Reports; OPCS, 1991.*

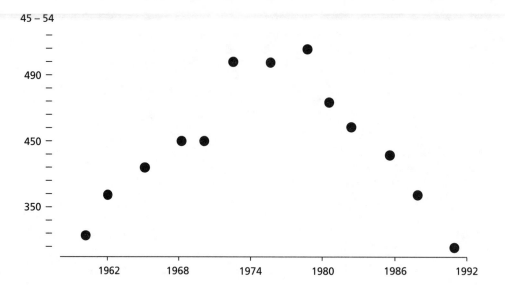

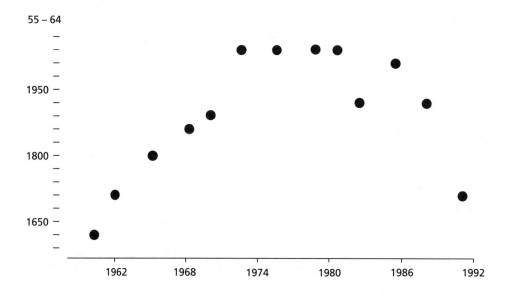

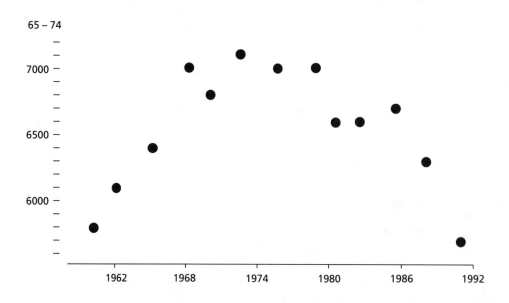

The following have been identified as problems in these trials:

1) There is a problem of 'contamination' of the control groups. Most trials occur in countries where the trial participants have considerable knowledge as to risk factors so that behaviour changes in both intervention and control groups, considerably weakening the power of the trial.

2) Drugs used to treat high blood pressure may have deleterious side effects on other risk factors; some for example increase lipid levels or have an adverse effect on glucose tolerance.

3) Early drugs used to treat hyperlipidaemias may have had adverse effects, increasing non-cardiac deaths so that whilst there may be a reduction of cardiac deaths the effect on total mortality was not significant. Smith and Pekkanen (1992) indeed ask if there should not be a moratorium on the use of cholesterol lowering drugs. Others consider that the early drug trials were too small to provide sufficiently precise estimates of the effects on total mortality. They argue that the potential benefits of the new HMG coenzyme A reductase drugs, which can produce a 20–30% reduction in serum cholesterol levels, are so great that a trial of sufficient size to settle the total mortality issue in high risk groups is of the highest priority.

4) It may be that interventions did not concentrate on sufficiently high risk groups. This not only reduces the power of trials to show a significant result but may shift the risk/benefit ratio for drug interventions so as to negate any benefit. However, trials apart, concentration only on high risk groups has two important disadvantages. Firstly one must identify the high risk group by screening or case finding. Secondly the high risk group will be a small minority and, though its IHD rates are higher than average, it may nonetheless only contribute a minority of total deaths because of the far larger size of lower risk groups. Thus the ability of such a strategy to make serious inroads into the mortality of the whole community will be considerably limited.

5) Intervention in middle age may be too late to be really effective. Far better results might occur if behaviours such as smoking and inadequate exercise could be avoided from youth. We have already noted that potentially reversible risk factors best predict IHD in the youngest age groups which lends support to this viewpoint. Risk factor modification may only be truly effective before IHD has developed, and at late ages, when IHD is more likely to be already established, it may be ineffective or less effective.

6) Interventions may have been insufficiently stringent as trial evidence does suggest that extremely rigorous intervention specifically to reduce smoking and high cholesterol values by diet may be effective (Oliver, 1992).

The present status of interventional policies is thus far from clear but it would seem prudent to promote measures to reduce smoking, avoid low exercise levels and eat diets with higher polyunsaturated/saturated fat levels on a whole community basis. Only by such a strategy are we likely to have significant effects on the lifestyle of the younger age groups, yet this would seem all important.

Of perhaps even greater importance, given the findings of the Barker group as to predisposition in foetal and infant life, is that care of pregnant women and infants is given high priority. Advice to mothers on avoidance of smoking and alcohol and good nutrition during pregnancy might have a considerable impact on future rates of IHD.

Familial IHD

Young victims of IHD commonly have a family history of IHD. In about a fifth of cases there are identifiable genetic defects leading to hypercholesterolaemia. Overall some 1% of the population has a genetic predisposition to premature IHD and correction of environmental risk factors would seem to be particularly important in such individuals (Royal College of Physicians, 1992).

Oestrogens and IHD

Pre-menopausal women have far lower levels of IHD than men as shown in Figures 5.2 and 5.3. However at ages past 50 rates in the two sexes converge. Mortality data suggest that this might be more due to a diminution in the rate of increase in men, perhaps due to reduction in androgenic hormone levels, than to an acceleration in the increase in age-specific rates in women due to loss of a protective effect of oestrogens (Fairweather, 1992). Hormone replacement therapy is thought however to have some potential as a preventive measure in post-menopausal women but would need to be continued long term. As discussed in Chapter 8 the observational data suggesting a reduction in IHD incidence by post-menopausal oestrogen therapy are suggestive but not convincing and randomised controlled trials are urgently needed.

Aspirin in the prevention of IHD

Aspirin in small daily dosage has effects on clotting factors, and has been shown to be capable of reducing IHD mortality by 44% in the American Physicians' Health Study (Steering Committee, 1989). However, protection was bought at an expense in bleeding complications which precludes the use of this preventive measure in low risk individuals.

Treatment of established IHD

IHD can be thought of as having two phases. Firstly vessels of the heart are compromised by deposition of fatty atheromatous deposits in their walls at which stage the disease is usually asymptomatic. Secondly these lesions may rupture and thrombosis be superimposed so that there is acute deterioration in blood supply to the heart and illness in the form of unstable angina, myocardial infarction and acute cardiac death. For many years medical treatment of such acute syndromes has relied on anticoagulant drugs (aiming to counteract further thrombosis) but recent years have seen the introduction of effective thrombolytic therapy (aiming to reverse thrombosis).

Thrombolytic therapy has been recently reviewed by Wilcox (1991). The combination of aspirin with streptokinase, anistreplase or alteplase can reduce mortality after myocardial infarction by 25–40% and this gain in early survival appears to be maintained for at least a year. This would not appear to be at the cost of survivals in a more functionally disabled state and so appears to be a real improvement. However, though valuable in terms of those who become victims of IHD, the impact of this teatment advance on mortality of the whole community from IHD is likely to be marginal as would appear to have been the case for other treatment advances in the past, for example the establishment of specialist coronary care units. In policy terms we would be wise to concentrate on prevention if we wish to achieve the greatest benefits from our efforts.

Future trends

As was shown in Figures 5.2 and 5.3, rates for IHD in the third age are in decline. Furthermore, if we are to judge from experience in countries such as the USA and Australia, the UK still has a long way to go in terms of further improvements. Osmond and Barker (1990) have made a detailed examination of present trends and cohort effects and have based forecasts extending to 2007 for all of England and Wales and for regions. They predict large falls in rates for IHD, particularly below the age of 65.

They do however caution that there is likely to be an increase in the present north/south divide so that the northern experience becomes even more unfavourable in comparison with that of the south. They suggest that preventive measures might thus be given highest priority in the north.

Extrapolating from their findings, it would seem prudent that this advice should be extended to Northern Ireland and Scotland which are similarly disadvantaged now and whose relative performance might also lag further behind in the future if there were no modification of present trends.

References

Barker DJP, Martyn CN. The maternal and fetal origins of cardiovascular disease. *J Epidemiol & Community Health*, 1992; 46: 8–11.

Barker DJP, Meade TW, Fall CDH, Lee A *et al*. Relation of fetal and infant growth to plasma fibrinogen and factor VII concentrations in adult life. *Br Med J*, 1992; 304: 148–152.

Barker DJP, Osmond C. Infant mortality, childhood nutrition, and ischaemic heart disease in England and Wales. *Lancet*, 1986; 1: 1077–1081.

Barker DJP, Osmond C, Winter PD *et al*. Weight in infancy and death from ischaemic heart disease. *Lancet*, 1989; 2: 577–580.

Doll R, Gray R, Hafner B, Peto R. Mortality in relation to smoking: 22 years' observations on female British doctors. *Br Med J*, 1980; 1: 967–971.

Doll R, Peto R. Mortality in relation to smoking: 20 years' observations on male British doctors. *Br Med J*, 1976; 2: 1525–1536.

Fairweather DS. The heart in ageing. *Rev Clin Gerontol*, 1992; 2: 83–103.

Fall CHD, Barker DJP, Osmond C, Winter PD, Clark PMS, Hales CN. The relation of infant feeding to adult serum cholesterol and death from ischaemic heart disease. *Br Med J*, 1992; 304: 801–805.

Grimley Evans J. Metabolic switches in aging. *Age Ageing*, 1993; 22: 79–81.

Hales CN, Barker DJP, Clark PMS *et al*. Fetal and infant growth and impaired glucose tolerance at age 64. *Br Med J*, 1991; 303: 1019–1022.

Kaplan GA, Salonen JT. Socioeconomic conditions in childhood and ischaemic heart disease during middle age. *Br Med J*, 1990; 301: 1121–1123.

Law CM, Barker DJP, Bull AR, Osmond C. Maternal and fetal infuences on blood pressure. *Arch Dis Childhood*, 1991; 66: 1291–1295.

MacMahon S, Peto R, Cutler J et al. Blood pressure, stroke, and coronary heart disease. Part 1, prolonged differences in blood pressure: prospective observational studies corrected for regression dilution bias. *Lancet*, 1990; 335: 765–774.

Marmot MG, Mann JI. Epidemiology of ischaemic heart disease. In Fox KM (ed.), *Ischaemic heart disease*, pp. 1–31. MTP Press, Lancaster, 1987.

Marmot MG, McDowall ME. Mortality decline and widening social inequalities. *Lancet*, 1986; 2: 274–276.

Meade TW, Chakrabarti R, Haines AP, North WRS, Stirling Y. Haemostatic function and cardiovascular death: early results of a prospective study. *Lancet*, 1980; 1: 1050–1054.

Oliver MF. Doubts about preventing coronary heart disease. *Br Med J*, 1992; 304: 393–394.

OPCS. Series DH2 No. 17, *1990 mortality statistics, cause, England and Wales*. HMSO, London, 1991.

Osmond C, Barker DJP. Ischaemic heart disease in England and Wales around the year 2000. *J Epidemiol & Community Health*, 1990; 45: 71–72.

Robinson RJ. Is the child father of the man? *Br Med J*, 1992; 304: 789–790.

Royal College of Physicians. *Preventive medicine*, pp. 55–68. Royal College of Physicians, London, 1992.

Shaper AG, Wannamethee G. Physical activity and ischaemic heart disease in middle-aged British men. *Br Heart J*, 1991; 66: 384–394.

Smith DS, Pekkanen J. Should there be a moratorium on the use of cholesterol lowering drugs? *Br Med J*, 1992; 304: 431–434.

Smith WCS, Kenicer MB, Tunstall-Pedoe H et al. Prevalence of coronary heart disease in Scotland: Scottish heart health study. *Br Heart J*, 1990; 64: 295–298.

Steering Committee of the Physicians' Health Study Research Group. Final report on the aspirin component of the ongoing physicians' health study. *New Engl J Med*, 1989; 321: 129–135.

Wannamethee G, Shaper AG. Physical activity and stroke in British middle aged men. *Br Med J*, 1992; 304: 597–601.

Wilcox RG. Coronary thrombolysis: round two and beyond. *Br Heart J*, 1991; 65: 175–176.

Chronic bronchitis

Malcolm Hodkinson

Chronic bronchitis remains a major contributor to deaths from respiratory diseases, the third largest category of deaths in those aged 55–64, behind cancers and heart disease and a close fourth in those aged 65–74, behind heart disease, cancers and cerebrovascular disease (OPCS, 1991).

Yet mortality rates for chronic bronchitis have shown impressive declines in Britain, for example total deaths in England and Wales falling from a peak level of 30,001 in 1963 to 11,793 in 1984 and to 4,934 in 1990 (Registrar General's Statistical Returns, 1964–1974; OPCS, 1991). These dramatic falls in total deaths have greatly benefited those in the third age, especially men in whom rates have always been far higher than women. Figure 6.1 shows the very dramatic nature of this decline for men aged 55–64, similar changes having taken place for mortality rates for both sexes and in the age groups 45–54 and 65–74.

It does not seem likely that advances in medical treatment could account for these dramatic changes; rather we should look to the known risk factors for development of the disease: smoking, childhood respiratory tract infections, adequacy of foetal growth and atmospheric pollution.

Chief among these is smoking. The studies of Doll and Peto (1976) and Doll *et al.* (1980) on British doctors found that the relative risks in smokers as compared with non-smokers were highest for chronic bronchitis as compared with other smoking-related diseases. Indeed Burrows *et al.* (1988) found virtually no evidence of decline in respiratory function such as results from chronic bronchitis in middle-aged non-smokers when asthmatics were excluded, whereas they found that the decline in smokers could be related to pack-years of smoking experience. Declines in population rates for smoking are thus major contributors to falling mortality rates for chronic bronchitis but do not appear to be the whole reason.

The remaining risk factors have also shown improvements which can be presumed to have played their part. The importance of childhood chest infections has been shown for 20-year-olds by Colley *et al.* (1973) to be second only to smoking and has been confirmed in the middle aged by Barker and Osmond (1986). Barker (1991) has also found that low birth weight indicative of poorer maternal nutrition and health and poor foetal growth is associated with higher rates for chronic bronchitis in middle life. Air pollution may not be a particularly strong factor in adult life (Colley *et al.*, 1973; Barker and Osmond, 1986) but atmospheric pollution may be important as a cause of childhood chest infections. So too may passive smoking experience, children of smoking parents having a greater likelihood of chest infections (Leeder *et al.*, 1976).

If population smoking rates continue to fall, we can expect the steep decline in chronic bronchitis to continue. This will have effects on mortality in the third age

Figure 6.1
Male deaths per
million per year from
chronic bronchitis for
England and Wales.
Age groups 45–54,
55–64 and 65–74.

*Sources: Registrar
General's Statistical
Reports; OPCS, 1991.*

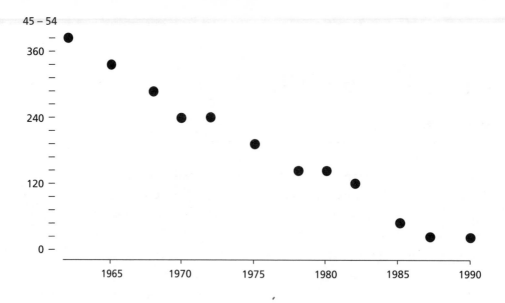

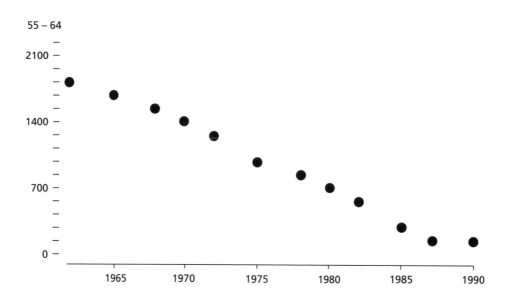

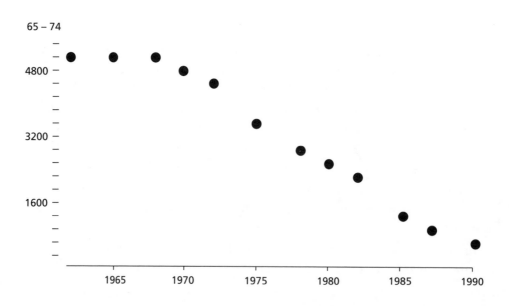

but the even more striking effects on morbidity in the age group should be borne in mind, for sufferers typically have many years of disability before their deaths.

References

Barker DJP. The intrauterine origins of cardiovascular and obstructive lung disease in adult life. *J Roy Coll Phys Lond*, 1991; 25: 129–133.

Barker DJP, Osmond C. Childhood respiratory infection and adult chronic bronchitis in England and Wales. *Br Med J*, 1986; 293:1271–1275.

Burrows B, Knudson J, Cline MG, Lebowitz D. A reexamination of risk factors for ventilatory impairment. *Am Rev Resp Dis*, 1988; 138: 829–836.

Colley JRT, Douglas JWB, Reid DD. Respiratory disease in young adults: influence of early childhood lower respiratory tract illness, social class, air pollution, and smoking. *Br Med J*, 1973; 3: 195–198.

Doll R, Gray R, Hafner B, Peto R. Mortality in relation to smoking: 22 years' observations on female British doctors. *Br Med J*, 1980; 1: 967–971.

Doll R, Peto R. Mortality in relation to smoking: 20 years' observations on male British doctors. *Br Med J*, 1976; 2: 1525–1536.

Leeder SR, Corkhill R, Irwig LM, Holland WW, Colley JRT. Influence of family factors on the incidence of lower respiratory illness during the first year of life. *Br J Prev Soc Med*, 1976; 30: 203–212.

OPCS. Series DH2 No. 17, *1990 mortality statistics, cause, England and Wales*. HMSO, London, 1991.

Registrar General's Statistical Returns for England and Wales. *(1962–1972)—Part I Tables, Medical.* HMSO, London, 1964–1974.

Sobonya RE, Burrows B. The epidemiology of emphysema. *Clinics in Chest Medicine*, 1983; 4: 351–358.

Osteoarthritis

J. Grimley Evans

Rheumatic complaints, arthritis and soft-tissue symptoms rank highly among the conditions causing lost days of work and leisure in middle life and beyond. By far the commonest of this group of disorders causing symptoms and disability is osteoarthritis. The majority of people have some degree of osteoarthritis by the age of 65 and more than 80% by the age of 75. The epidemiology is complicated by the fact that there is a poor correlation between the signs and the symptoms of osteoarthritis and an even poorer correlation between symptoms and radiological evidence of the condition. For example less than half of the people with radiological evidence of osteoarthritis of the knee complain of pain. Such findings suggest that the factors causing osteoarthritis may differ to some degree from the factors causing symptoms, usually pain, in osteoarthritis.

One of the fundamental questions about osteoarthritis is whether each joint is affected as a separate entity or whether there is a tendency for subjects with osteoarthritis of one joint to be at higher risk for changes at others also. There appears to be broad acceptance in the literature that some patients show a greater propensity for multiple joint involvement than do others, and that some manifestations of osteoarthritis such as Heberden's nodes have a genetic component. Several suggestions have been made for the mechanisms underlying generalised osteoarthritis. These include the possibility that osteoarthritis may be caused by metabolically determined crystal deposition in joints or that minor abnormalities of collagen may predispose to osteoarthritis. It is has also been suggested that generalised osteoarthritis may come about because of secondary changes in joints slightly damaged by previous episodes of unrelated polyarthropathy.

While osteoarthritis may affect most joints, particularly as a secondary effect of injury or nearby fracture, in terms of morbidity the joints of the spinal column, the knee and the hip produce the most morbidity. In the third age the last two are the most significant.

Osteoarthritis of the knee

Table 7.1 lists prevalence rates from a variety of studies of radiographic osteoarthritis of the knees. The broad picture that emerges is of increasing prevalence of osteoarthritis of the knees in both sexes over the age range 55–74. The data suggest that the condition may have a higher prevalence in England than elsewhere in the world. The English data (Lawrence et al., 1966) are somewhat older than the two USA studies which relate to 1971–75 (NHANES I) and 1983–85 (Framingham). The Leigh and Wensleydale samples may also have differed in social class and occupation from the USA subjects.

In the Framingham Study (Felson, 1990) the ratio of symptomatic osteoarthritis to all grades of radiographic osteoarthritis was 0.22 in men and 0.33 in women, and for the more severe grades 3 and 4, was 0.43 in men and 0.74 in women. In men but not in women there was a tendency for these ratios to fall with age. Presumably the prevalence of symptoms in osteoarthritis will be determined to some extent by the pattern of use of the affected joint. Conceivably men with osteoarthritis in later life are more able than women to adopt social roles that produce fewer symptoms.

If we take an average, weighted by total sample size from the data in Table 7.1, together with the ratios derived above we can arrive at the broad estimates of the likely prevalence of radiological and symptomatic osteoarthritis of the knee in people of the third age set out in Table 7.2. These figures must be regarded as speculative but give a broad order-of-magnitude estimate of the proportion of people whose wellbeing is in some degree impaired as a result of osteoarthritis of the knee. The figures give an upper limit to the proportions who might be candidates for knee replacement surgery should that reach the satisfactory stage of technical development of hip replacement.

Risk factors for osteoarthritis of the knee

Age

As the data above indicate, age is a potent risk factor for osteoarthritis of the knee. The simplest explanation for this might be the progressive accumulation of minor trauma in the presence of imperfect repair mechanisms—in the view of many the basic paradigm of ageing.

Sex

The prevalence of radiologically defined osteoarthritis at young adult ages is somewhat higher in men and usually involves one or two joints possibly reflecting sporting or occupational injuries. At later ages women are more frequently affected and typically several joints are involved (Davis et al., 1988).

No association was found in the NHANES I data between osteoarthritis of the knee and parity or an early onset menopause. Nonetheless the age-associated increase in prevalence ratio for osteoarthritis of the knee in women has suggested that post-menopausal reduction in endogenous oestrogens might be a risk factor for a generalised propensity to osteoarthritis. Data from some animal models, however, suggest that oestrogens may increase the susceptibility of articular cartilage to stress-induced damage.

Race

In the NHANES I data there was evidence of a greater susceptibility to knee osteoarthritis in black women compared with white. This was not observed in men and remained after adjustment for possible confounding variables in multiple logistic regression (adjusted risk ratio, 2.12; 95% CI, 1.39–3.23).

Table 7.1

Age-specific prevalence rates (%) of radiographic knee osteoarthritis (definite osteophytes) in various population groups. Data from Felson (1988)

	Age group					
	25–34	35–44	45–54	55–64	65–74	75–USA
(NHANES I)						
Men	0.0	1.7	2.3	4.1	8.3	—
Women	0.1	1.5	3.6	7.3	18.0	—
USA (Framingham)						
Men	—	—	—	—	30.8	30.5
Women	—	—	—	—	30.8	41.8
Sweden (Malmö)						
Men	—	0.0	3.0	4.5	4.5	4.5
Women	—	7.0	4.0	11.0	26.5	36.0
Bulgaria (Sofia)						
Men	3.1	3.6	7.0	10.0	9.6	—
Women	1.6	4.7	9.6	11.3	9.6	—
England						
Men	—	7.0	12.1	28.7	42.3	—
Women	—	6.0	17.4	48.6	56.3	—
Holland (Zoetermeer)						
Men	—	—	9.3	16.8	20.9	22.1
Women	—	—	13.9	18.5	35.2	44.1

Table 7.2

Estimated age-specific prevalence (%) of radiologically (R) and symptomatically (S) defined osteoarthritis of the knee

	Men		Women	
Age group	R	S	R	S
35–44	2.7	0.6	3.4	1.1
45–54	5.6	1.2	8.2	2.7
55–64	10.0	2.2	14.1	4.6
65–74	14.9	3.3	23.4	7.7
75–	20.5	4.5	41.8	13.8

Obesity

In prevalence studies there is a consistent association of osteoarthritis of the knee with obesity. For some years there was debate over three possible explanations. The first was that obesity caused the osteoarthritis, the second suggestion was that the immobility caused by osteoarthritis led to obesity, the third hypothesis was that some metabolic process underlay both the arthritis and the obesity. A prospective examination of the issue in the Framingham study demonstrated a strong and consistent link in individuals between being overweight in 1948 to 1952 and having osteoarthritis of the knee 36 years later (Felson *et al.*, 1988). Observational study shows that women who give a history of weight loss are less likely than others to have symptomatic osteoarthritis of the knee (Felson *et al.*, 1992). This is compatible with the view that obesity causes symptomatic osteoarthritis.

Table 7.3 presents data from the NHANES I study relating body mass index (BMI) to the prevalence of radiographic osteoarthritis of the knee. The distributions of BMI in men and women aged 55–64 in the OPCS survey of heights and weights of adults in Great Britain in 1983 (Knight, 1984) are also shown in Table 7.3. The data indicate that approximately 9% of men and 14% of women will be at enhanced risk of osteoarthritis of the knee on account of obesity.

Occupation and trauma

The association of osteoarthritis of the knee with previous trauma seems well established. Anderson and Felson (1988) report an analysis of occupational data in the NHANES I sample of people aged 35–64 using data from the US Department of Labor Dictionary of Occupations in which the strength required for particular jobs and the use of knee bending were coded. The results suggested that prolonged years in an occupation requiring knee bending may predispose to osteoarthritis of the joint in both sexes. A similar relationship with strength exerted in occupations was only significant in women.

Smoking

In the NHANES I data (Felson *et al.*, 1989a) smoking appeared to be negatively associated with osteoarthritis and the association was independent of age, sex and body weight. In a prospective analysis of the Framingham Study there appeared to be a lower risk of osteoarthritis in smokers than in non-smokers (risk ratio 0.74, and 0.70 for severer grades). These ratios resisted adjustment for age, sex, weight, knee injury, sports and general physical activity, coffee and alcohol consumption. On the other hand, smoking did not seem to protect against symptomatic osteoarthritis. One possible interpretation of these data is that smoking protects against radio-graphically detectable changes of osteoarthritis. An alternative explanation would be a defect in the adjustment for physical and sporting activity due to downward biassing of estimated regression coefficients by measurement error or, conceivably by systematic overestimation by smokers of their activity levels.

Table 7.3

Odds ratio (OR) of radiographic osteoarthritis of the knee in NHANES I (age and race adjusted) and distribution (%) of BMI in Great Britain of adults aged 55–64 in 1983

	Men		Women	
BMI	*OR*	*%*	*OR*	*%*
≤20	0.96	7	0.85	7
>20 to ≤25	1.00	41	1.00	44
>25 to ≤30	1.69	43	1.89	35
>30 to ≤35	4.78	8	3.87	11
>35	4.45	1	7.37	3

Chondrocalcinosis

Linear calcification of articular cartilage due to deposits of calcium pyrophosphate dihydrate (CPPD) increases with age. In the Framingham data (Felson *et al.*, 1989b) the prevalence of chondrocalcinosis increased from 3.2% at ages under 70 to 27.1% at ages over 85. The risk ratios for radiographically defined osteoarthritis in the presence of chondrocalcinosis were of the order of 1.5 for both sexes, while for symptomatic osteoarthritis the ratios were 2.3 for men and 1.6 for women. However, in terms of attributable risk chondrocalcinosis was not an important factor. The proportion of osteoarthritis possibly attributable to chondrocalcinosis was only of the order of 4%.

Bone mass

There has long been a clinical tradition that osteoarthritis and fracture of the hip rarely occur together. This has been partly explained in terms of local changes around the hip joint produced by osteoarthritis including supportive osteophytes and cervical buttresses. A more generalised effect has been suggested in that dense bone is less compliant than osteoporotic bone which will be better at absorbing deforming forces and so reduce stress on joints. There was no support in the NHANES I data for any effect of bone density on the prevalence of osteoarthritis of the knee when controlled for body weight index (Davis *et al.*, 1990).

Osteoarthritis of the hip

Table 7.4, adapted from Felson (1988) sets out prevalence data from a number of studies in white and black populations. The rates in the black populations are consistently lower than in the white. For purposes of planning orthopaedic surgery services it may be argued that radiographic criteria for hip osteoarthritis are unhelpful since it is well known clinically that the relationship between radiographic changes and functional limitation in the condition is not always close. Wilcock (1979) carried out a survey of 838 people aged 65 and over in Oxfordshire based on postal

Table 7.4

Prevalence of radiographic hip osteoarthritis, grades 2–4 and 3–4 (Felson, 1988)

			Men			Women	
	Age	n	*2–4 (%)*	*3–4 (%)*	n	*2–4 (%)*	*3–4 (%)*
England	55+	377	23	7	452	15	7
Germany	55+	50	16	6	69	10	5
Czechoslovakia	55+	180	17	3	196	10	3
Switzerland	55+	93	17	7	130	7	4
Jamaica	55–64	87	1	0	91	4	4
Nigeria	55+	66	3	2	60	2	1
Bantu	55+	61	3	1	138	3	0
All surveys	55+	914	17	6	1136	10	4
All surveys	55–64	576	14	4	664	8	2

questionnaires and examination of general practice records. He concluded that the prevalence of functionally significant osteoarthritis of the hip was 5.5% including 1.2% who were suitable for, or had received surgery and 1.7% unfit for surgery.

The epidemiology of osteoarthritis of the hip differs in several ways from that of the knee and several other joints. It affects predominantly men and shows a distinct pattern of geographical variation. For example it is much rarer in Chinese than in Western European populations even though there is little difference between the two races in the prevalence of osteoarthritis of other joints.

In general, osteoarthritis of the hip is much less related to factors such as obesity and repetitive use which are risk factors for osteoarthritis of other joints, particularly the knee. The consensus is that except for a minority of cases involved in a polyarticular diathesis, osteoarthritis of the hip mainly arises as a secondary response to some deformity of the joint surfaces and that the main determinants of the wide variation in prevalence observed between some geographically and racially distinguished population groups are developmental irregularities of the hip joint particularly affecting the femoral head. The three major deformities are congenital dislocation of the hip, Perthes disease and slipped femoral capital epiphysis. None of these is common in the UK.

Requirements for hip and knee replacement

Frankel *et al*. (1990) have reviewed the data on hip and knee replacement surgery in the UK. They note that rates of hip replacement have reached a plateau but that increasing numbers of operations are for revision. There are also problems arising from the increasing use of hip arthroplasty as an immediate treatment for fractures of the proximal femur, a factor that also makes international comparisons of operation rates difficult to evaluate. Frankel *et al*. (1990) estimate current operation rates for total hip replacement in England at 54/100,000 per year compared with 108 in France, 84 in Denmark and 116 in Belgium. They conclude that a modest increase in present rates of hip replacement to approximately 70 per 100,000 per year would be sufficient to meet the needs arising from incident cases and revision procedures, but as there has been no study of incidence of the disease this comfortable conclusion must be regarded as provisional. Certainly, rates of operation have stabilised in recent years but as Frankel *et al*. (1990) point out it is not clear whether this is because of satisfied demand or saturated capacity. Since one operation in eight at present is a revision procedure, it is also possible that rates are stabilising because of more stringent criteria being adopted for the initial replacements as part of clinical cost-utility adjustments.

Rates for knee replacement are rising steeply. Comparison of the data in Table 7.2 on symptomatic knee osteoarthritis with the estimates of functionally significant hip osteoarthritis derived by Wilcock (1979) shows that the levels of morbidity from the two conditions are similar. One might expect the operation rates for the two conditions to converge if, as seems plausible, the incidence rates as well as the prevalence rates of the two conditions are similar. For both procedures a good outcome in terms of pain relief can be expected in 80% of cases. There is at present only limited experience of the problems of revision procedures in total knee replacement and this will need to be one of the factors to be considered in identifying appropriate operation rates.

Conclusions

Osteoarthritis of the weight-bearing joints is an important source of discomfort and functional limitation in later life. Around 5% of people aged over 55 will have problems with knees and a slightly smaller proportion with the hip. Except where secondary to previous joint damage, disease will tend to be bilateral. There is nothing to suggest significant changes in incidence or prevalence and there appears to be little scope for a preventive approach to osteoarthritis of the weight-bearing joints except through the control of obesity and occupational damage to knee joints. Important issues lie with the provision of replacement surgery, its accessibility and durability. Available data are inadequate for health service planning. There is a need for studies to reassess the prevalence and incidence of hip and knee osteoarthritis and their associated morbidity, and to identify whether available surgical treatment is actually reaching the people who could benefit from it.

References

Anderson JJ, Felson DT. Factors associated with osteoarthritis of the knee in the First National Health and Nutrition Examination Survey (NHANES I): evidence for an association with weight, race and physical demands of work. *Am J Epidemiol*, 1988; 128: 179–189.

Davis MA, Ettinger WH, Neuhaus JM, Hauck WW. Sex differences in osteoarthritis of the knee. *Am J Epidemiol*, 1988; 127: 1019–1030.

Davis MA, Ettinger WH, Neuhaus JM. Obesity and osteoarthritis of the knee: evidence from the National Health and Nutrition Examination Survey (NHANES I). *Semin Arthritis Rheum*, 1990; 20(3) Suppl. 1: 34–41.

Felson DT. Epidemiology of hip and knee osteoarthritis. *Epidemiol Rev*, 1988; 10: 1–28.

Felson DT, Anderson JJ, Naimark A *et al*. Obesity and knee osteoarthritis. *Ann Int Med*, 1988; 109: 18–24.

Felson DT, Anderson JJ, Naimark A *et al*. Does smoking protect against osteoarthritis? *Arthritis Rheum*, 1989a; 32: 166–172.

Felson DT, Anderson JJ, Naimark A *et al*. The prevalence of chondrocalcinosis in the elderly and its association with knee osteoarthritis: the Framingham Study. *J Rheumatol*, 1989b; 16: 1241–1245.

Felson DT. The epidemiology of knee osteoarthritis: results from the Framingham osteoarthritis study. *Semin Arthritis Rheum*, 1990; 20(3) Suppl. 1: 42–50.

Felson DT, Zhang Y, Anthony JM, Naimark A, Anderson JL. Weight loss reduces the risk for symptomatic knee osteoarthritis in women. The Framingham Study. *Ann Int Med*, 1992; 116: 535–539.

Frankel S, Williams M, Nanchahal K, Coast J. *DHA Project: Epidemiologically based needs assessment. Report 2: total hip and knee joint replacement*. Health Care Evaluation Unit, University of Bristol, Bristol, 1990.

Knight I. *The heights and weights of adults in Great Britain*. HMSO, London, 1984.

Lawrence JS, Bremner JM, Bier F. Osteoarthrosis: prevalence in the population and relationship between symptoms and X-ray changes. *Ann Rheum Dis*, 1966; 25: 1–24.

Wilcock GK. The prevalence of osteoarthrosis of the hip requiring total hip replacement in the elderly. *Int J Epidemiol*, 1979; 8: 247–250.

Osteoporosis, falls and fractures

J. Grimley Evans

In osteoporosis bone tissue is weak but structurally normal and there is, in essence, a reduced amount of bone tissue per volume of anatomical bone. Bone is constantly being reabsorbed and reformed and osteoporosis comes about because of an imbalance in the rates of replacement and absorption.

Weakness of bone is only one of the factors determining the risk of fractures. In Western societies most osteoporotic fractures in later life result from simple falls. Whether a fall results in a fracture depends not only on bone strength but also on what protective factors may be acting. Some of these factors may be active neuro-muscular responses to falling (Grimley Evans, 1982), others may be more passive factors such as the cushioning effects of subcutaneous fat.

Possible importance of bone structure and dynamics

The standard method of assessing the status of bone is now through single- or dual-energy radiation absorption. These methods essentially measure the amount of calcium salt per unit volume (strictly per unit length or area) of bone. Other factors may make an important contribution to the weakness of bone tissue, including defects in matrix or abnormally large bone crystals. The dynamics of bone may also be significant. One function served by the continuous absorption and replacement of bone (imbalance of which leads to osteopororosis) is to remove fatigue microfractures which accumulate in any rigid material subjected to continuous fluctuating stresses. If this remodelling process were to become slower microfractures would accumulate in the skeleton which would be weaker than would be predicted from its calcium content.

Finally we need to consider the architecture of the bone tissue. Cancellous bone is a three-dimensional latticework of struts (trabeculae). The strength of the bone depends on the pattern of the lattice and at present there is no easy non-invasive method of assessing details of bone structure. The trabeculae of the proximal femur contribute about 70% to the strength of the bone but make only a small contribution to overall bone mineral density measurement (Lotz *et al.*, 1990).

Osteoporotic fractures

Although osteoporosis may be considered to contribute to the incidence of all fractures in later life, the three common fractures most closely associated with the condition are those of the forearm, the vertebrae and the proximal femur.

Distal forearm fractures

Distal forearm fractures are common among adolescents of both sexes but thereafter in men rates remain fairly low and constant throughout life. In women there is a large stepwise increase in risk in middle life. One important determinant of the injury is freezing weather and each year the onset of icy conditions underfoot causes a mini-epidemic of distal forearm fracture which usually quickly fades (Miller and Grimley Evans, 1985).

Although there is some variation in the absolute levels of incidence for distal forearm fracture, there is a high degree of consistency in the pattern of association with age. In women a regular pattern of fluctuation in rates in later life is partly due to an interaction between bone weakness from osteoporosis and a localised peak in the age-specific incidence of falls among women aged 45–60 (Winner *et al.*, 1989).

Vertebral fractures

The impact of vertebral fractures upon quality of life in the third age has been underestimated. Apart from the usually short-lived pain associated with the acute fracture, the subsequent deformity of the thoracic cage, 'Dowager's hump' is seen as one of the disfigurements of ageing. Deformity may also impair respiratory function and muscular ability, thus impairing leisure activities.

The most comprehensive epidemiological data on vertebral fractures come from Rochester USA (Melton *et al.*, 1989). Table 8.1 sets out incidence and prevalence rates from that study. The estimates include 3% of women who had suffered their fractures due to definable severe trauma; the remainder had suffered spontaneous 'osteoporotic' fractures. In this study the bone mineral density of lumbar spine vertebrae was also measured. A 0.1 gm per cm^2 reduction in bone mineral density (about the amount lost in ten years on average) was associated with a 44% increase in age-adjusted risk. The prevalence of vertebral fractures in women with lumbar vertebral bone density greater than 1 gm per cm^2 was only 9%. This level of bone mineral density is widely regarded as approximating the fracture threshold (to ordinary levels of trauma) for bone at other sites.

Table 8.1

Smoothed prevalence (%) and estimated incidence (per 1000 per annum) of one or more vertebral fractures

White women in Rochester Minnesota (Melton et al., *1989)*

Age group	Prevalence %	Incidence/1000/year
50–54	5.9	5.2
55–59	8.3	7.3
60–64	11.7	10.1
66–69	16.2	13.8
70–74	21.9	18.2
75–79	29.0	23.4
80–84	37.4	28.9
85–89	46.5	34.0
⩾ 90	55.9	

Proximal femoral fractures

At ages up to about 55 proximal femoral fractures (PFF) are more common in men than in women and are usually associated with severe degrees of trauma, particularly as incurred in road traffic accidents. From around the age of 55 rates start to rise in women and from the age of 65 increase exponentially, doubling with every seven years of age. In men there is also an exponential increase in incidence rates, and of approximately similar slope, at ages over 65 but the absolute rates lag by around ten years of age behind those of women. Approximately 2% of men and 3% of women in contemporary Britain will experience a PFF before the age of 75 (Law *et al.*, 1991). It is a serious fracture carrying considerable mortality and long-term morbidity. Although the most severe effects are seen in the very aged (Grimley Evans *et al.*, 1979; Greatorex, 1988), PFF can precipitate restriction of lifestyle at any age.

Increasing incidence of femoral fracture

The incidence of proximal femoral fracture has been increasing in the UK over the last 30 years (Boyce and Vessey, 1985). Hospital admission rates in both sexes may have levelled off since 1979 (Spector *et al.*, 1990) but this needs to be validated by incidence studies.

The rise in incidence of femoral fractures may have been due to an increase in the prevalence of osteoporosis and there is some archaeological evidence for this in the UK (Lees *et al.*, 1993). Studies of 70-year-old Swedish men suggest a secular increase in the prevalence of osteoporosis. Environmental and lifestyle changes affecting the frequency and consequences of falls could also have been relevant.

Osteoporosis and femoral fractures

In clinical studies, measurement of bone mineral density, particularly in association with other factors such as presence of previous fractures, provides useful information about risk of future fractures (e.g. Ross *et al.*, 1991). Population screening by measurement of bone mineral density does not offer a useful basis for a preventive programme for PFF. The differences between people with fractures and those without are on average small, amounting to approximately 0.5 of a standard deviation of the population bone density distribution, and diminishes with age (Law *et al.*, 1991). This is insufficient for use in a population screening programme.

These observations have led some authors to suggest that osteoporosis is irrelevant to the genesis of PFF and that therefore preventive measures should focus on the other factors (falls and protective responses, and factors in falling—see above) rather than osteoporosis. While this deduction might be true for prevention in late life, it could be a misapprehension to apply it across the age range. Osteoporosis is underestimated as a risk factor for PFF at later ages because bone density falls with age to a degree where nearly all women past the age of 80 have bones below the fracture threshold. The variance between cases and controls will therefore be explained by factors other than bone density. Nonetheless, the overall incidence of fractures is determined by the proportion of the population whose bone strength lies below fracture threshold, in other words the prevalence of osteoporosis. A means of preventing bone loss in middle age or earlier could be expected to have a greater impact on the incidence of proximal femoral fracture in later life than relative risks suggest.

Falls

There is a considerable literature on the epidemiology of falls and of fallers, mostly in populations of people aged over 65. The use of some forms of medication, notably hypnotic and sedatives emerges with some consistency as a risk factor (Prudham and Grimley Evans, 1981; Cumming *et al.*, 1991). Probably the longer-acting drugs are particularly hazardous in falls generating fractures (Ray *et al.*, 1989a) but tricyclic antidepressants are also a risk factor (Ray *et al.*, 1991). Alcohol does not emerge as an important factor in British populations. While much attention is paid to possible identifiable hazards in the environment such as loose mats and trailing electric leads, attention to these seems to offer little preventive scope. In a prospective study in New Zealand, more than 1000 loose mats were identified in the homes of a sample of elderly people but only 5 of them caused a fall in the following twelve months (Campbell *et al.*, 1990).

Perhaps more promising as an approach to preventing falls is to focus on hazards in the public environment. Falls involving steps and stairs are particularly hazardous and Archea (1985) and others have studied the effect of stair design on the risk of falls. Confusing visual cues, and stairs that break a natural rhythm of walking can cause unnecessary problems. There is scope for British architects to become more sensitive to the perceptual and motor limitations of an ageing population.

Risk factors, treatment and prevention of osteoporosis

Alcohol and smoking

Alcoholics have low bone density but moderate alcohol intake is not associated with demonstrable variation in bone density. Cigarette smoking is associated with lower bone density and with increased rate of loss of bone density in post-menopausal women (Krall and Dawson-Hughes, 1991). It is also associated with lower bone density in 70-year-old men (Mellström *et al.*, 1982). While there appears to be no association between smoking and bone density in pre-menopausal women, women who smoke experience the menopause earlier than non-smoking women by an average of up to two years. Part of the effect of smoking on bone density is presumably due to the lower average body weight of smokers but there is also evidence that smoking has an anti-oestrogenic effect.

In terms of relative risk smoking does not emerge as a very powerful risk factor for proximal femoral fracture, relative risk being of the order of 1.2–1.3 (Law *et al.*, 1991). Relative risks may underestimate the potential effect of stopping smoking on the incidence of the fracture however. Because smoking is associated with femoral fractures through its effect on osteoporosis, measurements of its relative risk will be subject to the bias discussed above for osteoporosis in general. Study of the literature shows that smoking is associated with higher relative risks of femoral fracture at younger ages. It is also associated with higher relative risks, of the order of 3.0, in its association with vertebral fractures which occur at a younger age than femoral fractures. We may therefore expect that reduction in smoking among women would produce a greater beneficial effect on fractures in later life than would be estimated from the relative risk calculations for PFF.

Genetic factors

There is some evidence that women whose mothers suffered from one or more manifestations of osteoporosis are more likely than the average population to develop the condition. It is not known whether this is due to genetic factors or to habits of diet and lifestyle. There are clearly genetic factors which contribute to the determination of peak bone mass and which seem largely responsible for the lower incidence of osteoporotic fractures in black Americans than in white.

Medication

As already noted some forms of medication are associated with risk of falling and may therefore be expected to emerge as risk factors for fractures. In the Framingham study caffeine intake seemed to be positively linked with the risk of PFF (Kiel *et al.*, 1990), but in Swedish data it was found that when adjustment was made for cigarette smoking and other factors the effect of coffee drinking on bone loss and fractures was very small (Johansson *et al.*, 1992). On the positive side, several studies have demonstrated that thiazide diuretics have a favourable effect on bone density and on the incidence of fractures (Ray *et al.*, 1989b; LaCroix *et al.*, 1990). This effect is of sufficient magnitude (a reduction of a third in the risk of hip fracture in older people) that it is a reason, where clinically appropriate, for choosing thiazides as first-line treatment for hypertension in patients in middle age and beyond.

Hormone replacement therapy (HRT)

It is now generally accepted that there is a period of accelerated bone loss during the five to ten years immediately following natural menopause or surgical oophorectomy. This loss can be retarded by exogenous oestrogen therapy. Case-control studies and prospective studies of natural menopause suggest that exogenous oestrogen therapy reduces the incidence of proximal femoral fracture. It is also generally accepted that when the exogenous oestrogens are withdrawn there follows a phase of accelerated bone loss analogous to that seen after an unmodified menopause. At issue is the question of whether this loss takes the bones to where they would have been if no exogenous oestrogen had been given (Model 1) or to where they would have been at the end of the natural menopausal process (Model 2). If Model 1 is correct, protection against fractures will not outlast the taking of the oestrogen. if Model 2 is correct the risk of fracture in a woman who took oestrogens for *x* years after the menopause will always be that of a woman *x* years younger with the same age of menopause who had not taken oestrogens. A recent review summarises various studies which suggest that the benefits of oestrogen therapy on relative risk of hip fracture diminish with time since taking the oestrogens (Law *et al.*, 1991). At first sight this seems to support Model 1 but it must be recognised that time since taking oestrogens also correlates with age and with steeply rising incidence rates, a constant rightward shift in incidence rate as postulated by Model 2 will be associated with diminishing benefit as expressed in relative risk even though the absolute benefit is constant. It also needs to be borne in mind that HRT may reduce the risk of fractures by means other than an effect on bone density. Oestrogens have been shown to increase muscle strength and it may turn out that the enhanced risk of falls in the peri-menopausal period identified by Winner *et al.* (1989) is oestrogen dependent.

Under the simplest form of Model 2 outlined above, one would not predict benefit from starting oestrogen therapy more than 5–10 years after the menopause. In a randomised controlled trial Lindsay and Tohme (1990) found evidence of increased vertebral bone mass following oestrogen or oestrogen–progestogen therapy in women who were an average of 14 years post-menopausal. This finding suggests that the loss of bone seen in later life which is slower than that immediately after the menopause may be sex-hormone dependent.

The type of hormone replacement offered may also be important. Most of the data in the literature relate to oestrogen therapy without progestogens which is no longer given to women with intact uteri because of its increasing the risk of endometrial carcinoma. One prospective study suggests that the taking of progestogens does not inhibit the beneficial effects of oestrogen on bone, but the potency of different oestrogen preparations is a significant factor (Naessén *et al.*, 1990).

Most studies have claimed a benefit of post-menopausal oestrogen therapy on the incidence of coronary heart disease and, less consistently, stroke (e.g. Stampfer *et al.*, 1991). Studies have shown that the menopause is associated with changes in blood lipids that would be expected to increase the risk of coronary heart disease and that these are potentially ameliorable by HRT (Mathews *et al.*, 1989). The serious methodological problem with the empirical data linking HRT with the incidence of coronary heart disease is that the studies have been observational and based on women who self-selected themselves for peri-menopausal oestrogen therapy. The selection bias towards peri-menopausal oestrogen therapy in women who were destined for lower than average incidence of vascular disease anyway must be assumed to be substantial. Barrett-Connor (1991) has demonstrated that women who report peri-menopausal oestrogen therapy had more physician contacts and undertook significantly more preventive health care procedures than women who did not take HRT.

If HRT were to be considered as an intervention to be encouraged as a public health measure aimed at reducing the incidence of 'osteoporotic fractures' and their associated disability it would need to be acceptable to the generality of women. Wallace *et al.* (1990) found an uptake of only 36% among women aged between 50 and 70 years offered HRT following a distal forearm fracture. Even in the age group 50–54 the uptake was only 54%. Data from the USA, where a more positive attitude to preventive interventions with feminist implications might be expected, only 40% of women thought to be at higher than average risk for osteoporotic fractures were compliant with HRT 6 to 12 months after initiation (Ravnikar, 1987). The general public is confused by conflicting opinions about HRT, and there is no uniform policy among general practitioners (Wilkes and Meade, 1991). At present we must conclude that the encouragement of HRT as a public health measure aimed at reducing the incidence of 'osteoporotic fractures' seems unlikely to have a major effect. Similar conclusions have been drawn for the USA by Cummings *et al.* (1990).

Fluoride

Several studies in different countries have examined the frequency of osteoporosis and of osteoporosis related fractures in areas with varying fluoride content in the drinking water. There have been findings of both positive and negative correlations between PFF rates and drinking water fluoride and there are considerable technical difficulties in such studies. Cooper *et al.* (1990) linked hospital discharge rates for PFF in 39 county districts of England and Wales with water fluoride concentrations measured a decade earlier. The correlation coefficient was only 0.16 ($p = 0.34$). This study suggests that water fluoridation to levels of around 1 mg per litre currently being advocated for the prevention of dental caries would be unlikely to have a major impact on hip fracture incidence in the UK. This view is in keeping with the conclusions of a workshop which reviewed the world literature on the topic in 1991 (Gordon and Corbin, 1992).

Fluoride has also been used therapeutically as a means of retarding bone loss in women with symptomatic osteoporosis, but most workers in the field now consider fluoride to have a very limited therapeutic applicability (Riggs *et al.*, 1990).

Physical activity

A range of studies, recently summarised by Law *et al.* (1991) have shown a relationship between habitual exercise levels and risk of hip fractures. In broad terms, compared with the risk in women with low levels of activity, moderate activity is associated with a 40–50% lower risk and high levels of activity with a 70% lower risk. Several intervention studies have shown short-term benefits from exercise regimes. The benefit might be mediated by reducing falls or improving protective responses as well as through an effect on bone strength. However, animal work has shown that even small loading stresses applied to bones in immobilised limbs can bring about measurable reductions in disuse bone loss (Lanyon, 1990).

A recent study by Prince *et al.* (1991) concluded that post-menopausal bone loss could be slowed by an exercise regime associated with either HRT or with dietary calcium supplementation. The exercise–HRT regime was the more effective but caused more side-effects than exercise and calcium supplementation.

Low body weight

Osteoporosis is associated with low body weight. This is presumably partly due to lower stress on bones but in post-menopausal women adipose tissue has a significant hormonal effect through the conversion of adrenal steroids into oestrogenic forms. The hazards of being overweight must offset the benefits of a lower prevalence of osteoporosis, so average body weight seems the desirable aim.

Dietary calcium

The relevance of dietary calcium levels to the genesis of osteoporosis remains unresolved, partly because of methodological difficulties. Epidemiological evidence suggests that dietary calcium intake in childhood contributes to peak bone mass (Cumming, 1990). It is likely that there is biological variability in the ability of individuals to adapt to low calcium diets in terms of establishing and preserving bone substance. It seems prudent to recommend dietary calcium intakes of the order of 800–1000 mg per day for the population as a whole, but the scope for affecting fracture incidence through the manipulation of dietary calcium or the prescription of calcium supplements in adult life seems limited.

Cyclical etidronate therapy

Several recent trials have shown that cyclical etidronate therapy has a beneficial effect on spinal bone density and the incidence of vertebral fractures (Storm *et al.*, 1990; Watts *et al.*, 1990; Miller *et al.*, 1991). So far the studies have been over periods of a few years and longer-term work is needed. Nonetheless etidronate therapy is coming into use in the UK as it employs a drug that has a low profile of adverse effects and which avoids the problems of HRT in older women. It is too early to assess its ultimate role in the prevention of vertebral fractures at a population level and it has not yet been shown to be efficacious in other osteoporotic fractures.

Conclusions

The incidence of osteoporotic fractures is clearly subject to powerful environmental and lifestyle factors. These factors have produced over a twofold increase in incidence of proximal femoral fractures over 25 years. The increase may now be ceasing and this is unlikely to be due to the use of HRT since the numbers of women of the age to suffer femoral fractures who have received HRT must still be extremely small in the UK. There is hope therefore that a public health approach to modification of lifestyle could reduce fracture incidence to its earlier levels, although it is only fair to note that there is no nation that has yet reported reductions in fracture rates. Falls are an important source of morbidity and even mortality, and architecture and urban planning have a role to play in preventing falls. The prevention of falls offers only limited scope for reducing the incidence of fractures in later life, for which it seems that the major hope lies with an attack on the prevalence of osteoporosis. The lifestyle factors identified as being of importance are giving up smoking, maintenance of average body weight, moderation of excessive alcohol intake, ensuring an adequate dietary calcium intake and, probably most important, maintaining physical exercise.

Population screening using currently available measures of bone density measurement is not justifiable. Given the uncertainties surrounding the risk–benefit ratio of hormone or other therapies for osteoporosis, bone density measurements have a place in the clinical assessment of someone who is of apparently high risk of osteoporotic fracture for other reasons. Indications might include an early menopause, an 'osteoporotic fracture' such as of the distal forearm, and a family history of osteoporosis. Facilities should be available for such clinical use of densitometry as it may reduce the use of therapy. The significance of HRT needs to be investigated further, in particular the issue of whether it produces long-term or only current effects. It seems that long-term large randomised controlled trials are both justified and necessary. The public should be educated in the need for trials and encouraged to participate.

References

Archea JC. Environmental factors associated with stair accidents by the elderly. *Clin Geriat Med*, 1985; 1: 555–568.

Barret-Connor E. Postmenopausal estrogen and prevention bias. *Ann Int Med*, 1991; 115: 455–456.

Boyce WJ, Vessey MP. Rising incidence of fracture of the proximal femur. *Lancet*, 1985; i: 150–151.

Campbell AJ, Borrie MJ, Spears GF, Jackson SL, Brown JS, Fitzgerald JL. Circumstances and consequences of falls experienced by a community population 70 years and over during a prospective study. *Age Ageing*, 1990; 19: 136–141.

Cooper C, Wickham C, Lacey RF, Barker DJP. Water fluoride concentration and fracture of the proximal femur. *J Epidemiol Community Health*, 1990; 44: 17–19.

Cumming RG. Calcium intake and bone mass: a quantitative review of the evidence. *Calcif Tissue Int*, 1990; 47: 194–201.

Cumming RG, Miller JP, Kelsey JL, Davis P, Arfken CL, Birge SJ, Peck WA. Medications and multiple falls in elderly people: the St Louis OASIS study. *Age Ageing*, 1991; 20: 455–461.

Cummings SR, Rubin SM, Black D. The future of hip fractures in the United States. Numbers, costs, and potential effects of postmenopausal estrogen. *Clin Orthop*, 1990; 252: 163–166.

Gordon SL, Corbin SB. Summary of workshop on drinking water fluoride influence on hip fracture and bone health (National Institutes of Health, 10 April 1991). *Osteoporosis Int*, 1992; 2: 109–117.

Greatorex IF. Proximal femoral fractures: an assessment of the outcome of health care in elderly people. *Commun Med*, 1988; 10: 203–210.

Grimley Evans J. Epidemiology of proximal femoral fracture. In Isaacs B (ed.), *Recent advances in geriatric medicine 2*, pp. 201–214. Churchill Livingstone, Edinburgh, 1982.

Grimley Evans J, Prudham, D, Wandless I. A prospective study of proximal femoral fracture: incidence and outcome. *Publ Health (Lond)*, 1979; 93: 235–241.

Johansson C, Mellström D, Lerner U, Österberg T. Coffee drinking: a minor risk factor for bone loss and fractures. *Age Ageing*, 1992; 21: 20–26.

Kiel DP, Felson DT, Hannan MT, Anderson JL, Wilson PWF. Caffeine and the risk of hip fracture: the Framingham study. *Am J Epidemiol*, 1990; 132: 675–684.

Krall EA, Dawson-Hughes B. Smoking and bone loss among post-menopausal women. *J Bone Miner Res*, 1991; 6: 331–337.

LaCroix AZ, Wienpahl J, White LR, Wallace RB, Scherr PA, George LK, Cornoni-Huntley J, Ostfeld AM. Thiazide diuretic agents and the incidence of hip fracture. *New Engl J Med*, 1990; 322: 286–290.

Lanyon LE. Bone loading—the functional determinant of bone architecture and a physiological contributor to the prevention of osteoporosis. In Smith R (ed.), *Osteoporosis 1990*, pp. 63–78. Royal College of Physicians of London, London, 1990.

Law MR, Wald NJ, Meade TW. Strategies for prevention of osteoporosis and hip fracture. *Br Med J*, 1991; 303: 453–459.

Lees B, Molleson T, Arnett TR, Stevenson JL. Differences in proximal femur bone density over two centuries. *Lancet*, 1993; 341: 673–675.

Lindsay R, Tohme JF. Estrogen treatment of patients with established postmenopausal osteoporosis. *Obstet Gynecol*, 1990; 76: 290–295.

Lotz JC, Gerhart TN, Hayes WC. Mechanical properties of trabecular bone from the proximal femur: a quantitative study. *J Comput Assist Tomogr*, 1990; 14: 107–114.

Mathews KA, Meilahn E, Kuller LK, Kelsey SF, Caggiula AW, Wing RR. Menopause and risk factors for coronary heart disease. *New Engl J Med*, 1989; 321: 641–646.

Mellström D, Rundgren D, Jagenburg R, Steen B, Svanborg A. Tobacco smoking, ageing and health among the elderly: a longitudinal population study of 70-year old men and an age cohort comparison. *Age Ageing*, 1982; 11: 45–48.

Melton LJ III, Kan SJ, Frye MA, Wahner HW, O'Fallon WM, Riggs BL. Epidemiology of vertebral fractures in women. *Am J Epidemiol*, 1989; 129: 1000–1011.

Miller PD, Neal BJ, McIntyre DO, Yanover MJ, Anger MS, Kowalski L. Effect of cyclical therapy with phosphorus and etidronate on axial bone mineral density in postmenopausal osteoporotic women. *Osteoporosis Int*, 1991; 1: 171–176.

Miller SWM, Grimley Evans J. Fractures of the distal forearm in Newcastle: an epidemiological survey. *Age Ageing*, 1985; 14: 155–158.

Naessén T, Persson I, Adami H-O, Bergström R, Bergkvist L. Hormone replacement therapy and the risk for first hip fracture. A prospective, population-based cohort study. *Ann Int Med*, 1990; 113: 95–103.

Prince RL, Smith M, Dick IM, Price RI, Webb PG, Henderson NK, Harris MM. Prevention of postmenopausal osteoporosis. A comparative study of exercise, calcium supplementation and hormone-replacement therapy. *New Engl J Med*, 1991; 325: 1189–1195.

Prudham D, Grimley Evans J. Factors associated with falls in the elderly: a community study. *Age Ageing*, 1981; 10: 264–270.

Ravnikar AZ. Compliance with hormone therapy. *Am J Obstet Gynecol*, 1987; 1565: 1332–1334.

Ray WA, Griffin MR, Downey W. Benzodiazepines of long and short elimination half-life and the risk of hip fracture. *JAMA*, 1989a; 262: 3303–3307.

Ray WA, Griffin MR, Downey W, Melton LJ III. Long-term use of thiazide diuretics and risk of hip fracture. *Lancet*, 1989b; i: 687–690.

Ray WA, Griffin MR, Malcolm E. Cyclic antidepressants and the risk of hip fracture. *Arch Int Med*, 1991; 151: 754–756.

Riggs BL, Hodgson SF, O'Fallon WM, Chao EYS, Wahner HW, Muhs JM, Cedel SL, Melton LJ III. Effect of fluoride treatment on the fracture rate in postmenopausal women with osteoporosis. *New Engl J Med*, 1990; 322: 802–809.

Ross PD, Davis JW, Epstein RS, Wasnich RD. Pre-existing fractures and bone mass predict vertebral fracture incidence in women. *Ann Int Med*, 1991; 114: 919–923.

Spector TD, Cooper C, Fenton Lewis A. Trends in admission for hip fracture in England and Wales, 1968–85. *Br Med J*, 1990; 300: 173–174.

Stampfer MJ, Colditz GA, Willett WC, Manson JE, Rosner B, Speizer FE, Hennekens CH. Postmenopausal estrogen therapy and cardiovascular disease. Ten-year follow-up from the nurses' health study. *New Engl J Med*, 1991; 325: 756–762.

Storm T, Thamsborg G, Steiniche T, Genant HK, Sorensen OH. Effect of intermittent cyclical etidronate therapy on bone mass and fracture rate in women with postmenopausal osteoporosis. *New Engl J Med*, 1990; 322: 1265–1271.

Wallace WA, Price VH, Elliot CA, MacPherson MBA, Scott BW. Hormone replacement therapy acceptability to Nottingham post-menopausal women with a risk factor for osteoporosis. *J Roy Soc Med*, 1990; 83: 699–701.

Watts NB *et al.* Intermittent cyclical etidronate treatment of postmenopausal osteoporosis. *New Engl J Med*, 1990; 323: 73–79.

Wilkes HC, Meade TW. Hormone replacement therapy in general practice: a survey of doctors in the Medical Research Council's general practice framework. *Br Med J*, 1991; 302: 1317–1321.

Winner SJ, Morgan CA, Grimley Evans J. Perimenopausal risk of falling and incidence of distal forearm fracture. *Br Med J*, 1989; 298: 1486–1488.

Stroke

J. Grimley Evans

Stroke is one of most important causes of death over the age range 55–74 and is one of the most important causes of disability. Mortality rates from stroke have been falling in the USA since 1900 (Whisnant, 1984). Dobson (1981) has reported on mortality rates from cerebrovascular disease in Australia which fell from 1950 in all age groups above 35. Bonita and Beaglehole (1982) have demonstrated a decline in mortality from cerebrovascular disease in New Zealand, greater in men than in women, which accelerated in the late 1970s.

In England and Wales, also, mortality rates for stroke have been falling during this century (Grimley Evans, 1986). Rates among men aged 45–84 have been falling at a rate of approximately 2–3% per annum since the early 1950s. At ages 25–44 rates were constant until the late 1960s and have been falling since then. At ages 85 and above rates were constant or still rising until the early 1970s since when they have been falling at the same proportional rate as at younger ages. The picture is essentially similar in women except that there is more suggestion of declining rates prior to 1950 in the middle-aged group 45–64. At ages under 45 there is little evidence of the decline seen in men except in the most recent years. For the age group 85 and above (and to a smaller extent the 75–84 year age group) the rise in incidence rates from the 1940s to the 1970s may partly reflect an increasing precision of diagnosis among older people.

In the USA and New Zealand, but not in Britain, there was a biphasic decline in stroke mortality rates with a steady background decline followed by a more rapid decline of rather abrupt onset in the 1970s. Ostfeld (1980) calculates the decline between 1975 and 1977 as 4% per annum compared with 1.5% per annum between 1951 and 1974, and 1% per annum between 1900 and 1950. Some authors have attributed this rapid recent decline to community programmes for the control of hypertension (Whisnant, 1984) which have become much more effective in the USA in recent decades (Borhani, 1979). The mortality decline which preceded the advent of effective therapy for hypertension is attributed by Whisnant (1984) to changes in certification practice and other artefacts. There is no direct evidence for this and it may be that dietary and lifestyle risk factors for hypertension or stroke may have been undergoing change before hypertension detection and treatment programmes became widely spread. Several suggestions have been made to explain this. One has been a decline in nephritis as a cause of hypertension (Reid and Grimley Evans, 1969). A second is the suggestion of Joossens (1973) that a secular decline in dietary sodium has reduced the prevalence of hypertension (Joossens et al., 1979). Barker et al. (1989) have linked regional mortality rates for stroke to maternal and perinatal mortality rates half a century earlier. They suggest that one of the determinants of stroke lies in the mechanisms of fetal adaptation to maternal malnutrition. The adaptation may lead to permanent metabolic consequences through its effect on development of tissues that do not change after birth. Thus stroke incidence rates may have been falling because of improvements in maternal nutrition over the earlier years of this century.

On the other hand, the decline in mortality rates from stroke might not be due to changes in incidence at all. Changes in death certification practice or improved treatment leading to a fall in case fatality might be responsible. Rochester NY offers the only long-term dataset linking incidence to mortality data over a prolonged period (1949–84). The data (Broderick *et al.*, 1989) show a decline in 30-day fatality of all forms of stroke combined from 33% in 1945–49 to 20% in 1975–79. The improvement seems to have particularly affected survival over the period of 5–21 days after the onset of stroke (Garraway *et al.*, 1983). These changes presumably reflect at least to some degree improvements in management but there may also have been changes in diagnostic criteria. At earlier stages in the period reviewed fatality may have been an implicit criterion for the diagnosis of cerebral haemorrhage. Nonetheless, taken with the Framingham finding that the longer a patient survives following a stroke the less likely is stroke to appear on his or her death certificate (Corwin *et al.*, 1982), a prolongation of average survival due to improved care would have reduced the proportion of strokes appearing as cause of death.

The Rochester data also, however, show a decline in incidence rates of stroke. Over the study period, standardised annual incidence rates of stroke per 100,000 in Rochester fell from 209 for men and 155 for women to 124 and 68, respectively. Broderick *et al.* (1989) have noted that the decline in incidence in Rochester ceased in the late 1970s and rates actually began to rise after 1980. The authors attribute this rise to the increased use of computerised tomographic scanning and the consequent increased detection of minor forms of cerebrovascular disease. Their interpretation of the data is that the stabilisation of stroke incidence had antedated this effect of increased detection.

Incidence rates in the United Kingdom

Direct estimates of stroke incidence in the UK are sparse. One of the most recent and most widely quoted studies is the Oxfordshire Stroke Registration project which monitored cases of possible stroke arising within a group of co-operating general practices in Oxfordshire during 1981 to 1984 (Bamford *et al.*, 1990). Incidence rates in the Newcastle Age Research Project (Grimley Evans, 1987) relating to ages 65 and over were some 40% higher in men and 60% higher in women than in the Oxfordshire study (Figure 1). These related to a region of England with higher mortality rates from stroke (and most other causes of death) than Oxfordshire and were collected some five years earlier. Furthermore the cases were not so rigorously assessed as in Oxfordshire, particularly in the women, although in the men 89% of the cases were ascertained on the basis of hospital notes or clinical examination. It should be noted, moreover, that the predictive value of a clinical diagnosis of stroke in hospital series is around 95% (Allen, 1983).

Bonita (1992) has estimated that the cumulative risk of stroke for a person of 45 is 3% in both sexes by the age of 65, and 10% for men and 6% for women by the age of 75. In looking to the future in the UK it seems reasonable to expect that the decline in stroke mortality does indicate in part an underlying decline in incidence. We may expect this decline to continue at least while the detection and treatment of hypertension become more effectively deployed in the general population. If the Rochester experience is a foreshadowing of our own, stroke incidence is likely to stabilise during the 1990s.

Risk factors

Blood pressure

In terms of population attributable risk high blood pressure emerges in most studies as the most important risk factor. Whisnant (1984) has suggested that high blood pressure may account for as many as 70% of strokes. Control of blood pressure has been shown to reduce the risk of stroke in middle-aged and elderly subjects but the cost–benefit ratio of hypertension detection and treatment remains rather undefined for the milder forms of 'hypertension'. In middle age, where incidence rates of stroke are low, many people will have to receive treatment for several years in order to prevent one stroke. Blood pressure treatment also carries a burden of side-effects that complicate management and reduce compliance. It is not clear that the quality of supervision of blood pressure treatment will be as good in the context of British primary care as it was in the relevant controlled trials. In later life where incidence rates are higher the cost–benefit ratio of treatment might be more favourable from a public health point of view.

Heart disease

There is clear epidemiological association between the presence of heart disease, and specifically of coronary heart disease and stroke. Whether the relationship is cognate or causal is uncertain except in the acute situation where a recent myocardial infarct leads to mural thrombus and cerebral embolism. Rheumatic valve disease is also a source of cerebral embolism in some situations but is no longer a major cause of stroke in the UK. It is to be hoped that a fall in coronary heart disease incidence, similar to that seen in the USA may be beginning in the UK and that this will be associated with a decline in stroke risk. The increasing use of aspirin prophylaxis in patients following myocardial infarction may be expected to have modest beneficial effect on stroke incidence. In general it seems that aspirin reduces the risk of thromboembolic stroke but increases the risk of cerebral haemorrhage. In healthy population groups not at enhanced risk of thromboembolic stroke aspirin may have a net harmful effect by producing more cerebral haemorrhages than the thromboembolic strokes it prevents. In those groups who through previous episodes of coronary heart disease or transient ischaemic attacks are at demonstrably above average risk of thromboembolic stroke, aspirin produces net benefit.

Atrial fibrillation

In the contemporary British population one cardiac feature of concern for direct preventive action is atrial fibrillation. In insured populations of young adults there does not appear to be a significant increased risk of stroke associated with 'lone' atrial fibrillation (Kopecky et al., 1987). 'Lone' fibrillation implies its presence without detectable underlying heart disease, particularly valvular disease. In middle age and beyond, however, the relative risk of stroke in people with atrial fibrillation is of the order of 3–5 and approximately 15% of strokes occur in subjects with fibrillation (Wolf et al., 1987). The prevalence of atrial fibrillation in British people aged 65 and over is of the order of 5% (Grimley Evans, 1985). Data from the USA suggest that over the age range 55–74 the annual incidence increases from around 1 to 10 per thousand in men and from 0.5 to 6 per thousand in women (Wolf et al., 1987). The risk of stroke appears to be particularly high at the time of onset of atrial fibrillation (Wolf et al., 1983). Atrial fibrillation seems in part to be a feature of generalised vascular disease and is associated with an increased risk of cerebral haemorrhage as well as of thromboembolism so there has long been doubt about the potential for reducing the risk of stroke in atrial fibrillation by anticoagulant or antiplatelet therapy. Recent large randomised controlled trials indicate that anti-coagulant therapy can reduce the risk of stroke in atrial fibrillation by approximately 30–40% (The Stroke Prevention in Atrial Fibrillation Investigators, 1991). The degree of anticoagulation required is only moderate (The Boston Area Anticoagulation Trial for Atrial Fibrillation Investigators, 1990) and the incidence of important side-effects correspondingly low. The length of follow-up has been short in the reported trials, and there remains the possibility that the risk–benefit ratio may change with increased duration of follow-up as the cumulative incidence of haemorrhagic side-effects increases. In some subjects in whom anticoagulation is contraindicated aspirin in doses of 325 mg daily may be associated with some benefit (The Stroke Prevention in Atrial Fibrillation Investigators, 1991) although not all studies have demonstrated this.

Diet

In contrast with coronary heart disease stroke is not powerfully related to blood lipids, particularly in later life. There is growing evidence that blood pressure, the most powerful risk factor for stroke, can be influenced by the dietary intake of sodium and potassium. Dahl et al. demonstrated that genetically susceptible rats could be made hypertensive by a diet high in sodium and low in potassium. Some population groups with a low prevalence of hypertension were shown to have unusually low intakes of dietary sodium (Prior et al., 1968). It was technically difficult to demonstrate a relation between sodium and potassium intake and blood pressure on a within-population basis because of a high measurement variance in both intake and blood pressure compared with the within-population variance. Acute experiments of modifying sodium and potassium intake gave conflicting results and were of dubious relevance since the mechanisms of long-term effects of dietary electrolytes on blood pressure are not necessarily those activated in an acute experiment and the long-term effects may not be readily reversible. Wald et al. (1991) have reviewed the data on the subject and conclude that there is no longer reasonable doubt that diets high in sodium and low in potassium will on a population basis lead to higher blood pressures. It may be that there is a genetically defined susceptible subgroup in most human populations. Unexpectedly the dietary effect seems to be more pronounced in later life. There are good grounds for recommending a reduction in the average levels of sodium consumption in the population and such recommendations have been made by the World Health Organisation and endorsed by the Department of Health.

Smoking

An overview by Shinton and Beevers (1989) showed relative risks of stroke associated with smoking to decline with age. Nonetheless, British data (Shaper *et al.*, 1991) and reviews by Bonita *et al.* (1986) indicate that smoking is an important modifiable risk factor for stroke during the years of middle life. The potential for prevention of stroke by control of smoking depends on the mechanism connecting the two. Smoking is associated with increase in haematocrit and hence blood viscosity and this has been associated with increase in risk of stroke in some studies and with the size of cerebral infarcts in the presence of carotid stenosis (Harrison *et al.*, 1981). Smoking also has effects on platelet function and fibrinogen which may favour thrombosis. On the other hand smoking may be linked indirectly with stroke through its stronger association with coronary heart disease which is a powerful risk factor for stroke. However, as already noted it is not clear whether the association between coronary heart disease and stroke in the non-acute situation is cognate or causative. There are no data from randomised controlled trials that could provide an adequate basis for estimating the magnitude of the benefit of smoking control on stroke risk.

Alcohol

The relationship between alcohol consumption and stroke is controversial. Alcohol intake appears to be related monotonically though not necessarily linearly with blood pressure, and men in alcohol-related occupations show generally high standardised mortality rates for stroke. Some epidemiological studies suggest that the association with stroke is due to the confounding effect of smoking. On the other hand the relationship might be the inverse. The fact that alcohol rather than smoking disappears in multivariate analysis of their joint association with stroke (Wolf, 1986) may reflect the accuracy with which the two variables are estimated rather than their true relationship with the disease.

In addition to the chronic association of alcohol with stroke, possibly as implied in the previous paragraph mediated through hypertension, there is also the issue of an acute effect of 'binge' drinking and stroke. This was originally postulated in studies from Finland (Hillbom and Kaste, 1981) drawing attention to the high incidence of stroke in young men on the traditional drinking days (Friday and Saturday) of Finnish urban society. Studies elsewhere have provided little support for the concept, and it has not been demonstrated in women or older men, but this may reflect a lower frequency of drinking of the periodicity and intensity of the young Finnish male population.

The future

As indicated earlier, survival following stroke has probably improved since the 1950s but mostly through improved supportive therapy and non-specific facilitation of spontaneous recovery. While more can be done for stroke victims than commonly is done, a major advance in rehabilitation could only be expected from some means of reconstructing damaged brain tissue. Research into nerve growth factors offers this as a distant hope, but seems unlikely to bear fruit within the present decade. For the foreseeable future, reductions in stroke-associated disability can only be achieved through primary prevention.

It seems likely that a modest reduction in the incidence of stroke contributes to the decline in stroke mortality in the UK. If, as seems likely, the situation in the USA foreshadows what will happen here,this spontaneous decline may be expected to cease during the decade of the 1990s. We may expect that further decline might be achieved by improved detection and treatment of high blood pressure as public and professional awareness increase and a wider range of effective and more acceptable drugs becomes available. Modification of diet to reduce salt intake may produce further falls in average population blood pressures. A reduction in smoking would contribute to a decline in stroke incidence through other mechanisms. A further modest reduction in incidence of the order of 5% might be expected from a programme of detection and anticoagulant treatment of atrial fibrillation. It is not realistic to try to make firm estimates of the effects of all these factors but given that present trends seem to be in a positive direction we can perhaps expect a 20–30% reduction in stroke incidence in the age range 55–75 by the year 2001. In the anticipated absence of major developments in rehabilitative measures during this period the reduction in disability from stroke will be of the same order.

References

Allen CMC. Clinical diagnosis of the acute stroke syndrome. *Q J Med*, 1983; 52: 205–211.

Bamford J, Sandercock P, Dennis M *et al.* A prospective study of acute cerebrovascular disease in the community; the Oxfordshire Community Stroke Project—1981–1986. 2. Incidence, case fatality rates and overall outcome at one year of cerebral infarction, primary intracerebral haemorrhage and subarachnoid haemorrhage. *J Neurol Neurosurg Psychiatry*, 1990; 53: 16–22.

Barker DJP, Osmond C, Golding J, Kuh D, Wadsworth MEJ. Growth *in utero*, blood pressure in childhood and adult life, and mortality from cardiovascular disease. *Br Med J*, 1989; 298: 564–567.

Bonita R, Scragg R, Stewart A, Jackson R, Beaglehole R. Cigarette smoking and risk of premature stroke in men and women. *Br Med J*, 1986; 293: 6–8.

Bonita R. Epidemiology of stroke. *Lancet*, 1992; 339: 342–344.

Bonita R, Beaglehole R. Trends in cerebrovascular disease mortality in New Zealand. *NZMJ*, 1982; 95: 411–414.

Borhani N. Mortality trends in hypertension, United States, 1950–1976. In Havlik R, Feinleib M (eds), *Proceedings of the conference on the decline in coronary heart disease mortality*, NIH publication No. 79-1610, pp. 218–233. US Department of Health Education and Welfare, Washington DC, 1979.

Broderick JP, Phillips SJ, Whisnant JP, O'Fallon WM, Bergstrahl EJ. Incidence rates of stroke in the eighties: the end of the decline in stroke? *Stroke*, 1989; 20: 577–582.

Corwin LI, Wolf PA, Kannel WB, McNamara PM. Accuracy of death certification of stroke: the Framingham study. *Stroke*, 1982; 13: 818–821.

Dobson AJ. Age-specific trends in mortality from ischaemic heart disease and cerebrovascular disease in Australia. *Am J Epidemiol*, 1981; 113: 404–412.

Garraway WM, Whisnant JP, Drury I. The changing pattern of survival following stroke. *Stroke*, 1983; 14: 699–703.

Grimley Evans J. *Risk factors for stroke in the elderly*, MD Dissertation. University of Cambridge, 1985.

Grimley Evans J. The decline of stroke. In Rose FC (ed.), *Stroke: epidemiological, therapaeutic and socioeconomic aspects*, pp. 33–38. Royal Society of Medicine, London, 1986.

Grimley Evans J. Blood pressure and stroke in an elderly English population. *J Epidemiol Community Health*, 1987; 41: 275–282.

Harrison MJG, Pollock S, Kendall BE, Marshall J. Effect of haematocrit on carotid stenosis and cerebral infarction. *Lancet*, 1981; ii: 114–115.

Hillbom M, Kaste M. Ethanol intoxication a risk factor for ischaemic brain infarction in adolescents and young adults. *Stroke*, 1981; 12: 422–425.

Joossens JV. Salt and hypertension, water hardness and cardiovascular disease. *Triangle*, 1973; 12: 9–16.

Joossens JV, Kesteloot H, Amery A. Salt intake and mortality from stroke. *New Engl J Med*, 1979; 300: 1396.

Kopecky SL, Gersh BJ, McGoon MD *et al*. The natural history of lone atrial fibrillation. A population-based study over three decades. *New Engl J Med*, 1987; 317: 669–674.

Ostfeld AM. A review of stroke epidemiology. *Epidemiol Rev*, 1980; 2: 136–152.

Prior IAM, Grimley Evans J, Davidson F, Lindsay M. Sodium intake and blood pressure in two Polynesian populations. *New Engl J Med*, 1968; 279: 515–520.

Reid DS, Grimley Evans J. New drugs and changing mortality from non-infectious disease. *Br Med Bull*, 1970; 26: 191–196.

Shaper AG, Phillips AN, Pocock SJ, Walker M, Macfarlane PW. Risk factors for stroke in middle-aged British men. *Br Med J*, 1991; 302: 1111–1115.

Shinton R, Beevers G. Meta-analysis of relation between cigarette smoking and stroke. *Br Med J*, 1989; 298: 789–794.

The Boston Area Anticoagulation Trial for Atrial Fibrillation Investigators. The effect of low-dose warfarin on the risk of stroke in patients with nonrheumatic atrial fibrillation. *New Engl J Med*, 1990; 323: 1505–1511.

The Stroke Prevention in Atrial Fibrillation Investigators. Stroke prevention in atrial fibrillation study. Final results. *Circulation*, 1991; 84: 527–539.

Wald NJ, Frost CD, Law MR. By how much does dietary salt reduction lower blood pressure? *Br Med J*, 1991; 302: 818–824.

Whisnant JP. The decline of stroke. *Stroke*, 1984; 15: 160–168.

Wolf PA, Kannel WB, McGee DL, Meeks SL, Bharucha NE, McNamara PM. Duration of atrial fibrillation and imminence of stroke: the Framingham Study. *Stroke*, 1983; 14: 664–667.

Wolf PA. Cigarettes, alcohol and stroke. *New Engl J Med*, 1986; 315: 1087–1088.

Wolf PA, Abbott RD, Kannel WB. Atrial fibrillation: a major contributor to stroke in the elderly. The Framingham study. *Arch Int Med*, 1987; 147: 1561–1564.

Cancers

M.J. Goldacre

In this chapter we provide brief descriptions of the epidemiology of the numerically most important cancers in the third age. In so far as risk factors for individual cancers have been established, they are similar in the third age to those for cancers at other times in adult life.

Oesophagus

Cancer of the oesophagus accounts for about 2% of all cancers in the third age. Incidence rates of oesophageal cancer vary considerably internationally. Britain is not a particularly high-risk area. In Britain, as in western Europe generally, the cancer is aetiologically related to smoking and alcohol consumption. Its occurrence fell progressively in the first half of the present century with the decline in alcohol consumption. However, it has risen in recent decades, notably in middle-aged men, as alcohol consumption has risen again.

Stomach

On a worldwide scale, cancer of the stomach is one of the commonest causes of death from malignant disease. In Britain it accounts for about 5% of all cancers in the third age. There is wide geographical variation in its incidence internationally (with particularly high rates in Japan and parts of China). Within Britain its incidence tends to be higher in the north than south and higher in the west than east. It is considerably more common in social classes 4 and 5 than 1 and 2. Its incidence in Britain has been gradually declining. Genetic factors play some part in its aetiology and diet is almost certainly important. However, despite a number of clues, there is no firm evidence about the major causes of this cancer.

Large bowel

Cancers of the colon and rectum account for about 11% of all cancers in the third age. International variation in the incidence of these cancers is marked. It is considerably more common in developed than developing countries. There is some epidemiological evidence which indicates an association with 'western' diet but specific causes are unknown.

Lung

Lung cancer accounts for about 26% of all cancers in males and 12% of cancers in females in the third age in Britain. Until the 1920s it was an uncommon disease. By the 1950s the age-standardised mortality rates for lung cancer in Britain in men had increased 20-fold. It is now well recognised that over 90% of all lung cancers in Britain are attributable to tobacco smoking.

Incidence rates have been considerably lower in women than men (reflecting the fact that in the past the prevalence of smoking was much lower in women than men). In the last couple of decades, however, the incidence of lung cancer in men has started to decline (as has that in young women) whilst the incidence in older women is increasing. These trends reflect trends in tobacco consumption in earlier years.

Occupational exposures (e.g. to asbestos and polycyclic hydrocarbons) are also recognised risk factors for a minority of cases of lung cancer.

Pancreas

Cancer of the pancreas accounts for about 3% of cancers in the third age. It is about twice as common in regular cigarette smokers than in non-smokers. In addition, the incidence of the disease appears to be correlated with high standards of living but, otherwise, its aetiology is unknown.

Breast

Cancer of the breast accounts for over 20% of cancers in women in the third age in Britain. There is striking geographical variation in its incidence internationally. In general, it is much more common in the developed than the developing world. The incidence of breast cancer has increased in recent decades in the developed world. Dietary factors have been implicated in its aetiology but it has not been possible yet to define them precisely. Similarly, hormonal factors are recognised as important but have not been defined specifically. The lifetime duration of ovarian activity appears important as the disease is more common in women who have an early menarche and a late menopause than in others. An early age of first full-term pregnancy also seems protective against breast cancer later in life. There is conflicting evidence about whether long duration of use of oral contraceptives, particularly prior to the birth of the first child, is a risk factor. Despite various clues about aetiology, for the most part it remains unknown.

Cervix

Cancer of the cervix accounts for 2% of cancers in women in the third age in Britain. Squamous cell carcinoma, the common type, is associated with a number of indicators of sexual activity of which the number of sexual partners (either of the woman or her partner), is probably the common denominator. Other factors which may contribute to the disease include cigarette smoking and, possibly, the use of oral contraceptives.

Endometrium

Cancer of the endometrium (body of the uterus) accounts for about 4% of all cancers in women in the third age. The risk of the disease is higher in nulliparous women than others. Its risk is unrelated to the number of sexual partners. Like cancer of the breast, it is associated with early menarche and late menopause. Exposure to the intake of oestrogens is also a recognised risk factor.

Ovary

Cancer of the ovary accounts for about 5% of cancers in women in the third age. The incidence of the disease is decreased by the use of oral contraceptives. In rare instances ovarian cancer occurs in families and is considered to have a genetic component. Its causes are otherwise unknown.

Prostate

Cancer of the prostate accounts for about 8% of cancers in men in the third age. Its aetiology is unknown.

Bladder

Bladder cancers account for about 5% of all cancers in the third age. The most important known aetiological agent is cigarette smoking. A range of other chemical exposures (e.g. in the dye and rubber industries) have been implicated in its aetiology but the total contribution of recognised industrial carcinogens to the overall incidence of bladder cancer is fairly small.

Leukaemias and lymphomas

These conditions account for about 5% of cancers in Britain in the third age. Ionising radiation is a recognised risk factor for leukaemia but accounts for small numbers of cases. Other recognised causes in a minority of cases include certain chemicals and medicinal agents. However, the cause of the majority of cases is unknown.

Registration rates

Registration rates for newly diagnosed cancers at common sites are shown in Table 10.1.

Table 10.1

Cancer registrations of newly diagnosed cases of cancer, selected sites. Trends 1971–1986: rates per 100,000 population

Site description	(ICD codes)	Age group	Males				Females			
			1971	1976	1981	1986	1971	1976	1981	1986
All malignant neoplasms	140–209	50–54	392.4	411.3	372.9	342.9	424.9	465.1	436.8	443.1
		55–59	650.3	665.8	662.5	613.4	536.8	584.5	610.0	596.7
		60–64	1013.1	1076.3	1029.5	1048.9	657.3	756.9	764.7	807.5
		65–69	1429.9	1570.0	1534.7	1529.5	790.5	909.9	955.6	992.3
		70–74	1918.1	2117.7	2116.1	2145.8	957.4	1104.4	1159.0	1232.9
Stomach	151	50–54	26.7	27.4	23.8	18.3	11.3	11.0	7.8	7.1
		55–59	52.0	44.1	43.6	38.5	17.8	17.2	16.5	10.6
		60–64	88.6	77.5	70.1	64.2	33.7	28.8	23.7	22.3
		65–69	129.4	132.2	115.7	99.9	51.6	47.1	40.3	32.6
		70–74	173.8	180.6	167.2	144.3	75.7	77.8	69.1	53.0
Large intestine, except rectum	153	50–54	19.5	24.7	22.3	20.8	25.4	23.1	22.9	24.8
		55–59	35.6	35.9	38.0	39.1	34.5	39.1	36.5	37.5
		60–64	52.8	58.2	61.5	61.1	52.9	58.5	54.4	58.1
		65–69	77.5	96.4	93.6	91.6	72.1	81.6	81.7	73.0
		70–74	122.4	142.3	134.1	134.9	94.6	111.8	116.2	103.5
Rectum and rectosigmoid colon	154	50–54	17.9	19.6	19.9	19.3	12.7	15.7	13.4	12.3
		55–59	31.6	34.9	34.6	32.4	19.7	22.6	23.0	20.8
		60–64	50.0	53.9	48.2	56.3	30.2	31.1	29.7	30.4
		65–69	76.4	79.9	81.0	77.1	37.9	44.3	41.7	40.1
		70–74	109.8	111.1	111.2	108.2	51.9	56.6	56.4	56.2
Trachea, bronchus and lung	162	50–54	126.0	127.2	97.5	64.9	35.2	39.3	40.8	29.3
		55–59	221.6	221.9	200.0	152.3	49.8	56.5	71.7	61.9
		60–64	377.6	376.3	372.0	282.6	61.4	86.8	98.9	107.9
		65–69	503.6	526.6	472.6	415.2	72.6	95.3	121.8	141.2
		70–74	621.8	678.0	629.6	559.8	77.9	102.1	132.4	159.7
Female breast	174	50–54	–	–	–	–	123.6	144.5	139.1	154.4
		55–59	–	–	–	–	141.0	153.8	162.2	167.7
		60–64	–	–	–	–	161.3	184.9	171.8	197.9
		65–69	–	–	–	–	163.2	193.3	201.7	204.6
		70–74	–	–	–	–	180.8	203.1	208.7	221.3
Prostate	185	50–54	4.9	5.6	7.2	7.2	–	–	–	–
		55–59	18.8	19.4	25.0	25.9	–	–	–	–
		60–64	44.6	56.2	54.9	64.6	–	–	–	–
		65–69	92.6	114.8	124.3	139.2	–	–	–	–
		70–74	180.7	206.4	221.6	259.4	–	–	–	–
Bladder	188	50–54	22.4	23.9	23.0	21.7	6.4	7.9	8.0	8.6
		55–59	41.7	36.5	43.0	40.6	8.6	10.9	13.7	13.4
		60–64	61.2	63.0	69.0	71.3	15.8	14.9	20.3	21.9
		65–69	97.2	94.9	101.6	101.8	21.2	22.7	28.8	29.6
		70–74	132.6	139.1	146.0	148.7	30.9	32.6	34.0	42.1

Source: OPCS, series MB1.

Acknowledgements

This chapter includes analyses from studies undertaken by the author with funding from the Department of Health. I thank Joanna Norton and Kate Hey for their help in preparing the tables and graphs; and Pamela Evans for typing the manuscript.

Depression

11

Margaret Savory

Prevalence

Depression has been called the epidemic of old age (Coleman, 1988). It is one of the most common conditions found to prevail in surveys of older persons (Brayne and Ames, 1988). However, amongst the older population it has proved difficult to estimate prevalence. Rates range from 7.6% to 20.9% for males and from 13.6% to 29.4% for females. Table 11.1 summarises results from recent studies for the prevalence of depression in the community.

Several reasons account for the varying estimates. Firstly, it has proved difficult to define depression precisely. It is an umbrella term, referring to a continuum that extends from the normal reactions of sadness at life's adverse events through to major disorders for which there are strict diagnostic criteria. In addition, depression can often accompany and be secondary to other psychiatric disorders such as dementia, or psychosis (Blazer and Williams, 1980). All depressions have features in common such as deflated mood, increased worry, apathy, tension, but severity and combinations of symptoms are variable. As stated in *The Oxford textbook of psychiatry*, 'There is no general agreement about the best method of classifying depressive disorders' (Gelder *et al.*, 1989). Thus, rates vary according to where the 'cutoff' point for classifying a person as depressed is placed. For example, a study of 997 community-residing persons over the age of 65 in south-east USA found that whereas in total 14.7% of the sample had symptoms of depression, just 3.7% met the diagnostic criteria for a major depressive disorder. Other persons categorised as depressed were either dysphoric (i.e. of lowered mood), but did not meet the diagnostic criteria of the depressive disorder (4.5%), or their symptoms were considered to be related to impaired physical health (6.5%) (Blazer and Williams, 1980). Other studies have considered affective disorders together and not separated out depression from other neuroses (e.g. Kay *et al.*, 1964).

A second source of discrepancy lies in the methodology used to gather data. Results vary according to the samples under study—whether they are community- or hospital-based—and according to whether self-report or clinical diagnostic criteria are used to ascertain levels of depression. Studies that have used clinical diagnostic criteria (such as an interview with a psychiatrist) yield lower prevalence rates than those which use self-report questionnaires, usually encompassing a broader definition of depression. Meaningful comparison across different studies is also made difficult by the wide variety of self-report questionnaires in use.

There are no consistent age trends for prevalence of depression. Some studies suggest an increased prevalence with advancing age (Murrell *et al.*, 1983; Livingston *et al.*, 1990), whereas other show a decline (Myers *et al.*, 1984; Evans *et al.*, 1991; Blazer, 1989). Blazer *et al.* (1991) found a positive association between age and depressive symptoms amongst 3998 community dwellers age 65+, although they argue that the association was relatively weak. There appears to be no satisfactory study which compares the prevalence of depression across the entire lifespan, such studies as have been reported invariably having too few older subjects for the results

Table 11.1

Prevalence of depression: UK and US community samples

Authors	Sample	Age	Location	Assessment measure	Prevalence
Kay et al., 1964	115 M 194 F	65+	Newcastle, UK	Psychiatrist interview	20.9% M (8.7% mild, 12.2% severe) 29.4% F (20.6% mild, 8.8% severe)
Blazer and Williams, 1980	373 M	65+	SE USA	OARS-depressive scale	13.1% M 15.7% F 14.7% overall
Murrell et al., 1983	962 M 1555 F	55+	Kentucky, USA	CES-D Scale (Score ≥ 16)	18.5% M 23.8% F
Gurland et al., 1983	396 445	65+ 65+	London, UK New York, USA	CARE CARE	12.4% 13.0%
Myers et al., 1984	3350	65+	USA—3 different centres	DIS/DSMIII	0.1–0.5% M-major depression 1.0–1.6% F-major depression
Berkman et al., 1986	2806	65+	New Haven, USA	CES-D Scale (Score ≥ 16)	11.31% M 19.21% F
Copeland et al., 1987a	410 M 660 F	65+	Liverpool, UK	AGECAT	7.6% M 13.6% F 11.3% overall
Copeland et al., 1987b	396 445	65+	London, UK New York, USA	AGECAT AGECAT	19.4% 16.2%
Morgan et al., 1987	406 M 636F	65+	Nottingham, UK	Symptoms of Anxiety and Depression scales (SAD)	9.8% (or 4.9% meeting stricter clinical criteria)
Lindesay et al., 1989	357 M 533 F	65+	London, UK	CARE	8.4% M (2.8% M meet stricter criteria) 16.9% F (5.3% F meet stricter criteria)
Livingston et al., 1990	258 M 447 F	65+	London, UK	CARE	15.9%

M = male; F = female

to be meaningful. Studies specifically looking at those aged 65 or more may provide data, but then it is difficult to make comparisons with younger age groups. Furthermore, many studies restrict themselves to a global description of all those in the 65+ category, without closer scrutiny of separate age bands. In addition, longitudinal (or prospective) studies are scarce. Such studies need to be carried out in order to eliminate the possible confounding of age with cohort effects. For example, there has been some indication that certain cohorts have been protected against depressive symptoms, which could possibly introduce an artefactual age effect in cross-sectional comparisons (Blazer *et al.*, 1991).

Acknowledging the difficulties mentioned above, Table 11.2 lists the results from two studies where smaller age-band data are provided. It is difficult to describe any clear pattern. For males, there appears to be a steady increase in prevalence with advancing age. However, the situation appears more mixed for females, with rates decreasing in 'early' old age before increasing once more. There is, perhaps, a clearer pattern between the sexes. Many studies find higher overall rates of depression amongst women (e.g. Lindesay *et al.*, 1989; Copeland *et al.*, 1987a; Evans *et al.*, 1991), although the differences are not always statistically significant (e.g. Livingston *et al.*, 1990). Women also appear to report milder depression more commonly than men (Kay *et al.*, 1964).

Risk factors for depression

Advanced age, *per se*, may not necessarily be the predominant risk factor for depression. Changes in prevalence rates for depression could result from a relative increase in the distribution of other risk factors known to be associated with depression, all of which are thought to have greater occurrence in later years. These include a previous history of depression, physical illness and disability, recent life events (such as bereavement) and social and economic circumstances. Indeed, Blazer *et al.* (1991) found that by taking into account such factors as physical disability, social support and income, a previously positive association between age and depressive symptoms disappeared.

Physical illness, pain and disability

There is a well-established association between physical illness and depression. Murrell *et al.* (1983) found that depression increased with poor health and that this

Table 11.2

Prevalence of depression across age groups

Murrell et al. (1983), Kentucky			Livingston et al. (1990), London		
Age	Males (%)	Females (%)	Age	Males (%)	Females (%)
55–59	13.2	19.0	65–69	13.6	21.4
60–64	11.1	15.0	70–74	13.3	16.5
65–74	12.9	14.5	75–79	12.9	21.5
75+	17.5	26.0	80+	16.4	16.5

relationship was unaffected by age in both sexes. Likewise, depressive symptoms are often reported by patients with chronic pain (Magni *et al.*, 1990). In the UK, *The health and lifestyle survey* (Huppert *et al.*, 1987) found that those self-reporting greater numbers of symptoms associated with physical illness had higher mean scores on the General Health Questionnaire, a screening questionnaire devised to detect psychiatric illness (Table 11.3). Turner and Noh (1988) reported that the disabled have three times the risk of depression than the non-disabled (35% *vs* 12%).

Often it is difficult to distinguish between physical illness and depression, as there are symptoms which are common to both. For example, many scales used to assess depressive symptoms contain several questions concerning somatic complaints, such as loss of appetite, sleeplessness, lack of energy etc. Higher scores on depression scales, therefore, may reflect declining physical health rather than a depressed mood state. Alternatively, older persons may not report depressive symptoms *per se*, but tend to present physical symptoms that mask the depressive symptoms. Gurland (1976) compared older with younger depressives and found that the only statistically significant difference was the more frequent somatic symptoms reported by the older persons.

Unclear is the extent to which age is a mediating factor in the relationship between physical illness and depression. Gurland *et al.* (1988) suggest that there is a weakening in the relationship between depression and disability as age advances, and provide several reasons including: the effect of survivorship; selection bias, as surveys of those in the community, by definition, exclude those admitted to institutions; changes in the nature of disability with advancing age; normative expectations, making it easier to accept disability; cohort differences in coping strategy; practice effects of previous experience; greater support from family and friends; a reduction in other life events; and neurobiological changes.

Whereas physical illness is a common predictor of depression, it also appears that the converse is true. Depressed people are also more likely to report physical illness and disability. In a study of recovery from stroke, Feibel and Springer (1982) reported that 24 out of 91 cases were also suffering from depression. After six months, the depressed group had a significantly reduced chance of returning to their normal social functioning, losing 67% of their prior social activities, compared with 43% in the non-depressed group. Pitt (1988) also suggests that older depressive persons are prone to hypochondriasis and cites De Alarcon (1964) who found

Table 11.3

Scores on 30-item General Health Questionnaire and illness symptoms

Mean number of symptoms declared by responders with low, average or high scores

Age	Males			Females		
	Low	Average	High	Low	Average	High
18–39	2.98	3.63	5.40	3.27	4.41	6.57
40–64	2.64	3.77	5.55	2.66	4.00	6.19
65+	2.49	3.54	5.22	2.83	3.57	7.38

Source: Huppert et al. *(1987). In* The health and lifestyle survey. *Health Promotion Research Trust, London.*

hypochondria in approximately two-thirds of depressed elderly patients admitted to hospital.

However, the absence of longitudinal studies makes it difficult to uncover the direction of causality between physical illness and depression.

Life events

Murphy (1982) compared 100 depressed inpatients with a group of community-dwelling controls, matched for age and sex. In the year preceding illness onset, the depressed patients experienced significantly more 'severe' life events (80 per 100 subjects) than the healthy counterparts (26 per 100 subjects). Of the severe life events, the most frequently occurring was physical illness (28 per 100 patients) followed by separation from or death of a spouse or child (18 per 100 patients).

Bereavement is a relatively common occurrence in the older person's life and is considered to be an important risk factor. It has been shown to lead to a sixfold elevation in depressive symptomatology in widows at one month post-bereavement (Harlow et al., 1991). However, loss of a loved one by itself is not usually sufficient to cause long-term depression. Coleman (1988) argues that depression rates observed in later life are remarkably low given the increased prevalence of bereavement. The majority of older people cope relatively well with their losses. In their longitudinal study, Harlow and colleagues (1991) found that those widows who continued to suffer prolonged depression at 12 months post-bereavement, were best predicted by their pre-bereavement scores. That is, the risk factors for depression were the same for both widows and non-widows and factors other than bereavement were important.

Social factors

Social circumstance appears to be a strong predictor of depression. Murphy (1982) found that whereas none of the sample classified as 'middle' class were depressed, 17% of those categorised as 'working' class were. Furthermore, 'working' class members suffered a higher rate of severe life events, social difficulties and health problems, sufficient to account for the increased prevalence of depression. However, Evans et al. (1991) found no significant link between the presence of depression and financial problems.

Lack of a confiding relationship may be important in increasing vulnerability to depression. Murphy (1982) found that the chances of developing a depression after a severe life event without a confiding relationship were considerably higher than with one. A similar result was also obtained by Harlow et al. (1991) in their study of bereavement. Other studies have also highlighted the importance of social support in reducing vulnerability to depression (Brown et al., 1986, 1987). Feeling lonely (rather than living alone) has also been found to correlate with depression, although the presence of a home help was negatively correlated with depression, possibly indicating an important role for this service in meeting older persons' physical and emotional needs (Evans et al., 1991).

Addition of risk factors

Murphy (1982) provides some evidence that the risk factors are additive, i.e. poor health and deprived social circumstances increase the risk of depression following a major life event. Of 51 community-dwelling subjects who experienced a 'severe' event, 25% became depressed subsequently. Of 18 who had both poor health and a severe event, 44% became depressed. Of 12 who had a major social difficulty and a severe event, 50% became depressed. Finally, of the five subjects who possessed all three risk factors, four (80%) became depressed.

Summary

There still remains considerable confusion as to the exact prevalence rates of depression in the older population. Estimates vary according to the stringency of diagnostic criteria, the measuring instruments used, and the samples under consideration. Prevalence studies have reported rates that range from around one in ten to one in four of the elderly population suffering some form of depression. There appears to be little consensus as to whether rates increase or decrease with advancing age, although it is a common illness amongst the older population.

Perhaps the most striking risk factor for depression is disability and physical illness, although life events such as bereavement and social and economic status are also considered important. Prevalence of these risk factors all increase with advancing age, yet the evidence for prevalence of depression increasing is inconsistent. Given the reduced economic and social circumstances, the ill health and bereavement that older persons face, Jarvik (1976) questions 'why is not every old person in a profound state of depression?' Yet, most older persons live out their lives without major depressive symptomatology. Future research that establishes the factors that enable the majority to cope successfully with bereavement, physical illness and reduced social and economic circumstances may be of as great importance as establishing risk factors for depression.

References

Berkman LF *et al.* Depressive symptoms in relation to physical health and functioning in the elderly. *Am J Epidemiol*, 1986; 124: 372–388.

Blazer D. The epidemiology of depression in late life. *J Geriat Psych*, 1989; 12: 35–52.

Blazer D, Williams C. Epidemiology of dysphoria and depression in an elderly population. *Am J Psych*, 1980; 137: 439–444.

Blazer, D. *et al.* The association of age and depression among the elderly: an epidemiologic exploration. *J Gerontol*, 1991; 46: 210–215.

Brayne C, Ames D. The epidemiology of mental disorders in old age. In Gearing B, Johnson M, Heller T (eds), *Mental health problems in old age*, pp. 10–26. Wiley, Chichester, 1988.

Brown GW *et al.* Social support, self-esteem and depression. *Psychol Med*, 1986; 16: 813–831.

Brown GW, Bifulco A, Harris TO. Life events, vulnerability and onset of depression. *Br J Psych*, 1987; 150: 30–42.

Coleman P. Mental health in old age. In Gearing B, Johnson M, Heller T (eds), *Mental health problems in old age*, pp. 36–41. Wiley, Chichester, 1988.

Copeland JRM *et al.* Range of mental illness among the elderly in the community: prevalence in Liverpool using the GMS-AGECAT Package. *Br J Psych*, 1987a; 150: 815–823.

Copeland JRM *et al.* Is there more dementia, depression and neurosis in New York? *Br J Psych*, 1987b; 151: 466–473.

De Alarcon RD. Hypochondriasis and depression in the aged. *Gerontol Clin*, 1964; 6: 266–277.

Evans ME *et al.* Depression in the elderly in the community: effect of physical illness and selected social factors. *Int J Geriat Psych*, 1991; 6: 787–795.

Feibel JH, Springer CJ. Depression and failure to resume social activities after stroke. *Arch Phys Med Rehabil*, 1982; 63: 276–278.

Gelder M, Gath D, Mayou R. *The Oxford textbook of psychiatry*. Oxford University Press, Oxford, 1989.

Gurland B. The comparative frequency of depression in various adult age groups. *J Gerontol*, 1976; 31: 283–292.

Gurland B *et al.* *The mind and mood of aging*. Croom Helm, London, 1983.

Gurland B *et al.* Depression and disability in the elderly: reciprocal relations and changes with age. *Int J Geriat Psych*, 1988; 3: 163–179.

Harlow SD *et al.* A longitudinal study of risk factors for depressive symptomatology in elderly widowed and married women. *Am J Epidemiol*, 1991; 134: 526–538.

Huppert FA *et al.* Psychological function. In Cox B *et al.* (eds), *The health and lifestyle survey*. Health Promotion Research Trust, London, 1987.

Jarvik L. Aging and depression: some unanswered questions. *J Gerontol*, 1976; 31: 324–326.

Kay DWK, Beamish P, Roth M. Old age mental disorders in Newcastle upon Tyne. *Br J Psych*, 1964; 110: 146–158.

Lindesay J, Briggs K, Murphy E. The Guy's/Age Concern Survey: prevalence rates of cognitive impairment, depression and anxiety in an urban elderly community. *Br J Psych*, 1989; 155: 317–329.

Livingston G *et al.* The Gospel Oak study: prevalence rates of dementia, depression and activity limitation among elderly residents in inner London. *Psychol Med*, 1990; 20: 137–146.

Magni G *et al.* Chronic musculoskeletal pain and depressive symptoms in the general population. An analysis of the first National Health and Nutrition Examination Survey data. *Pain*, 1990; 299–307.

Morgan K *et al.* Mental health and psychological well-being among the old and very old living at home. *Br J Psych*, 1987; 150: 801–807.

Murphy E. Social origins of depression in old age. *Br J Psych*, 1982; 141: 135–142.

Murrell S, Himmelfarb S, Wright K. Prevalence of depression and its correlates in older adults. *Am J Epidemiol*, 1983; 117: 173–185.

Myers JK *et al.* Six-month prevalence of psychiatric disorders in three communities. *Arch Gen Psych*, 1984; 41: 959–967.

Pitt B. Characteristics of depression in the elderly. In Gearing B, Johnson M, Heller T (eds), *Mental health problems in old age*, pp. 114–122. Wiley, Chichester, 1988.

Turner RJ, Noh S. Physical disability and depression. *J Health Soc Behavior*, 1988; 29: 23–37.

Dementia

12

J. Grimley Evans

The term 'dementia' has been used with a variety of meanings over the years but has in common usage now come to imply an acquired irreversible global impairment of cognitive function. 'Global' implies that all higher brain functions are impaired including memory, perception, attention and reasoning. Not all functions are necessarily affected to an equal degree at all stages of the common forms of dementia, and in the early stages of Alzheimer's disease, for example, memory problems are usually dominant. The memory problems in this condition are due to damage to a particular part of the brain and such damage may occur from some other causes which do not progress to damage other parts of the brain as happens in Alzheimer's disease. The demonstration of global impairment is therefore of crucial diagnostic importance.

Demonstration that a patient's cognitive impairment is acquired usually depends on reports from friends or relatives or may be deduced from a decline in occupational performance. Dementia is not the only cause of acquired impairment, however, and other problems such as depression and drug or alcohol abuse need to be excluded in a clinical assessment. One psychological approach to diagnosis is to compare scores on verbal tests with those on 'performance' tests such as manipulating shaped blocks into specified patterns or other tests of non-verbal reasoning. Tests such as the Wechsler Adult Intelligence Scale (WAIS) have been standardised so that people in good mental health tend to score similarly on both sets of subtests. In early dementia performance scores drop before verbal scores while in depression and some other conditions the two tend to fall together. In late dementia verbal skills are also lost. Criteria for the diagnosis of dementia drawn up by the American Psychiatric Association (1987) have come into general use (DSM-III-R).

Causes of dementia

The International Classification of Diseases lists the specific types of dementia under three main heads. The commonest in the UK is Alzheimer's disease (AD). Second commonest is vascular dementia due to disease in the blood vessels supplying the brain. The third group comprises an assemblage of rather rarer conditions including Huntington's disease, Pick's disease and Creutzfeld-Jakob disease which tend to follow a more distinctive clinical course than the two commoner groups of dementing diseases. It may prove difficult without invasive tests to distinguish between vascular dementia and AD in a particular patient, and mixed forms are not uncommon. In the absence of specific and effective therapy for either condition the distinction is important mainly for prognostic purposes. McKhann *et al.* (1984) have drawn up a widely accepted set of criteria for the clinical diagnosis of AD and the common

109

clinical features of multi-infarct dementia (MID), the commonest form of vascular dementia have been embodied in the Hachinski scale (Hachinski *et al.*, 1975). Recently there has been growing scepticism about the usefulness of this scale in clinical practice.

There are some rarer causes of a dementia syndrome that can be treated, although the benefit may only be to arrest progression rather than to restore function. Such conditions include neurosyphilis, hypothyroidism, hyperparathyroidism, vitamin B12 deficiency and cerebral tumours. Good clinical practice therefore demands that a patient who is suspected of early dementia should be assessed for the accuracy of the diagnosis and to exclude treatable factors. Until recently computed tomography (CT) scanning and other sophisticated radiological techniques have been considered likely to be useful only in cases where the clinical picture was somehow atypical and the possibility of a tumour existed. Some radiological methods are now becoming useful as a means of providing direct evidence of AD and so yielding prognostic information of value to the patient and his or her family.

The epidemiology of dementia

In the UK, USA and Scandinavia, MID is less common as a cause of dementia than is AD but the opposite is found in Japan and Russia. It is generally assumed that the epidemiology of MID follows that of stroke although there has been no clear demonstration that this is so. Thus the condition is thought to increase in incidence with age, to affect men more than women and to be related to high blood pressure, coronary heart disease and other risk factors for stroke. One may also hope that if the incidence of stroke is falling, as seems likely, vascular dementia will follow suit.

Subjects with atrial fibrillation who have not had a stroke have been shown by CT scanning to have suffered more 'silent' brain infarcts than matched controls without atrial fibrillation (Petersen, 1987). This presumably implies that treatment with anticoagulants for people with atrial fibrillation is likely to prevent some cases of vascular dementia as well as bringing about a 30–40% reduction in the risk of stroke (The Stroke Prevention in Atrial Fibrillation Investigators, 1991). Other approaches to preventing multi-infarct dementia as distinct from stroke, for example by drugs claimed to increase brain blood flow, have not been convincing.

As reviewed by Jorm (1990), there are serious and only partly solved methodological problems in the epidemiological study of dementia. Some of these involve difficulties in standardising interviews and interviewers' techniques. Others are more fundamental and include, for example, the vexed issue of whether scores on mental function scales should be adjusted for educational status (Berkman, 1986). If this is not done social class differences emerge with higher rates in the lower social and educational classes. Some would argue that adjustment of scores for educational status will obscure genuine differences in the prevalence of dementia between social classes. Similar considerations presumably apply to the higher rates of cognitive impairment and clinically diagnosed AD found in blacks than in whites in some North American studies (Schoenberg *et al.*, 1985).

There are three possible explanations for a social class difference if it exists (Grimley Evans, 1992). The lower classes may have been differentially exposed to some environmental cause of AD or they may have a higher prevalence of other forms of brain damage, such as vascular disease, which enhances the functional impairment due to AD. The third possibility is that better brains, whether better because of their genetic endowment or made to function better by education, can compensate better and longer for the damage caused by AD or other forms of brain pathology. This last hypothesis has the intriguing implication that even if the incidence and prevalence of brain damage do not change, improving the nutrition and education of the population may reduce the incidence and prevalence of mental and social impairments. In Sweden such progressive improvements in the mental functioning of elderly people may in fact be occurring (Berg, 1980).

Prevalence data are also sensitive to differences in survival times and data from the UK suggest that over recent decades the survival times of patients with dementia have been increasing, presumably through improved nursing care (Blessed and Wilson, 1982).

A rigorous attempt was made by Gurland et al. (1984) to compare the prevalence of dementia and AD in New York and London. The results suggested lower rates in London and in a subsequent comparison Kay et al. (1985) noted that Hobart, Tasmania had rates comparable with those of New York. There is a general problem in defining an appropriate sampling frame for elderly people in urban centres in the UK since demented subjects may be withdrawn into residential care some distance from their original abode and be omitted from community samples.

Because of such methodological uncertainties it is generally agreed that there is no unequivocal evidence of consistent geographical differences in the many prevalence studies that have been carried out. Several attempts have therefore been made to merge findings into some form of composite model of age-specific prevalence. The data suggest an exponential relationship of prevalence to age and Jorm et al. (1987) have proposed a specific formula implying that prevalence rates double every 5.1 years of age.

Illustrative data based on the average for published studies are shown in Table 12.1 (Jorm, 1990). There are no consistent sex differences in prevalence rates for dementia of all types (Table 12.1) but fairly consistent differences between the sexes emerge in the studies separating AD and vascular disease. The M:F ratio of prevalence of AD is of the order of 0.5 and of vascular dementia 1.8. This epidemio-

Table 12.1

Age-specific prevalence rates (%) of dementia (all forms)

Age group	Median age	Prevalence
60–64	62.5	0.7
65–69	67.5	1.4
70–74	72.5	2.8
75–79	77.5	5.6
80–84	82.0	10.5
85–89	87.0	20.8
90–95	91.5	38.6

Source: Jorm (1990).

logical evidence that AD is more common in women is supported by many, although not all necropsy studies.

The methodological difficulties in prevalence studies of dementia are compounded in the measurement of incidence by the need to stabilise techniques over a period of time. There are no incidence data relating to the third age from the UK, although an annual incidence of 1.4% has been reported for a population sample of people aged 75 and over (Jagger et al., 1989). Hagnell et al. (1983) have presented data from the Lundby study which is unusual in having made observations over a long period of time and in having involved an unusually wide age range. Table 12.2 sets out the estimated age-specific cumulative incidence of dementia from Lundby.

Risk factors for Alzheimer's disease

A general heuristic model for AD postulates that in the genesis of damage to brain cells there is an interaction between one or more environmental agents and a genetic susceptibility (Grimley Evans, 1992). Most people have a genetic make-up which allows them to live out a long life without accumulating enough damage to become functionally demented. A minority of people have an unfortunate genetic endowment, or have Down syndrome, and will accumulate damage faster. Thus the genetic component in AD will be much more apparent in early-onset than in late-onset disease. Nonetheless in large bodies of data evidence for a familial link in late-onset can be detected (Breitner, 1991). Indeed it has been suggested that the risk of AD in first degree relatives of sufferers may approach 50% by the age of 90 (Breitner, 1991) but this is in the relatives of selected cases with highly specific features such as aphasic difficulties. Such may represent the genetics of early- rather than late-onset disease. It is already clear that early-onset disease is genetically heterogeneous. Presumably there will also be in the population some people who are immune to the putative environmental agents and the genetic make-up of undemented centenarians may prove to be as interesting as that of people dementing in middle life. The study of the phenotypic actions of genes producing early-onset AD may give a clue to the environmental factors involved. At present the absence of any clear evidence of geographic or occupational variation in AD incidence may indicate that the environmental factors are ubiquitous. It could also indicate that there are no environmental factors involved and AD is entirely autotoxic. Since environmental manipulation offers more immediate prospect of control of AD than does gene

Table 12.2

Incidence rates per 1000 per year for AD and MID in Lundby 1957–72

	Men		Women	
Age	AD	MID	AD	MID
0–49	0	0	0	0
50–59	0	0.4	0	0
60–69	0	4.1	1.7	1.3
70–79	7.0	4.4	12.3	5.1
80–89	18.9	20.5	25.3	9.3
90–99	13.2	40.2	17.8	0

Source: Hagnell et al. (1983).

therapy it seems prudent to maintain a search for such factors in addition to pursuing the AD genes.

Aluminium is one candidate as a relevant and ubiquitous environmental agent since it has been found in the brain lesions of AD (Candy *et al.*, 1986) although a later report based on a different method of analysis has been unable to confirm this (Landsberg *et al.*, 1992). Doll (1993) has reviewed the epidemiological evidence linking AD with environmental sources of aluminium. He concludes that evidence from high levels of industrial exposure shows that aluminium can be neurotoxic but that there are insufficient grounds at present for concluding that it can cause AD. Attempts to link AD prevalence with aluminium in drinking water have not been convincing in themselves (Flaten, 1989; Martyn *et al.*, 1989) but Doll (1993) points out that positive associations between AD and aluminium content of drinking water may be restricted to areas where the pH of the water is low.

It could be that differences in the metabolism of aluminium make it more toxic for some individuals than for others. Data suggesting that there might be differences in the protein-binding of aluminium in blood between patients with AD and controls (Farrar *et al.*, 1990) have come under methodological criticism. A recent report has suggested that there may be differences in the absorption of aluminium in early-onset (but not late-onset) AD patients compared with controls (Taylor *et al.*, 1992). A further piece of evidence possibly implicating aluminium is the report that injections of desferrioxamine which removes aluminium (and other things) from the body may retard the rate of deterioration in patients with AD (McLachlan *et al.*, 1992). It would be premature to implicate aluminium in the aetiology of AD but its pursuit exemplifies the various approaches that could be brought to bear on possible environmental agents.

Several studies have suggested a higher parental age at birth for AD patients than for controls. Jorm (1990) lists 15 studies on maternal age of which only four found a statistically significant difference but 11 found higher ages in the patients than in the controls. Given the powerful effect of publication bias (Easterbrook *et al.*, 1991) these published findings may not be representative of all the studies that have been done.

A number of studies have found a higher frequency of previous head injury in patients with AD than in controls or patients with multi-infarct dementia (Mortimer *et al.*, 1985). The basis for such an association remains obscure and in most cases the injuries reported have not been of sufficient severity to destroy a significant amount of brain tissue. For the time being the finding has to be regarded as provisional.

Conclusions

With regard to the total risk of dementia the only active approach that seems justifiable at present is an attack on the lifestyle factors linked with cerebrovascular disease. Research on Alzheimer's disease is actively pursuing a number of promising leads. For the third age the cumulative risk of dementia is low and its horrors are largely reserved for later life. It could perhaps be argued that the main challenge of AD for the third age will be the burden it places on people in middle life in looking after more aged relatives with the disease.

References

American Psychiatric Association. *Diagnostic and statistical manual of mental disorders*, 3rd edn. American Psychiatric Association, Washington DC, 1987.

Berg S. Psychological functioning in 70- and 75-year-old people. *Acta Psychiatr Scand*, 1980; Suppl 288:

Berkman LF. The association between educational attainment and mental status examinations: of etiologic significance for senile dementias or not? *J Chron Dis*, 1986; 39: 171–174.

Blessed G, Wilson ID. The contemporary natural history of mental disorder in old age. *Br J Psychiat*, 1982; 141: 59–67.

Breitner JCS. Clinical genetics and genetic counselling in Alzheimer disease. *Ann Int Med*, 1991; 115: 601–606.

Candy JM, Oakley AE, Klinowski J *et al.* Aluminiosilicates and senile plaque formation in Alzheimer's disease. *Lancet*, 1986; i: 354–357.

Doll R. Alzheimer's disease and environmental aluminium. *Age Ageing*, 1993; 22: 138–153.

Easterbrook PJ, Berlin JA, Gopolan R, Mathews DR. Publication bias in clinical research. *Lancet*, 1991; 337: 867–872.

Farrar G, Altman P, Welch S *et al.* Defective gallium-transferrin binding in Alzheimer disease and Down syndrome: possible mechanism for accumulation of aluminium in brain. *Lancet*, 1990; 335: 747–750.

Flaten TP. Mortality from dementia in Norway. *J Epidemiol & Community Health*, 1989; 43: 285–289.

Grimley Evans J. From plaque to placement; a model for Alzheimer's disease. *Age Ageing*, 1992; 21: 77–80.

Gurland B, Copeland J, Kuriansky J *et al. The mind and mood of aging.* Croom Helm, London, 1983.

Hachinski VC, Iliff LD, Zilhka E *et al.* Cerebral blood flow in dementia. *Arch Neurol*, 1975; 32: 632–637.

Hagnell O, Lanke J, Rorsman B, Öhmann R, Öjesjö L. Current trends in the incidence of senile and multi-infarct dementia. A prospective study of a total population followed over 25 years. The Lundby Study. *Arch Psychiatr Nervenkr*, 1983; 233: 423–438.

Jagger C, Clarke M, Cook AJ. Mental and physical health of elderly people: five-year follow-up of a total population. *Age Ageing*, 1989; 18: 77–82.

Jorm AF. *The epidemiology of Alzheimer's disease and related disorders.* Chapman and Hall, London, 1990.

Jorm AF, Korten AE, Henderson AS. The prevalence of dementia: a quantitative integration of the literature. *Acta Psychiatr Scand*, 1987; 76: 465–479.

Kay DWK, Henderson AS, Scott R *et al.* Dementia and depression among the elderly living in the Hobart community: the effect of the diagnostic criteria on the prevalence rates. *Psychol Med*, 1985; 15: 771–788.

Landsberg JP, McDonald B, Watt F. Absence of aluminium in neuritic plaque cores in Alzheimer's disease. *Nature*, 1992; 350: 65–68.

Martyn CN, Barker DJP, Osmond C *et al.* Geographical relation between Alzheimer's disease and aluminium in drinking water. *Lancet*, 1989; i: 59–62.

McKhann G, Drachman D, Folstein M *et al.* Clinical diagnosis of Alzheimer's disease: report of the NINCDS-ADRDA Work Group under the auspices of Department of Health and Human Services Task Force on Alzheimer's Disease. *Neurology*, 1984; 34: 939–944.

McLachlan DR, Dalton AJ, Kruck TP *et al.* Intramuscular desferrioxamine in patients with Alzheimer's disease. *Lancet*, 1991; 337: 1304–1308.

Mortimer JA, French LR, Hutton JT, Schuman LM. Head injury as a risk factor for Alzheimer's disease. *Neurology*, 1985; 35: 264–267.

Petersen P. Silent cerebral infarction in chronic atrial fibrillation. *Stroke*, 1987; 18: 1098–1100.

Schoenberg BS, Anderson DW, Haerer AF. Severe dementia: prevalence and clinical features in a biracial US population. *Arch Neurol*, 1985; 42: 740–743.

Taylor GA, Ferrier IN, McLoughlin IJ, Fairbairn AF, McKeith IG, Lett D, Edwardson JA. Gastrointestinal absorption of aluminium in Alzheimer's disease: response to aluminium citrate. *Age Ageing*, 1992; 21: 81–90.

The Stroke Prevention in Atrial Fibrillation Investigators. Stroke prevention in atrial fibrillation study. Final results. *Circulation*, 1991; 84: 527–539.

Incontinence

J. Grimley Evans

Incontinence of urine or faeces is an affliction with a wide range of severity. Estimates of its prevalence are therefore critically dependent on definition and methods of estimation. It is also a socially humiliating disability that many sufferers are unwilling to acknowledge even to their medical or nursing advisors. This fact adds to the difficulties in estimating prevalence rates and evaluating treatment.

Urinary incontinence

There are several different types of urinary incontinence and mixed forms are common in later life. Acute incontinence can occur in a number of situations including urinary infections, immobilising or delirious illnesses, and epilepsy. We are concerned here with chronic or established incontinence which is either continuous or recurrent. Table 13.1 offers one classification of the main forms of established urinary incontinence. Of these stress and urge incontinence are the commonest in the third age.

In a recent survey conducted by the Oxford Regional Health Authority, approximately 90% of people aged 65–74 claimed never to have episodes of urinary incontinence and 96% never to suffer from faecal incontinence (Oxford Regional Health Authority, 1991). A postal survey of people registered with 12 general practices distributed throughout the country revealed rather higher prevalence rates of urinary incontinence as shown in Table 13.2 (Thomas et al., 1980).

Stress incontinence was commonest in women at ages 45–54 while urge incontinence increased in prevalence with age up to 64. Stress incontinence became less common in later life. At ages under 65 the prevalence rates reported in this survey were lower than those found in some other studies where rates in women of over 40% have been reported (Jolleys, 1988).

Table 13.1

Forms of chronic incontinence

Stress	– loss of urine on coughing or straining
Urge	– often due to precipitate bladder contractions
Overflow	– secondary to obstruction of bladder outflow
Fistulous	– e.g. fistula between bladder and vagina
Functional	– difficulty in getting to toilet
Disinhibitory	– occurs in some forms of brain damage
Behavioural	– (rare) form of social manipulation

Among women there was an association of incontinence with parity. Incontinence rates were lowest among the nulliparous and highest among women with four or more pregnancies. There was no consistent trend for parities 1–3. Although there is widely held to be a link between stress incontinence and childbirth injury the details of the connection seem not to have been critically evaluated.

In a subsample of 158 people reporting incontinence in the survey by Thomas *et al.* (1980) and who gave interviews, 22% had moderate or severe incontinence but only a third of these were receiving help from the health or social services for their incontinence.

Faecal or double incontinence

Faecal incontinence is likely to be subject to an even greater degree of under-reporting than is urinary incontinence. In a study of 76 patients with diarrhoea consulting a gastrointestinal clinic, 39 suffered from faecal incontinence but only 19 volunteered the fact spontaneously (Leigh and Turnberg, 1988). Thomas *et al.* (1984) have estimated the prevalence of faecal or double incontinence based on a report of two or more episodes in the preceding month. The results are summarised in Table 13.3. Overall 8% of cases of faecal incontinence were doubly incontinent. Only 44% of the cases identified were known to the health and social services and 71% of these were resident in institutions.

Faecal and double incontinence are associated with a range of anorectal and neurological disorders. In later life the commonest cause is rectal or sigmoid overloading due to constipation. In middle-aged women a pelvic neuropathy, sometimes possibly a consequence of childbirth, is encountered as a cause of faecal incontinence which may be improved by surgical intervention. As already implied, any form of chronic diarrhoea will also lead to incontinence in a proportion of cases.

Table 13.2

Prevalence (%) of occasional (occ) and regular (reg) urinary incontinence and 'uncertain' (unc) (Thomas *et al.*, 1980)

Age group	Men			Women		
	Occ	Reg	Unc	Occ	Reg	Unc
45–54	3.7	1.6	1.4	21.9	11.8	2.4
55–64	5.7	2.9	2.6	18.6	11.9	2.8
65–74	8.4	6.1	4.9	14.6	8.8	3.4
75–84	9.5	8.1	7.0	13.6	16.0	7.2

Table 13.3

Prevalence (per thousand) of faecal or double incontinence by sex and age group. Total and those cases known to the health or social services (Thomas *et al.*, 1984)

Age group	Men		Women	
	Total	Known	Total	Known
15–64	4.2	0.5	1.7	0.4
65–	10.9	4.9	13.3	8.8

Management

Recent reviews by Ouslander (1990) of urinary incontinence in elderly people, and by Cardozo (1991) of urinary incontinence in women, suggest that many sufferers do not receive what is thought to be the best care that is available. This is partly due to inadequate training of health and social service workers. A variety of training materials have been devised to overcome this problem and the majority of professionals are reported to have an interest in updating their training in continence work. It has been suggested, however, that 'the referral process may need to be opened up to sidestep uncommitted practitioners' (Social Policy Research Unit, 1989).

One reason for the lack of enthusiasm among medical professionals, and an important general issue in the management of incontinence, is the inadequacy of evaluation of many of the treatments currently deployed. This is particularly true for surgical approaches to the management of stress incontinence and to incontinence associated with early prostatic hypertrophy in men. A range of operative procedures are in common use and each surgeon is convinced of the efficacy of whatever technique he or she applies. This prevents the use of randomised controlled clinical trials to compare techniques. One way of overcoming this problem would be by a process of randomised allocation of patients to surgeons. In theory the new arrangements in the NHS for funding to follow patients should make such trials possible, but so far the bureaucratic difficulties associated with this approach have not been overcome. Most of the evaluations of treatment of incontinence, including surgical, behavioural, pharmacological and physiotherapy techniques have been uncontrolled or short-term or both.

Newer techniques including neurostimulatory implants are under development, particularly for victims of neurological disorders, but are unlikely to prove generally applicable to the majority of incontinent people in the population.

The cost of deploying what on present opinion would be adequate services for incontinent patients was calculated in 1987 as not less than £270,000 for a typical health district (population 250,000) with an estimated 40% for the unrecognised cases (Townsend, 1988). How much of the cost might be offset by reduced rates of institutionalisation and prosthetic costs is unclear, but without better evidence on efficacy health authorities might question outlays of this order. At present there seems to be a major need for a co-ordinated and systematic approach to the evaluation of methods of ascertainment, assessment and management of incontinence in the population. Incontinence services in health districts may or may not be usefully employed at present but could provide the infrastructure for the large evaluative trials that are clearly needed.

Benign prostatic hypertrophy

The prostate gland lies at the base of the male bladder surrounding the beginning of its outflow through the urethra. Although the prostate can be the origin of one of the commoner forms of cancer in elderly men, much more frequent during the third age is the condition of benign prostatic hypertrophy (BPH) which is present in the majority of men aged over 60 and causes at least minor symptoms in about 40% (Garraway et al., 1991). Hypertrophy of the gland can lead to obstruction to the passage of urine and in some cases to incomplete bladder emptying and back pressure on the kidneys. More commonly symptoms are 'irritative' in the form of urinary urgency, frequency and incontinence in the form of dribbling. The effect on quality of life can be considerable with men (and their spouses) suffering from disturbed nights and constant worrying about fluid intake and where the nearest toilet is to be found. The usual treatment is surgical and about one man in four can expect to undergo prostatic surgery. BPH is rarely fatal except where it leads to renal failure due to chronic obstruction to urine outflow. It is however a common cause of symptoms including urinary urgency and frequency and incontinence. It may also lead to sudden stoppage of urine outflow from the bladder necessitating emergency intervention.

The causes of BPH are not clear but are probably mediated through the action of sex hormones such as testosterone secreted by the testes. Considerable research is in progress on pharmacological means of blocking the effects of testosterone or modifying its metabolism into more active forms in the prostate itself. The effectiveness of these approaches in controlling symptoms with an acceptable level of side-effects and in reducing the need for surgery is not yet established.

There are several unresolved problems surrounding the deployment of surgery for BPH. Not least are uncertainties about the indications for surgical treatment and the choice of technique. There are two main surgical methods, open prostatectomy in which the gland is removed from within the bladder by an abdominal incision, and transurethral resection of the prostate (TURP) in which the passage through the gland is widened with a diathermy knife used through a urethral endoscope. A newer form of endoscopic operation in which a stent is lodged in the prostatic urethra to keep it patent is still being evaluated. Open prostatectomies are carried out by urologists or by general surgeons but TURP usually only by urologists. Over 90% of prostatectomies are now TURP. The great majority of patients undergoing prostatectomy are symptomatically improved or relieved (Neal et al., 1989). There is some evidence that spontaneous improvement in symptoms may occur in BPH so the true benefit of elective operation is difficult to quantify accurately.

Between a quarter and a half of all prostatectomies are performed as emergencies following acute urinary obstruction. There is controversy over the indications for elective operation. Prostatectomy rates vary more than sixfold between different western countries with the USA having rates more than twice those of the UK (K. McPherson, personal communication 1992). It is not known whether it is more cost-effective to offer operation early in the disease or to await the onset of more troublesome symptoms. Barry et al. (1988) have suggested that patient preferences should be the major determinant of the timing of operation. As a clinical policy this calls for more complex communication between doctors and patients than is common. The use of interactive video techniques to help patients with BPH to make their decisions is being explored both in the USA and the UK. Complications of prostatectomy include incontinence (in about 1%) and various problems of sexual function, particularly impotence. An informed patient decision requires a personalised evaluation of the risks and benefits of intervention which may be assisted by a device such as interactive video which permits self-pacing and repetition.

Because TURP seems a less invasive operation than open prostatectomy, and because it involves shorter hospital stays, it has generally been assumed to be the procedure of choice where it is feasible. However, follow up studies show higher re-operation rates following TURP and also higher long-term mortality rates (Roos *et al.*, 1989). The higher re-operation rates are not perhaps surprising given the more limited initial resection, although for technical reasons surgeons may be more ready to re-operate following TURP than open surgery. The explanation for the higher long-term mortality rates after TURP is not clear; hospital fatality rates for the two procedures are similar (Neal, 1990). The explanation may lie in the initial selection of patients where those with significant co-morbidity that might increase the risk of prolonged anaesthesia are more likely to be offered TURP rather than open surgery.

With the ageing of the population and an increase in expectations of health in later life a rise in the demand for prostatectomy can be expected. It is not possible to estimate how well present resources match need since waiting lists may be protected by low referral rates by general practitioners. In 1981/82 about a third of patients presenting with prostatic symptoms were referred on for specialist assessment. It has been suggested (Donovan *et al.*, 1991) that since operation rates have been rising this proportion may also have increased but so may have GP consultation rates. This low secondary referral rate may or may not be appropriate but clearly is only one of several issues that yet need to be resolved in the management of BPH.

References

Cardozo L. Urinary incontinence in women: have we anything new to offer? *Br Med J*, 1991; 303: 1453–1457.

Donovan JL, Frankel SJ, Nanchahal K, Coast J, Williams MH. *Prostatectomy for benign prostatic hypertrophy*. University of Bristol Health Care Evaluation Unit, Bristol, 1991.

Garraway WM, Collins GN, Lee RJ. High prevalence of benign prostatic hypertrophy in the community. *Lancet*, 1991; 338: 469–471.

Jolleys JV. Reported prevalence of urinary incontinence in women in a general practice. *Br Med J*, 1988; 296: 1300–1302.

Leigh RJ, Turnberg LA. Faecal incontinence: the unvoiced symptom. *Lancet*, 1982; i: 1349–1351.

Neal DE. Prostatectomy: an open or closed case. *Br J Urol*, 1990; 66: 449–454.

Neal DE, Ramsden PD, Sharples L et al. Outcome of elective prostatectomy. *Br Med J*, 1989; 299: 762–767.

Ouslander JG. The efficacy of continence treatment. In Kane RL, Grimley Evans J, Macfadyen D (eds), *Improving the health of older people: a world view*, pp. 273–295. Oxford University Press, Oxford, 1990.

Oxford Regional Health Authority. *Lifestyle survey*. Oxford Regional Health Authority, Oxford, 1991.

Roos NP, Wennberg J, Malenka DJ et al. Mortality and reoperation after open and transurethral resection of the prostate for benign prostatic hyperplasia. *New Engl J Med*, 1989; 320: 1120–1124.

Social Policy Research Unit. DHSS 560 5/89 TH, *Beyond plastic pants — improving care for incontinence sufferers*. University of York, Heslington, York, 1989.

Thomas TM, Egan M, Walgrove A, Meade TW. The prevalence of faecal and double incontinence. *Commun Med*, 1984; 6: 216–220.

Thomas TM, Plymat KR, Blannin J, Meade TW. Prevalence of urinary incontinence. *Br Med J*, 1980; 281: 1243–1245.

Townsend J. Costs of incontinence. *Commun Med*, 1988; 10: 235–239.

Risk factors

Margaret Savory

Smoking

The serious negative consequences of smoking on health have been consistently reported and are underlined by the reports of the Royal College of Physicians (1962, 1971, 1977, 1983a). Smoking has been associated with increasing morbidity and mortality from cancer (particularly of the lung, the mouth, larynx and oesophagus), coronary heart disease, stomach and duodenal peptic ulcers and chronic obstructive lung disease (also generally referred to as chronic bronchitis and emphysema).

Data on smoking in the UK are provided by the annual General Household Survey (GHS) (OPCS, 1972 onwards) and the Tobacco Advisory Council (TAC) (Wald and Nicolandes-Bowman, 1990) from 1948 onwards. The data from the TAC tend to indicate greater prevalence rates than the GHS, due mainly to differences in methodology. However, changes over time in the two surveys are remarkably consistent.

GHS data indicate that prevalence of cigarette smoking is lower for those in the third age groups (Table 14.1). In the most recent survey the prevalence for both men and women is greatest in the 20–30-year-old age bracket. There is currently little difference between the sexes in terms of age profiles.

Data from both sources suggest that since the 1970s the prevalence of smoking has been declining for both men and women across all age groups. Figures 14.1a and b present the data collected by the GHS since 1972. Before the present, women tended to have lower prevalence rates than men. However the decrease in prevalence has been greater for men, leading to the current similarities between the two sexes.

GHS data analysed by cohort across 10 years also indicate that smoking prevalence is decreasing, though at a slightly faster rate for men than women (Figures 14.2a and b). Continuation of the current trend would lead to a rough estimate of a

Table 14.1

The current prevalence of cigarette smoking in the UK

	Percentage	
Age	*Men*	*Women*
16–19	28	32
20–24	38	39
25–34	36	34
35–49	34	33
50–59	28	29
60 plus	24	20

Source: OPCS Monitor/GHS 1990.

Figure 14.1a
Prevalence of
cigarette smoking:
trends (men).

Source: GHS

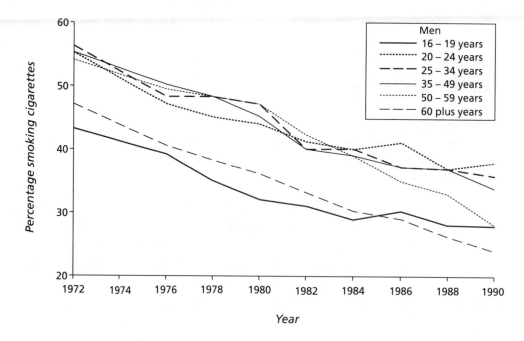

Figure 14.1b
Prevalence of
cigarette smoking:
trends (women).

Source: GHS

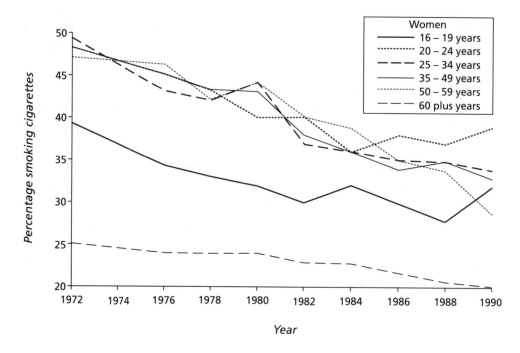

prevalence rate of around 20% in men over 60, and 15% in women over 60 in 10 years from now.

Weekly cigarette consumption per smoker appears to be related to age for both sexes, with those aged 60+ smoking less than other groups, with the exception of those aged 16–19 (Table 14.2). Figures 14.3a and b show the trends in weekly cigarette consumption. These are influenced by the overall decline in prevalence and whether the decline occurs amongst heavier or lighter smokers. Thus, since the 1970s there have been yearly fluctuations with no dramatic changes either upwards or down, although there is a slight upward trend.

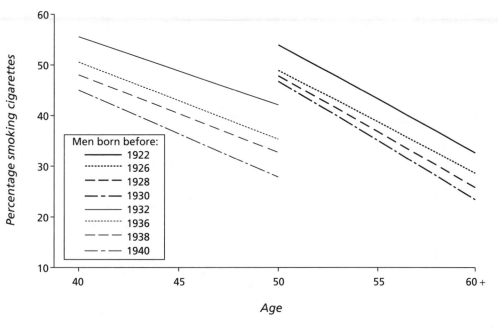

Figure 14.2a
Smoking behaviour –
successive cohorts
(men).

Source: GHS

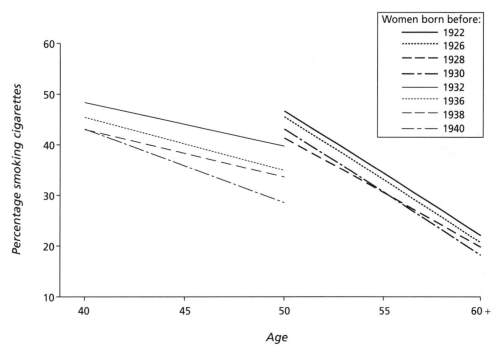

Figure 14.2b
Smoking behaviour –
successive cohorts
(women).

Source: GHS

Table 14.2

Current average weekly cigarette consumption per smoker in the UK

| Age | Numbers of cigarettes | |
	Men	Women
16–19	89	80
20–24	110	92
25–34	115	103
35–49	135	106
50–59	121	107
60 plus	106	81

Source: OPCS Monitor/GHS 1990.

Figure 14.3a
Average weekly cigarette consumption: 1972–1990 (men).

Source: GHS

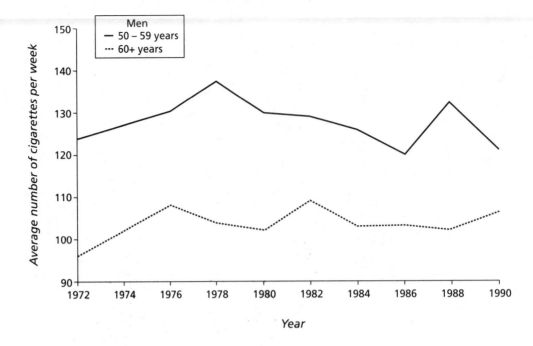

Figure 14.3b
Average weekly cigarette consumption: 1972–1990 (women).

Source: GHS

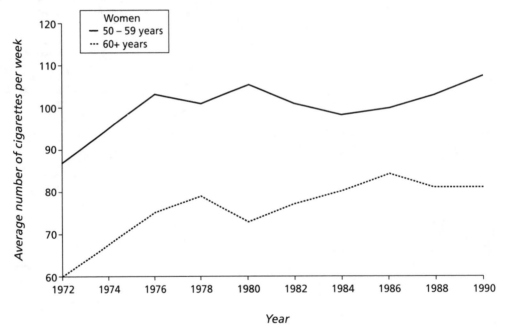

Obesity

Being overweight is generally agreed to be associated with increased health risk. Particular diseases for which the overweight or, more extremely obese person have greater risk include adult-onset diabetes, hypertension, coronary heart disease, certain cancers, gout, gall bladder disease and certain arthritic conditions (Royal College of Physicians, 1983b).

Body Mass Index (BMI, also known as Quetelet's index) is the ratio of weight/height² (kg/m²) and is generally used as the indicator of relative weight. In terms of defining obesity, three commonly used levels are:

$$BMI \leqslant 20.0 - underweight$$
$$BMI > 25.0 - overweight$$
$$BMI > 30.0 - obesity$$

In a prospective study of 7735 British men aged 40–59 years, it was found that mortality rates increased alongside raised BMI for values greater than 28.0, with the excess deaths being due primarily to cardiovascular causes (Wannamethee and Shaper, 1989). Similar findings have been reported for surveys of men in other countries. However, findings from the Whitehall Study (analyses based on 18,393 men), indicate that risk patterns associated with increased BMI were different according to age (Jarrett et al., 1982). For those aged between 50 and 60 years, there was an increased relative risk associated with obesity. For example, persons in the 55–59 age group with a BMI in the fourth quintile had a mortality rate of 14 per 100 persons per 10 years. This rose to 17 for those of the same age in the fifth and heaviest quintile. For men over 60, the relative risk of obesity disappeared, but one for excessively lean men appeared. Mortality rates for those aged 60–64 ranged from 26 per 100 persons per 10 years for the leanest quintile, to 22 per 100 persons per 10 years for the fourth quintile and 19 per 100 persons per 10 years for the fifth and heaviest quintile (Jarrett et al., 1982).

Studies of weight and mortality rates amongst women are conspicuous by their absence.

In terms of population distribution of BMI there have been few studies conducted that have been truly representative of Great Britain as a whole. Thus, comparisons over the years are difficult. The earliest studies were conducted during the 1940s, but were not considered to be nationally representative as data were derived from groups of civilian workers and housewives (Kemsley, 1950, 1952). The same criticism may be levied at a study of London-based British Petroleum office staff (Montegriffo, 1971). The first truly nationally-representative survey was conducted by the OPCS in 1981 (Rosenbaum et al., 1985). This has now been followed by the 1987 Dietary and Nutrition Survey (OPCS, 1990) and the Allied Dunbar National Fitness Survey (1992). Table 14.3 (a and b) presents some findings from the Dietary and Nutrition Survey and the National Fitness Survey. They reveal that the older age groups contain the highest proportions of men and women in the overweight category. According to the National Fitness Survey the worst age categories are men aged 55–64 (62% overweight) and women aged 65–74 (78% overweight). The evidence also suggests that the adult population is becoming fatter. Comparison between the 1981 and 1987 OPCS surveys shows a significant increase in mean BMI for both men and women across all age groups. In the 1981 survey mean BMI for men aged 16–64 was 24.3, compared with 24.9 in 1987. For women the respective figures were 23.9 and 24.6 (Rosenbaum et al., 1985; OPCS, 1990). Between the 1987 OPCS survey and the National Fitness Survey the percentage in the overweight and obese groups increased by about 7% for men and 11% for women.

Table 14.3(a)

Percentage distribution of Body Mass Index (BMI) across age groups

BMI		16–24 (%)	25–34 (%)	35–49 (%)	50–64 (%)
			Age		
Men					
<20	(Underweight)	15	4	4	5
20–25	(Normal)	64	60	44	33
25–30	(Overweight)	18	30	41	53
>30	(Obese)	3	6	11	9
Women					
<20	(Underweight)	25	17	8	5
20–25	(Normal)	52	56	52	49
25–30	(Overweight)	17	16	30	28
>30	(Obese)	6	11	10	18

Source: Data from the Dietary and Nutritional Survey of British Adults, OPCS and MAFF. HMSO, London, 1990.

Table 14.3(b)

Percentage distribution of Body Mass Index (BMI) across age groups

BMI		16–24 (%)	25–34 (%)	35–44 (%)	45–54 (%)	55–64 (%)	65–74 (%)
				Age			
Men							
≤20	(Underweight)	16	6	2	1	1	4
20.1–25	(Acceptable)	60	54	48	41	36	40
25.1–29.9	(Mildly overweight)	21	35	43	47	48	47
30+	(Obese)	3	5	7	11	15	9
Women							
≤18.6	(Underweight)	6	2	3	1	–	1
18.7–23.8	(Acceptable)	63	58	44	40	28	22
23.9–28.5	(Mildly overweight)	21	29	35	44	41	47
28.6+	(Overweight)	10	11	18	15	31	30

Source: Data from the Allied Dunbar National Fitness Survey, 1992.

Blood cholesterol levels

High levels of cholesterol in the blood are considered a risk factor in cardiovascular disease. In particular, the presence of high levels of cholesterol associated with one type of protein—low density lipoprotein (LDL)—is linked to increased risk. On the other hand, levels of cholesterol linked to high density lipoprotein (HDL) may have an inverse relationship with cardiovascular disease (OPCS, 1990).

Levels of serum cholesterol have been defined as follows:

Less than 5.2 mmol/l   – desirable

5.2 mmol/l–6.4 mmol/l – mildly elevated

6.5 mmol/l–7.8 mmol/l – moderately elevated

7.8 mmol/l or over   – severely elevated

Measures of serum cholesterol levels were obtained in the Dietary and Nutrition Survey of British Adults (OPCS, 1990). For both men and women total serum cholesterol level rose with increasing age. This was particularly marked for women in the 50–64 age group. In this age group the mean total cholesterol for women was significantly greater than for men. This was a reversal of the situation for younger ages where the mean values for men were significantly higher than the values for women. Table 14.4 shows the percentage distributions for total serum cholesterol across the age groups.

No direct measures of LDL cholesterol were taken. However, the total levels of serum cholesterol minus the total HDL cholesterol were used as an approximation. Again, the mean approximate LDL cholesterol concentration rose with age. Table 14.5 shows the percentage distributions for inferred LDL cholesterol across the ages.

Dietary cholesterol is just one factor affecting serum cholesterol. The major influence appears to be the amount of dietary saturated fatty acids consumed. An

Table 14.4

Percentage distribution of total serum cholesterol across age groups

Age	Total cholesterol (mmol/l)			
	Less than 5.2	*5.2–6.4*	*6.5–7.8*	*7.8+*
Males	%	%	%	%
18–24	75	21	4	0
25–34	41	43	12	4
35–49	21	45	25	9
50–64	13	45	32	10
Females				
18–24	66	32	4	2
25–34	61	37	1	1
35–49	35	44	18	3
50–64	10	31	38	21

Source: Dietary and Nutritional Survey of British Adults, OPCS and MAFF. HMSO, London, 1990.

Table 14.5

Percentage distribution of inferred LDL cholesterol across age groups

Age	LDL cholesterol (mmol/l)		
	Less than 3.4	*3.5–4.1*	*4.1+*
Males	%	%	%
18–24	45	30	25
25–34	22	22	56
35–49	8	17	75
50–64	3	13	84
Females			
18–24	47	32	21
25–34	40	35	25
35–49	19	27	54
50–64	5	11	84

Source: Dietary and Nutritional Survey of British Adults, OPCS and MAFF. HMSO, London, 1990.

indicator that is also often used is the ratio of polyunsaturated to saturated fats (P:S ratio), high levels being advantageous. Table 14.6 summarises the mean values for fat and cholesterol intake as revealed by the Nutritional and Dietary Survey of Adults (OPCS, 1990). There was no difference in the proportions of total food energy derived from fat across the age groups. However, in the older age groups there was a lower intake of polyunsaturated acids, resulting in a lower P:S ratio. The oldest age groups for both men and women also had significantly higher mean cholesterol intakes.

Trend data based on estimates from the National Food Survey (Chesher, 1990) for the past decade (i.e. 1979/80 and 1988/89) suggest that whereas the energy derived from fat has decreased slightly, the P:S ratio has risen over the decade (Table 14.7). However, the decreases in fat consumption and increases in P:S appear to be smaller for those in the older age groups. Despite the fact that, compared with other age groups, those in the third age are eating a diet with a higher proportion of saturated fats, they are following a more healthy diet than they were 10 years ago. Nevertheless, younger age groups have improved their eating habits to a greater extent.

Table 14.6

Fat and cholesterol intake, means: 1987

	Age: Males				*Age: Females*			
	16–24	*25–34*	*35–49*	*50–64*	*16–24*	*25–34*	*35–49*	*50–64*
Percentage of food energy from fat								
Mean	40.2	41.0	40.2	40.2	39.8	40.7	40.3	40.3
SEM	0.34	0.31	0.24	0.28	0.35	0.34	0.3	0.29
Percentage of food energy from saturated fatty acids								
Mean	16.1	16.5	16.3	17.2	16.4	16.9	16.9	17.5
SEM	0.19	0.18	0.16	0.19	0.21	0.21	0.18	0.19
Percentage of food energy from N-6 polyunsaturated acids								
Mean	5.54	5.72	5.58	4.94	5.31	5.50	5.32	4.99
SEM	0.12	0.12	0.13	0.12	0.13	0.13	0.11	0.12
Percentage of food energy from N-3 polyunsaturated acids								
Mean	0.79	0.81	0.79	0.73	0.77	0.77	0.74	0.74
SEM	0.02	0.02	0.02	0.02	0.02	0.02	0.01	0.02
Percentage of food energy from monounsaturated acids								
Mean	12.6	12.8	12.3	12.1	12.3	12.4	12.2	12.0
SEM	0.15	0.13	0.10	0.11	0.15	0.13	0.11	0.11
Ratio of polyunsaturated to saturated fatty acids (P:S)								
Mean	0.41	0.43	0.42	0.35	0.40	0.39	0.38	0.35
SEM	0.011	0.018	0.013	0.011	0.015	0.011	0.009	0.01
Average daily intake of cholesterol (mg)								
Mean	362	383	398	407	247	264	295	294
SEM	10.6	8.4	8.0	9.3	7.1	6.7	5.4	6.2

Source: Dietary and Nutritional Survey of British Adults, OPCS and MAFF. HMSO, London, 1990.

Blood pressure

Many studies have demonstrated that raised blood pressure levels (both systolic and diastolic) are associated with a raised risk of cardiovascular and cerebrovascular disease (Lichenstein *et al.*, 1985). Surveys have consistently indicated that in the developed world blood pressure levels increase with age (Whelton and Klag, 1989).

The World Health Organisation defines five blood pressure categories as follows:

140/90 mmHg and below – **normotensive**

141/91–159/94 mmHg – **borderline**

160/95 mmHg or higher, but with no treatment – **untreated hypertensive**

Actively treated with drugs, but various levels of blood pressure – **treated hypertensive**

Normotensive but being treated with drugs that may have blood pressure-lowering effects

Comparisons across studies are difficult because of differences in the samples under study, methods of measurement, different observers and whether those receiving treatment for hypertension are included or excluded. There have been few surveys of blood pressure levels in a nationally-representative UK sample. The Dietary and Nutrition Survey of Adults (OPCS, 1990) took blood pressure readings, but excluded respondents being treated for hypertension, whereas the Health and Lifestyle Survey (Cox *et al.*, 1987) included all blood pressure categories. Tables 14.8

Table 14.7

Decade changes in fat consumption: 1979/80–1988/89

Household member		Percentage change in	
		Energy derived from fat	P:S ratio
Males S	18–34	−4	44
Males M	18–34	0	40
Males A	18–34	2	84
Males S	35–64	−6	55
Males M	35–64	−1	41
Males A	35–64	13	104
Males	65–74	1	30
Males	75–	4	31
Females N	18–54	−9	57
Females P	18–54	−10	155
Females	55–59	−3	32
Females	60–74	−3	48
Females	75–	−9	−4

Source: Chesher A, Section 3 in Household food consumption and expenditure 1989, Annual Report of the National Food Survey Committee. HMSO, London, 1990.

The following abbreviations are used: S, sedentary occupation; M, moderately active occupation; A, very active occupation; N, not pregnant; P, pregnant.

and 14.9 present data from both surveys showing the percentage distribution of the various blood pressure categories by age group.

The UK data follow the general pattern of an increase in mean values for systolic and diastolic blood pressure with advanced age. This is true for both sexes. An increase in the prevalence of untreated hypertension is also revealed. This reaches

Table 14.8

Percentage distribution of blood pressure measures across age groups*

Age	Systolic blood pressure (mmHg)				Diastolic blood pressure (mmHg)					
	Less than 120	120–139	140–159	160+	Less than 65	65–74	75–84	85–94	95–104	105+
Males		%					%			
18–24	58	41	1	0	24	47	22	7	0	0
25–34	40	53	6	1	11	37	36	13	2	1
35–49	35	48	14	3	7	28	35	20	8	2
50–64	19	56	19	6	4	16	42	29	6	3
Females										
18–24	84	16	0	0	30	52	15	2	1	0
25–34	82	17	1	0	31	43	21	3	2	0
35–49	60	32	7	1	14	43	27	12	3	1
50–64	35	42	15	8	7	30	35	22	4	2

Source: Dietary and Nutritional Survey of British Adults, OPCS and MAFF. HMSO, London, 1990.
*Those receiving drugs for hypertension were excluded.

Table 14.9

Prevalence (in per cent) of blood pressure categories by age

Age	Categories (as defined by WHO)				
	Normotensive	Borderline	Untreated hypertension	Treated hypertension	Normotensive but on drugs with antihypertensive effects
Males	%	%	%	%	%
18–29	92.2	5.9	1.4	(2)	(2)
30–39	88.0	7.1	4.1	0.7	(1)
40–49	77.8	10.5	8.2	3.0	(3)
50–59	58.4	17.1	12.1	9.9	2.4
60–69	50.1	18.1	13.2	15.9	2.6
70–79	34.8	24.0	18.6	16.6	5.1
80+	43.5	22.6	11.3	16.1	6.7
Females					
18–29	98.5	1.0	(1)	(3)	0
30–39	94.8	3.2	0.9	0.6	(4)
40–49	87.1	5.0	2.8	4.1	1.0
50–59	66.2	13.0	8.5	10.8	1.5
60–69	54.0	17.6	11.5	14.2	2.7
70–79	33.6	15.9	22.9	24.6	3.0
80+	38.2	20.0	14.5	22.7	4.5

Source: Cox et al., The health and lifestyle survey. Health Promotion Research Trust, London, 1987.
(Parentheses indicate actual numbers, i.e. percentage <1%).

its peak in the third age, before a decline in the eighth decade and beyond. It appears that hypertension is more common in men than women up until the third age, whereupon the situation reverses.

Data from the Health and Lifestyle Survey provide an indication of the effectiveness of hypertensive therapy. Of those aged 60+ taking drugs for hypertension, 22% of men and 30% of women remained hypertensive. It is unclear what proportion of these figures represents non-compliance rather than efficacy.

There are no UK data available to indicate the secular trends in prevalence of hypertension.

Alcohol

Alcohol consumption presents several risks to public and personal health and is a major cause of premature death. However, it is difficult to estimate the excess mortality connected with alcohol consumption as death certificates rarely mention it as a cause. A current estimation of 28,000 excess deaths in England and Wales is based on five international longitudinal studies, four of which were conducted in the USA (Anderson, 1988). On a societal level alcohol is often a contributing factor in public disorder, violence, family disputes, child neglect, road accidents, fire, drowning, accidents in the home and employment problems amongst others (Faculty of Public Health Medicine, 1991).

In terms of disease, alcohol use is associated with conditions in almost every medical specialty, although mortality from alcoholism and liver cirrhosis are those which are specifically linked to alcohol consumption (Royal College of Physicians, 1987). The correlation between alcohol consumption and liver cirrhosis in epidemiological studies is between 0.8 and 0.9 (Anderson, 1991).

Alcohol has been implicated in cancer, with an estimation that it may cause 3% of all cancers (WHO/IARC, 1988). Epidemiological studies have reported that heavy drinkers have increased risks compared with non-drinkers for cancer of the oral cavity, larynx and pharynx. There is also evidence to suggest that alcohol is a contributing risk factor for strokes, hypertension and cardiovascular disease (Faculty of Public Health Medicine, 1991). Some population studies suggest that abstainers and those drinking large amounts are at greater risk than moderate drinkers; i.e. that moderate alcohol consumption has a protective effect (Marmot *et al.*, 1981). However, others have refuted this, suggesting that abstainers may be those that have stopped drinking as a result of pre-existing disease, hence the higher mortality rates (Shaper *et al.*, 1988).

Estimates of consumption levels are derived from two sources, population surveys and data from Customs and Excise. Population surveys typically underestimate consumption levels as people, particularly heavy drinkers, tend to underreport the amount they consume (Smith, 1981). Figures from Customs and Excise show that consumption in England and Wales rose steadily from the 1950s onwards, but is now tailing off in the 1980s and 1990s, with average consumption per person estimated as 9.6–9.8 litres of pure alcohol per person per year (Anderson, 1991). According to the 1988 General Household Survey 27% of men and 11% of women drink more than the recommended limits of 21 and 14 units of alcohol per week respectively (1 unit contains 8 grams of absolute alcohol) (OPCS, 1988). Drinking patterns by age and sex suggest that smaller proportions of the older population drink large amounts of alcohol (Table 14.10). A comparison between two national surveys conducted in 1978 and 1987 suggest that consumption is falling among younger men, but increasing among older men (Goddard, 1991). Consumption is rising among all women except the youngest age groups. However, overall, there was no change between 1978 and 1987 in average weekly consumption, men drinking three times as much as women—18.5 units compared with 7.2 units per week (Goddard, 1991).

Changes in mean per capita alcohol consumption in a population are mirrored by the prevalence of alcohol's ill effects, both medical and social. Indicators such as cirrhosis mortality, drunkenness conviction, accident rates, drink-drive offences all rise if alcohol consumption rises; these rates also fall if it falls (Kendell, 1984a). In England and Wales from 1860 to 1978 mortality rates due to cirrhosis of the liver rose and paralleled the rise in alcohol consumption (Royal College of Physicians, 1987). From 1979 to 1982 there was a subsequent slight fall in consumption (11%) and this was reflected by a decline of annual alcoholism admissions (19%), cirrhosis mortality (4%), drunkenness convictions (16%) and drink-driving convictions (7%) (Kendell, 1984b; Table 14.11). Therefore, from a public health point of view, anything that influences per capita consumption of alcohol must be important (Kendell *et al.*, 1983).

Several factors influence alcohol consumption. Cultural/religious traditions, advertising and health promotion all influence demand for alcohol, whereas importation and production controls, licensing hours of outlets, age limits and price

Table 14.10

Alcohol consumption levels by sex and age, England and Wales 1988

	Age			
	18–24	25–44	45–64	65+
Alcohol consumption level (units per week)	(%)	(%)	(%)	(%)
Men				
Non-drinker	5	4	7	14
Very low (<1)	6	5	11	19
Low (1–10)	30	33	37	40
Moderate (11–21)	24	25	21	14
Fairly high (22–35)	15	16	11	8
High (36–50)	9	9	6	3
Very high (51+)	11	9	6	2
Women				
Non-drinker	8	7	12	23
Very low (<1)	12	18	27	37
Low (1–7)	42	44	41	29
Moderate (8–14)	21	18	12	7
Fairly high (15–25)	10	9	6	3
High (26–35)	4	2	2	1
Very high (36+)	3	2	1	0

Source: General Household Survey, 1988.

influence availability (Kendell, 1984a). Influences on demand are important, although there is little documented evidence on the efficacy of health education or advertising. In contrast, there is considerable evidence showing that consumption can be manipulated most easily by controls on availability. For example, during the First World War, beer consumption was reduced by 63% and spirits by 52%, through reducing the number of outlets and their opening hours (Smart, 1974).

Price of alcohol relative to income is the most powerful influence on consumption (Semple and Yarrow, 1974; Popham *et al.*, 1975; Table 14.12) and direct taxation is the most obvious means for governments to exert price control and influence the prevalence of alcohol abuse. Taxation should, therefore, be considered as a positive public health measure and the UK Government could do more to reduce alcohol consumption through a deliberate taxation policy, with duties being based on the alcohol content of a drink (Cook, 1982; Faculty of Public Health Medicine, 1991). The UK Treasury suggests that a 1% rise in the real price of alcohol leads to a fall in consumption of beer by 0.25%, spirits by 1.5% and wine by 1% (Faculty of Public Health Medicine, 1991). Following the 1981 budget in the UK, when there was an increase in excise duty, such that the price of alcohol rose faster than the retail price index for the first time in 30 years, a study of 'regular drinkers' showed that their weekly alcohol consumption fell by 18% and their 'adverse effects score' fell by 16% (Kendell *et al.*, 1983).

Unfortunately, integration into the Common Market may force the Government to reduce taxes on alcohol as the UK currently has higher rates (especially for wine) than other member states (Maynard and O'Brien, 1982). This would result in price reductions for all types of alcoholic drink, increasing UK consumption by around 46% and doubling the numbers consuming more than 50 units per week (Baker and McKay, 1990). There would also be a rise in the frequency of alcohol-related

Table 14.11

The relationship between per capita consumption of alcohol and medical ill-effects, England and Wales

Year	Alcohol consumption (litres ethanol per year)	Alcoholism admissions per 100,000 population aged 15+ per year (ICD 303)	Cirrhosis mortality per 100,000 population aged 15+ per year (ICD 571)
1970	7.03	5.17	3.71
1971	7.37	5.7	4.19
1972	7.79	6.19	4.41
1973	8.61	7.34	4.77
1974	8.85	8.11	4.63
1975	8.82	8.40	4.82
1976	9.28	8.68	4.94
1977	8.81	9.17	4.73
1978	9.5	9.13	4.97
1979	9.79	9.74	5.6
1980	9.33	10.96	5.64
1981	8.89	10.55	5.59
1982	8.67	8.91	5.42

Source: Kendell (1984b).

Table 14.12

Consumption of alcohol and its relative price Ontario, Canada 1928–67

Year	Per capita alcohol consumption litres of absolute alcohol	Relative price
1928	2.81	0.102
1931	2.64	0.112
1934	2.09	0.137
1937	3.36	0.086
1940	3.64	0.074
1943	4.91	0.064
1946	5.82	0.069
1949	7.18	0.058
1952	7.32	0.051
1955	7.55	0.047
1958	7.96	0.043
1961	8.14	0.043
1964	8.73	0.039
1967	8.91	0.035

Source: Popham et al. *(1975).*

Table 14.13

Relevant 'Health of the Nation' risk factor targets

Smoking

To reduce the prevalence of cigarette smoking to no more than 20% by the year 2000 in both men and women (a reduction of a third)

To reduce consumption of cigarettes by at least 40% by the year 2000

In addition to the overall reduction in prevalence, at least 33% of women smokers to stop smoking at the start of their pregnancy by the year 2000

To reduce smoking prevalence of 11–15-year-olds by at least 33% by 1994

Obesity

To reduce the proportion of men and women aged 16–64 who are obese by at least 25% and 33% respectively by 2005 (to no more than 6% of men and 8% of women)

Diet and cholesterol levels

To reduce the average percentage of food energy derived from total fat by the population by at least 12% by 2005 (to no more than about 35% of total food energy)

To reduce the average percentage of food energy derived by the population from saturated fatty acids by at least 35% by 2005 (to more than 11% of food energy)

Hypertension

To reduce mean systolic blood pressure in the adult population by at least 5 mmHg by 2005

Alcohol

To reduce the proportion of men drinking more than 21 units of alcohol per week and women drinking more than 14 units per week by 30% by 2005 (to 18% of men and 7% of women)

Source: The health of the nation. HMSO, London, 1992.

problems. Several bodies are, therefore, recommending that the Government ensures that integration into the European Community does not result in significant price reductions for alcoholic drinks (Faculty of Public Health Medicine, 1991).

The health of the nation

The UK Government's White Paper, *The Health of the Nation* (1992), acknowledges the role that is played by the above risk factors in contributing towards major causes of premature death or avoidable ill-health. It has set specific targets to reduce the prevalence of the risk factors by the year 2000. These are outlined in Table 14.13.

References

Allied Dunbar. *National fitness survey.* Sports Council, London, 1992.

Anderson P. Excess mortality associated with alcohol consumption. *Br Med J*, 1988; 297: 824–827.

Anderson P. Alcohol as a key area. *Br Med J*, 1991; 303: 766–769.

Baker P, McKay S. IFS Commentary No. 21, *The structure of alcohol taxes. A hangover from the past.* Institute for Fiscal Studies, London, 1990.

Chesher A. Changes in the nutritional content of British household food supplies during the 1980s. In *Household food consumption and expenditure 1989, Annual Report of the National Food Survey Committee.* HMSO, London, 1990.

Cook PJ. Alcohol taxes as a public health measure. *Br J Addiction*, 1982; 77: 245–250.

Cox B et al. *The health and lifestyle survey.* Health Promotion Trust, London, 1987.

Faculty of Public Health Medicine of the Royal College of Physicians. *Alcohol and public health.* Macmillan, London, 1991.

Goddard E. *Drinking in England and Wales in the late 1980s.* OPCS, HMSO, London, 1991.

Jarrett M, Shipley MJ, Rose G. Weight and mortality in the Whitehall Study. *Br Med J*, 1982; 285: 535–537.

Kemsley WFF. Weight and height of a population in 1943. *Ann Eugenics*, 1950; 15: 161.

Kemsley WFF. Body weight at different ages and heights. *Ann Eugenics*, 1952; 16: 316.

Kendell RE et al. Effect of economic changes on Scottish drinking habits 1978–82. *Br J Addiction*, 1983; 78: 365–379.

Kendell RE. The determinants of per capita consumption. In *Alcohol: preventing the harm*, pp. 7–29. Institute of Alcohol Studies, London, 1984a.

Kendell RE. The beneficial consequences of the UK's declining per capita consumption of alcohol in 1979–82. *Alcohol Alcoholism*, 1984b, 19: 271–276.

Lichenstein MJ et al. Systolic and diastolic blood pressures as predictors of coronary heart disease mortality in the Whitehall Study. *Br Med J*, 1985; 291: 243–245.

Marmot MG et al. Alcohol and mortality: a U-shaped curve. *Lancet*, 1981; ii: 580–583.

Maynard A, O'Brien B. Harmonisation policies in the European Community and alcohol abuse. *Br J Addiction*, 1982; 77: 235–244.

Montegriffo VME. A survey of the incidence of obesity in the United Kingdom. *Postgrad Med J*, 1971; June (suppl): 418–422.

Office of Population Censuses and Surveys. *General household survey.* HMSO, London.

Office of Population Censuses and Surveys. *The dietary and nutritional survey of British adults.* HMSO, London, 1990.

Popham RE, Schmidt W, de Lint J. The prevention of alcoholism: epidemiological studies of the effect of government control measures. *Br J Addiction*, 1975; 70: 125–144.

Rosenbaum S. et al. A survey of heights and weights of adults in Great Britain: 1980. *Ann Human Biol*, 1985; 12(2): 115–127.

Royal College of Physicians. *Smoking and health: summary of a report on smoking in relation to cancer of the lung and other diseases.* Pitman, London, 1962.

Royal College of Physicians. *Smoking and health now: 2nd Report.* Pitman, London, 1971.

Royal College of Physicians. *Smoking or health: 3rd report.* Pitman, London, 1977.

Royal College of Physicians. *Health or smoking: follow-up report.* Pitman, London, 1983a.

Royal College of Physicians. Obesity. *J Roy Coll Phys*, 1983b; 17: 5–65.

Royal College of Physicians. *A great and growing evil: the medical consequences of alcohol abuse.* Tavistock, London, 1987.

Semple BM, Yarrow A. Health education, alcohol and alcholism in Scotland. *Health Bull*, 1974; 30: 31–34.

Shaper AG *et al*. Alcohol and mortality in British men: explaining the U-shaped curve. *Lancet*, 1988; ii: 1267–1273.

Smart RG. The effect of licensing restriction during 1914–1918 on drunkenness and liver cirrhosis deaths in Britain. *Br J Addiction*, 1974; 69: 109–121.

Smith R. The relationship between consumption and damage. *Br Med J*, 1981; 283: 895–898.

UK Government White Paper. *The health of the nation.* HMSO, London, 1992.

Wald N, Nicolandes-Bowman A. (eds). *UK smoking statistics*, 2nd edn. Oxford University Press, Oxford, 1990.

Wannamethee G, Shaper AG. Body weight and mortality in middle aged British men: impact of smoking. *Br Med J*, 1989; 299: 1497–1502.

Whelton PK, Klag MJ. The epidemiology of high blood pressure. *Clinics Geriat Med*, 1989; 5(4): 639–655.

WHO. *Arterial hypertension.* World Health Organisation (see Cox *et al.*, 1987).

WHO/IARC. IARC Monographs on the evaluation of carcinogenic risks to humans, Vol 44, *Alcohol drinking.* IARC, Lyon, 1988.

Physical fitness and the importance of exercise in the third age

15

Sarah Lamb

Introduction

Whether an increase in average life expectancy is at the expense of a good quality of life is a contentious issue that has yet to be resolved. However, it is evident that interventions which are aimed at minimising disability and maximising functional ability will assume increasing importance as the population ages.

Although the intrinsic process of ageing results in a decrease in physical fitness, or capacity for physical work, there is considerable individual variation in the rate and extent of decline (Elward and Larson, 1992). This suggests that other factors, apart from ageing are also responsible, one of the most important of which is a sedentary lifestyle (Bassey, 1978).

A growing consensus of opinion points to the significant role that exercise has in the maintenance of physical and mental health, and functional ability (Elward and Larson, 1992). Despite this, on average, the fitness of individuals in the third age, and their participation in exercise, is below that required to ensure good functioning in daily life (Bland and Williams, 1988). This should obviously be of considerable concern to all who are involved in providing care for people in the third age.

This chapter first investigates age-associated decline in physical fitness, emphasising the detrimental effect of a sedentary lifestyle. Secondly, the beneficial effect of exercise, specific guidelines and possible intervention strategies are discussed.

Section 1: Age associated changes in physical fitness, and their importance in everyday life

Physical fitness, or the capacity for physical work, is essentially dependent on the integrated action of four attributes—stamina, strength, suppleness and skill, as shown in Figure 15.1 (Gray *et al.*, 1987).

A phenomenon of ageing is a decline in each of these attributes, which eventually results in a loss of fitness. Although some of these age-associated changes do appear to be attributable to the intrinsic ageing process, there is considerable individual variation in the rate and extent of decline. This suggests that the decline is also dependent on a number of other factors, including co-existent medical illness, smoking, poor nutrition, and low levels of exercise (Elward and Larson, 1992).

A useful framework in which to consider changes in fitness with age, and effect of a sedentary lifestyle is shown in Figure 15.2 (Gray, 1982). The dotted line represents the loss of fitness that is a consequence of intrinsic ageing, and the solid and potentially reversible line, the accelerated loss that occurs as a consequence of a sedentary lifestyle.

Figure 15.1
Major components
of physical capacity.

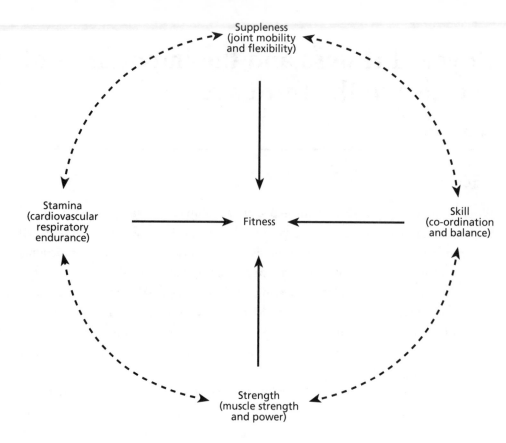

Figure 15.2
Change in physical
fitness with age
(Gray, 1982). - - - -,
decline due to
intrinsic aging;
———, the decline
compounded by
extrinsic factors.

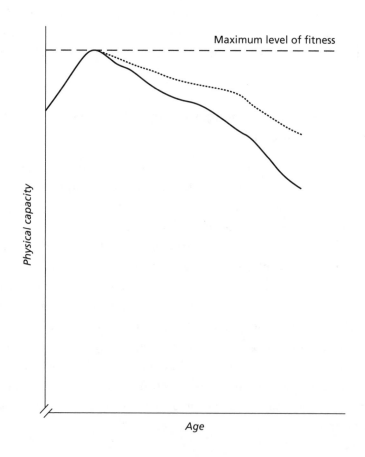

Many people do not realise that even simple everday activities require a minimum threshold of fitness for their completion. The body has to be sufficiently physically conditioned if it is to meet the challenges of ordinary life, and must also hold a 'reserve capacity' to meet additional requirements such as fighting infection (Young, 1989).

A model which demonstrates the importance of maintaining fitness in older age is shown in Figure 15.3 (Young, 1986). A healthy 20-year-old subject will require only 50–70% of the total strength of their thigh muscle to rise from a low armless chair, but a healthy 80-year-old female must make a maximal effort. Reserve capacity is lost and fitness falls to a critical 'threshold' level. Any further decline in fitness, or an increase in environmental stress, violates the threshold and jeopardises independence. If a person has a lower fitness level, the ability to stand up will be compromised at a much younger age. If fitness is high, performance can be sustained to a greater age, emphasising the fact that reduced fitness and poor performance in activities of daily living are not an inevitable consequence of ageing.

Age-associated changes in strength

There is a well-documented loss of muscle strength, power and mass with increasing age.

The decline in mass is the effect of a gradual reduction in the number of muscle fibres, a process which begins at birth (Lexell et al., 1983). The resultant loss of strength and power is accelerated from the age of 60 years onwards by a selective atrophy of stronger muscle fibres (Grimby and Saltin, 1983), and a decrease in the number of neuronal connections between the spinal cord and the muscles themselves (Green, 1986). As a consequence, the strength (averaged over all muscle groups) of subjects aged over 70 years, is at least 20% less than that of young adults (Vandervoort et al., 1986).

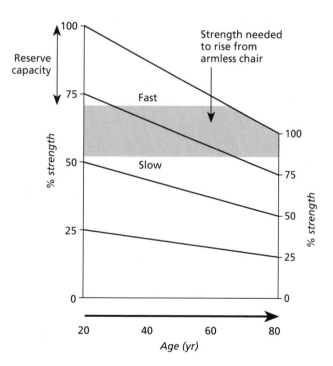

Figure 15.3 Effect of age on estimated percentage of strength required to rise from an armless chair (after Young, 1986).

Interestingly, some of the more functionally important muscle groups demon-strate an accelerated and much greater age-associated loss in strength. Lower limb muscles, notably the quadriceps muscle, are important in activities of daily living such as walking and climbing stairs, rising from a chair, and in maintaining balance. Larson *et al.* (1978), using a cross-sectional study design, reported the quadriceps to be particularly vulnerable to age-associated loss of strength from the fifth decade onwards, as shown in Figure 15.4. This was confirmed by a longitudinal study that found that the strength of the quadriceps fell between the ages of 70–75 by 9% in men and 14% in women at a rate of 1.8% and 2.8% per annum, respectively (Aniansson *et al.*, 1983).

Upper limb strength is essential for manual dexterity, and ability to wash, dress and feed oneself. Loss of hand grip strength has been shown to correlate positively with dependent living (Williams, 1984, 1987). Elbow flexion and extension strength, which enables the hand to be levered towards the face, declines rapidly between the age of 70 and 75 years, at a rate of 4.6 to 6.8% per annum (Aniansson *et al.*, 1983).

Muscle power determines how quickly strength can be generated, and appears to be much more sensitive to age-associated decline (Bassey *et al.*, 1992). Shook and Norris (1970) demonstrated that upper limb power output fades from about 40 years of age, whereas strength fades from 60 years onwards. Leg extensor power is important for walking, climbing and rising from a chair, and a threshold power of 0.5 W/kg of body weight has been suggested as essential for activities of daily living (Bassey *et al.*, 1992). A recent report suggests a rate of decline in leg extensor power of 3.5% per annum in healthy men and 3.7% per annum in healthy women between the ages of 65 and 84 years (Skelton *et al.*, 1992).

Encouragingly, loss of strength and power can be minimised by regular physical activity (Elward and Larson, 1992; Bassey *et al.*, 1992).

Figure 15.4
Change in quadriceps strength with age (cross-sectional data from Larson, 1978).

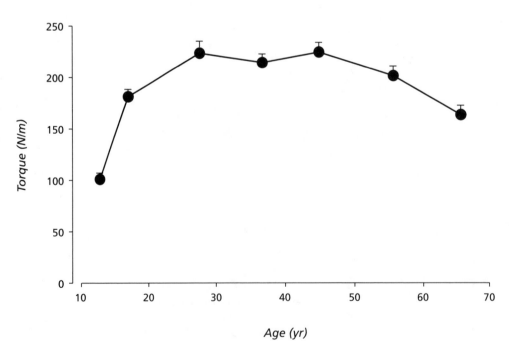

Age-associated changes in stamina

Stamina, or ability to sustain activity, is dependent on the rate at which oxygen can be removed from the atmosphere and delivered to the working tissues and, secondly, the ability of tissues to extract and utilise oxygen (Astrand and Rodahl, 1987).

Studies have shown that stamina decreases by up to 10% per decade regardless of habitual activity level (Lakatta, 1984), but the underlying mechanisms are not clearly understood. Possible explanations include a decreased ability to utilise oxygen caused by changes in cellular enzymes (Strandrell, 1964), or more likely, as a consequence of a reduced muscle mass (Asmussen, 1980). A decrease in the ability of the central circulation to transport oxygen cannot be excluded with any certainty, as ageing affects the structure and function of the heart, major vessels and lungs (Lakatta, 1990).

Cardiovascular system ageing is characterised by a decrease in vascular distensibility, and is associated with an increase in blood pressure (Lakatta, 1984). Heart valves become thicker and more rigid, further reducing the capacity for work and ability to tolerate a variety of stresses (Lakatta, 1984).

Changes in the structure of connective tissues affect the lung compliance. Additionally, the stiffness of the chest wall increases and respiratory muscle strength decreases with age, the combined effect of which is a reduction in lung capacity (Knudson, 1991). This loss of lung capacity is thought only to affect stamina in the older old, or in situations where the lungs have been subjected to cumulative insults such as those imposed by smoking (Shephard, 1987).

A reduction in stamina means that a task will require a greater effort to ensure completion. Certain activities may become unpleasant, or even impossible to perform. This was demonstrated in the Canadian fitness survey (Stephens *et al.*, 1986). By the age of 60–65 years the ability to walk uphill was significantly impaired in most older subjects, as shown in Figure 15.5(a). When those subjects who were below an acceptable threshold of fitness were examined separately, the situation was considerably worse as shown in Figure 15.5(b). In fact, many of these subjects were unable to walk up a hill. Decreased muscle strength and joint suppleness, which are commonly observed in older people, also increase the energy cost of completing a task, so that the amount of stamina required is even greater.

Stamina affects quality of life in many situations. Some occupations demand considerable stamina, as do heavy household chores and some leisure pursuits (Astrand and Rodahl, 1987). Consequently, if a person wishes to lead an active independent life, stamina is an essential prerequisite. The literature emphasises that the age-associated decline in stamina is accelerated by sedentary habits, the presence of occult coronary disease and/or smoking, all of which can be negated by a healthy lifestyle.

Age-associated changes in skill

The contribution of the central nervous system to fitness and ability in activities of daily living, might not at first seem apparent. However, the completion of any task

Figure 15.5
Age-associated
reduction in stamina
and the effect of
fitness levels. The
ability to walk uphill
(1 in 7 gradient and
on the level at 3 mph)
(Royal College of
Physicians, 1991).
(a) The stamina or
effort required to
walk uphill is age
associated. For
averagely fit men, at
age 25 years walking
uphill requires
moderate cardio-
vascular effort,
whereas at 65 years,
walking uphill
requires maximum
cardiovascular
effort.
(b) At age 25, for
unfit individuals,
walking uphill
requires severe
cardiovascular
effort. At age 65
years walking uphill
is impossible, and
even walking on the
level requires greater
effort.

(a) For averagely fit individuals

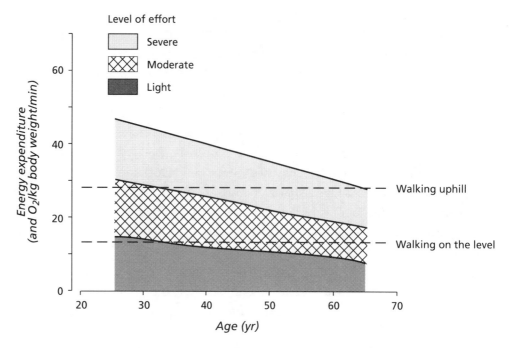

The stamina or effort required to walk uphill is age-associated. For averagely fit men, at age 25 years walking uphill requires moderate cardiovascular effort; whereas at 65 years, walking uphill requires maximum cardiovascular effort.

(b) For unfit individuals

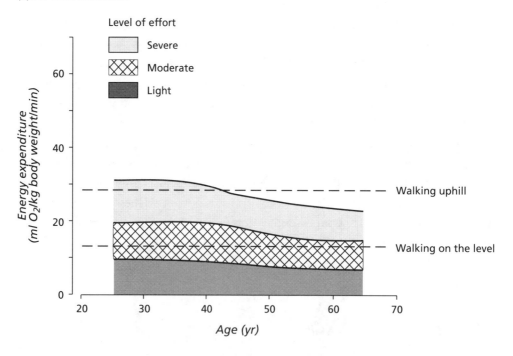

At age 25, for unfit individuals, walking uphill requires severe cardiovascular effort.
At age 65 years walking uphill is impossible, and even walking on the level requires greater effort.

142

requires skill, a characteristic of predominantly central nervous system origin (Astrand and Rodahl, 1987). Temporal factors such as motivation are also important (Astrand and Rodahl, 1987). The integrity of the central nervous system is essential if appropriate action is to be taken to avoid falls and accidents (Shephard, 1987). After stumbling, the likelihood of a fall is increased in the older person because of poor eyesight, a reduced leg lift when walking (Sheldon, 1960) and greater difficulty in restoring balance once stumbling has occurred (Shephard, 1987). Loss of cells in the brain stem and cerebellum, plus a diminution of peripheral proprioceptive function, limit the co-ordination of body movements, including the correction of externally imposed forces (Shephard, 1987). An increased movement and reaction time (Birren *et al.*, 1963; Stelmach and Diewart, 1977; Wright and Shephard, 1978), an alteration in the central processing of information (Birren *et al.*, 1979) and deterioration in vision, hearing and proprioception (Shephard, 1987) contribute to age-associated decline in skill.

These changes have been attributed predominantly to a progressive death of neurones in the central nervous system (Brody, 1980). On average 10–20% of cerebral mass is lost between the ages of 20 and 90 years (Dekoninck, 1982), with some areas of the brain demonstrating a much greater loss. However, it remains unclear to what extent the changes are a consequence of selective cell loss, cerebral ischaemia, viral infections, intoxication with metals such as aluminium, or a lack of antioxidants (Shephard, 1987).

Age-associated changes in suppleness

Connective tissue undergoes histochemical and structural change with advancing age (Grahame, 1978; Brandt and Palmoski, 1976). One result is a degeneration of joints, clinically known as osteoarthritis, which can be detected from the second decade of life, and thence with increasing frequency and severity as a person becomes older (Chung, 1966a,b; Calkins and Challa, 1985). Changes are not restricted to joints alone; tendons, ligaments and muscles are also affected (Shephard, 1987). Muscle stiffness is common and muscles become more susceptible to fatigue. The ability to recover from minor sprains and strains is lessened because of a reduction in blood supply to the soft tissues (Rothman and Parke, 1965), although it is possible that this phenomenon is associated with decreased activity levels (Rothman & Slogoff, 1967).

The common functional features of an ageing joint are loss of mobility and instability (Allman, 1974). Joint impairment increases the absolute energy cost of activities of daily living. Osteoarthritis of the upper limb can, in some people, lead to a painful restriction of movement (Shephard, 1987). Self-care ability, for example dressing, may be limited if range of movement in the shoulders is restricted. Figure 15.6 demonstrates the relationship between self-care ability and range of movement in the shoulder joint (Young, 1986). If the lower limbs are affected there may be a serious impairment of gait. Loss of suppleness in the hip may cause limping, and difficulty in performing some of the key activities of daily living such as climbing stairs, getting out of a bath, and rising from a low chair (Badley *et al.*, 1984). Involvement of the knee also causes difficulty in stair climbing (Badley *et al.*, 1984).

Figure 15.6
Relationship
between self-care
ability and range
of movement
(abduction) in the
shoulder joint
(Young, 1986).
Shaded area
indicates the amount
of movement
required to
complete each task.

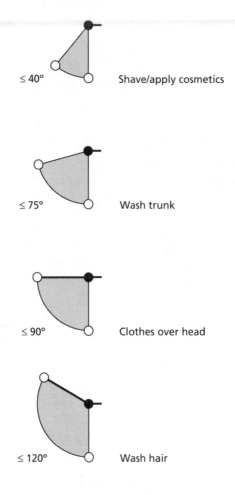

≤ 40°   Shave/apply cosmetics

≤ 75°   Wash trunk

≤ 90°   Clothes over head

≤ 120°   Wash hair

Barney and Neukom (1979) found that 37% of those over the age of 55 had some form of arthritis. In 24% of the sample this led to moderate or severe limitation in activities of daily living, emphasising the significance of degenerative joint changes. However, it should be noted that pain and limitation of activity are not inevitable sequelae of degeneration, as some people, despite radiographic evidence of degenerative change, do not experience any symptoms (Lee *et al.*, 1974).

Summary

Overall, evidence indicates that there is a gradual but consistent decline in physical fitness from early adulthood to old age. The literature indicates that the third age may present a critical point in the decline in physical fitness. With increased prevalence of impairments, compounded by decreasing habitual activity levels, it is the age at which physical performance of the sedentary person may become compromised.

Importantly, and on a positive note, the onset, rate and consequence of this decline varies greatly between individuals. Studies have repeatedly shown that decreased fitness, and struggling with tasks of everyday life are not an unavoidable consequence of ageing. An age-associated decline in physical fitness should not affect the functional ability of an older person, provided that he or she maximises their fitness, and pursues a healthy lifestyle. Even in the presence of pathologies, such as stroke, arthritis and cardiovascular disease, it is thought that the maintenance of fitness can maximise functional ability (Shephard, 1987; Elward and Larson, 1992). The importance of regular physical activity cannot be overstated.

Section 2: The importance of exercise in maintaining physical fitness

Interventions which are aimed at minimising disability and maximising functional ability are essential to ensure a good quality of life for people in the third age, and to relieve some of the fiscal burden of the ageing population. The literature indicates that regular physical activity plays a crucial role in the maintenance, and improvement, of fitness and physical and mental health (Elward and Larson, 1992). However, evidence suggests that the fitness and customary activity levels of individuals in the third age are below that required to ensure good functioning in activities of daily living (Bland and Williams, 1986; Dallosso *et al.*, 1988).

This section will emphasise the importance of regular and appropriate exercise. Current levels of exercise participation in the third age will be discussed in relation to those suggested by the literature as being appropriate for the maintenance of good health and functioning. The implications for government bodies, health professionals, leisure and urban planners, and the general public will be identified.

The importance of exercise

Regular exercise is fundamental to the maintenance of physical fitness at any age. This is demonstrated by the profound detrimental effect that immobilisation has on both young and older people (Saltin *et al.*, 1968). Individuals who exercise regularly throughout their lives tend to maintain a higher level of function and experience less decline in functional status than sedentary individuals (Elward and Larson, 1992).

Encouragingly, recent research suggests that the benefits of exercise of an appropriate nature accrue to sedentary elderly persons who begin exercise at an advanced age (Elward and Larson, 1992). Specific training effects that have been reported in sedentary elderly people are increased muscle strength and power (Deshin, 1969; Gore, 1972; Aniannson, 1980; Bassey *et al.*, 1992), increased stamina (Barry *et al.*, 1966; de Vries, 1970), and increased joint suppleness (Chapman *et al.*, 1972; Munns, 1981). Encouraging evidence indicates that exercise may also slow or prevent some of the intellectual and psychomotor decline which is associated with ageing, although further research is required to confirm these findings (Gray *et al.*, 1987; Elward and Larson, 1992). Important psychological benefits, namely a reduction in anxiety and a generalised sense of wellbeing have also been reported (Blumenthal and Williams, 1982).

The benefits of exercise are not limited to healthy older people. The judicious use of exercise can improve function in the presence of stroke, arthritis, peripheral vascular disease, and subsequent to a heart attack (Royal College of Physicians, 1991).

Epidemiological evidence also suggests that good physical fitness is associated with a reduction in all cause mortality in both men and women (Blair *et al.*, 1989). Vigorous exercise is related to a decreased risk of cardiovascular disease, and weight bearing exercise may have a role in the prevention of osteoporosis, and other conditions (reviewed by Elward and Larson, 1992).

Despite a growing consensus of opinion that exercise of appropriate intensity may benefit elderly persons in these complementary ways, participation in conditioning exercise remains low. Whether this is because the general public does not realise the potential benefits of exercise or what constitutes 'appropriate or conditioning' exercise, or that exercise is not being incorporated into the care of elderly persons by health professionals, are issues of great importance. These issues must be addressed if people in the third age are to be encouraged to participate in physical activity of an appropriate nature.

How much, and what type of exercise do we need to maintain or regain fitness?

Several studies have shown that a training effect will only occur if exercise is of an 'appropriate' intensity, duration, frequency and nature (Shephard, 1968). However, what constitutes 'appropriate' is a contentious issue, and a source of confusion to both those giving and taking advice. There has been minimal study of the exercise prescription required to ensure functional fitness in the third age. This is an almost impossible task due to the heterogeneous nature of the cohort. However, some authors have devised guidelines based on available research, but these have to be interpreted with some caution as they usually refer to healthy younger people (American College of Sports Medicine, 1990; Astrand, 1986). When deciding on suitable exercise regimes for older people careful consideration must be given to four factors—safety, effectiveness, enjoyment and cost.

Safety   It is a common belief that exercise carries an increased risk of a cardiac event and soft tissue injury (Shephard, 1987). On the contrary, data indicate that cardiac risk is lower in the 50–69-year-old age group than in the 40–49-year-old age group. Vouri *et al.* (1986) suggest, that for this group, the risk of a cardiac event is one in 11.7 million for walking, 6.7 million for jogging, 3.4 million for non-strenuous exercise and 1.2 million for strenuous exercise. It is difficult to identify those subjects who carry a greater cardiac risk, but indicators may be a higher prevalence of smoking, higher resting blood pressure, a type A personality, and specific changes on an exercise electrocardiogram (Shephard, 1984).

The use of exercise electrocardiographic testing as a screening method for all elderly people who undertake exercise has been advocated by some (Rousseau, 1989). However, this is a costly and time-consuming procedure, which has questionable efficacy (Shephard, 1987). It would seem sensible to ration this to persons in who symptomatic cardiac problems have been identified, or in who a cardiac risk is suspected. Questionnaires such as the 'Preparation for Activity Readiness Questionnaire' may provide a cheap alternative to formal exercise testing (Frior and Faulkner, 1988).

Musculo-skeletal injury occurs when the demand of an exercise regime has been too great, when there has been little or no 'warming up and down', when there has been poor attention to the flooring and lighting in the environment, or inappropriate footwear has been worn (Shephard, 1987). Obesity obviously increases the risk of injury (Shephard, 1987).

Individuals who are worried about their health and ability to undertake regular exercise should seek advice from their general practitioner or physiotherapist. This raises the issue that health professionals must be adequately trained to fulfil this role.

Effectiveness   In order to maximise functional ability in the elderly a general training regime which utilises specific exercises for stamina, skill, suppleness and strength is required. These exercises must be of sufficient intensity, duration and frequency if they are to have a beneficial effect. Concern over safety is often so great that exercise levels are moderated to such a point that they are no longer effective (Shephard, 1987). However, there are few complications associated with increasing activity, and thus exercise should be regarded as safe for most individuals (Elward and Larson, 1992).

Daily activity is essential to keeping fit. People should endeavour to walk for at least 60 minutes a day (Astrand, 1986). This need not be continuous, and can include moving, walking, and climbing the stairs. This should be interspersed with periods of greater activity designed to build up stamina. Stamina is increased in situations where heart rate is significantly increased (to between 120 and 150 beats per minute depending on initial fitness), for a minimum period of 15 minutes (Shephard, 1987). Two or three weekly sessions of brisk walking, swimming or similar activity, sustained for a period of 20–30 minutes, would fulfil this requirement (Astrand, 1986). These activities are also considered to be sufficient to maintain strength in the legs of an older person (Shephard, 1987). Isometric muscle contractions are useful for strengthening muscles which are especially weak, as long as they are not held against heavy resistance, and are not sustained for too long (Shephard, 1987). Heavy weight lifting or sustained efforts are not considered safe in older persons, as the exertion produces significant changes in blood pressure (Shephard, 1987). Suppleness can be improved by simple stretching exercises. Of special importance are the shoulders, hips, knees and ankles. Simple exercises in which a stretch is maintained at the end of the joint range, should be sufficient. As already discussed, skill may be compromised in an older person, and must be considered when prescribing exercise as this may predispose to injury. Exercises should be simple in the initial stages of training, and progress, with increased fitness, to more complex tasks.

These guidelines are appropriate for a healthy person in the third age. For the more frail or unfit individuals a regime which gradually builds up fitness is needed. People who have impairments such as stroke or diabetes should consult an exercise specialist, such as a physiotherapist, for individual advice and prescription. Older people should be advised to exercise to a degree that produces no more than a pleasant tiredness (Shephard, 1987). If they do experience tightness or excessive pounding of the chest they should stop exercising and seek professional advice (Shephard, 1987).

Enjoyment   To ensure motivation and compliance with an exercise programme an older person must both enjoy the experience and be able to identify gains in health and fitness (Shephard, 1987). Hobbies or interests that people currently enjoy, or have had previous experience of, can often be exploited. So for example, bowls, ballroom dancing or golf may be more attractive to an individual, but as equally effective as swimming, jogging or cycling. It is worthwhile finding out which pursuits are attractive to older persons, and encouraging the development of these activities.

Cost Group exercise has traditionally been thought more successful than an individual programme, both in arousing interest and maintaining motivation (Shephard, 1987). However, many older people cannot afford to join a fitness class or club, or purchase essential equipment such as training shoes. The Canadian fitness survey (Shephard, 1986) found that cost was an important factor in popularising exercise, the cheaper alternatives such as walking and gardening were preferable, and had a lower dropout rate. Clinical research supports the notion that vigorous weight bearing activity, such as brisk walking are the safest, cheapest, easiest and most beneficial form of exercise for the average senior citizen (Elward and Larson, 1992).

What are the customary activity levels of the third age and are they sufficient to maintain fitness?

The National Fitness Survey (The Sports Council and Health Education Authority, 1992) has provided the first comprehensive report concerning the fitness and activity levels of the UK population. In those aged 65–74, 30% of men and 56% of women had an inadequacy in quadriceps strength sufficient to make standing up from a chair unaided, difficult. Of those aged 55–64, 30% of men and 51% of women were not fit enough to sustain normal paced walking, rising to 45% and 79% respectively for those aged 65–74 years. These figures were in stark contrast to the self-assessment of fitness shown in Table 15.1. For example, 60% of women aged 55–74 reported themselves to be fairly fit, yet nearly all women in this age band would find it extremely difficult to walk up a hill with a 5% gradient.

Despite the fact that older people have an increased awareness of the importance of being physically fit (The Sports Council and Health Education Authority, 1992), only limited numbers participate in exercise appropriate to the maintenance of functional independence, as shown in Table 15.2. Even fewer undertake enough exercise to protect against heart disease. On a positive note, the percentage of people likely to experience difficulties with simple tasks of everyday life was consistently smaller in those subjects who exercised. Dallosso *et al.* (1988), in a study of community-dwelling people in Nottingham, found that only 47% of those aged

Table 15.1

Percentage distribution of self-assessment of fitness levels in those aged 55–74 years

	Men	Women
Very fit	23%	26%
Fairly fit	56%	60%
Not very fit	15%	11%
Not fit at all	6%	3%

Source: National Fitness Survey (The Sports Council and Health Education Authority, 1992).

65–74 participated in leisure activities such as swimming and cycling, with participation averaging only 2.2 hours/week. The total time spent walking averaged 55 minutes/day and only 29% had walked for more than an hour a day. Figure 15.7 shows the activity profile from this study.

When compared with the recommendations for exercise suggested in the previous section, it can be implied that, in general, exercise participation of the third age is below that required to ensure fitness. The reasons why older people do not participate in exercise need to be identified before any effective exercise promotion can be implemented.

Why do some people in the third age have low exercise participation?

Both the National Fitness Survey (Allied Dunbar, 1992) and the Health and Lifestyle Survey (Fenner, 1987) found that lower educational levels, being female, and of older age were associated with poor exercise participation. Gray (1987) discusses several philosophical and cultural factors which may discourage older people from participating in exercise. 'It's just my age', 'It's God's will', 'I don't want to wear out my body' or 'There's no point in trying', are verbalisations often heard by those involved in caring for older people. They reflect the cultural and religious beliefs held by much of the population of England, who regard retirement as a period of well-deserved rest, and the toils of everyday life as an irreversible consequence of ageing (Gray, 1987).

Elward and Larson (1992) suggest that many people do not know what constitutes 'healthful' regular exercise, i.e. the kind of exercise that induces a conditioning effect. In a study of 100 elderly people enrolled in a health co-operative, factors which prevented participation in an exercise programme were boredom with the exercise programme, an unawareness of how to get started, a lack of discipline, an unawareness of community opportunity, transportation problems, concerns about proper preparation or exercising in poor weather, and medical concerns (Elward and Larson, 1992). Shephard (1987) also suggests the provision of cheap, adequate and suitable facilities and personnel are vitally important.

Clearly, it is essential that elderly people regard healthy ageing as a realistic and achievable goal, and are able to identify the importance of exercise, and how much and what type of exercise is appropriate. A greater appreciation of the reasons why people do not exercise is needed so that intervention can be targeted effectively. It is

Table 15.2

Levels of participation in exercise

	Age (years)	
	55–64	*65–74*
Level 1	34%	23%
Level 2	37%	33%
Level 3	29%	44%

Source: National Fitness Survey (The Sports Council and Health Education Authority, 1992).

Key Amount of exercise in the last four weeks: Level 1, exercise at a frequency and intensity appropriate to the maintenance of good functioning in everyday life. Level 2, exercise insufficient to improve health or function. Level 3, no exercise.

Figure 15.7
Customary activity
levels in a sample of
people aged 65–74
years (Dallosso *et al.*,
1988).

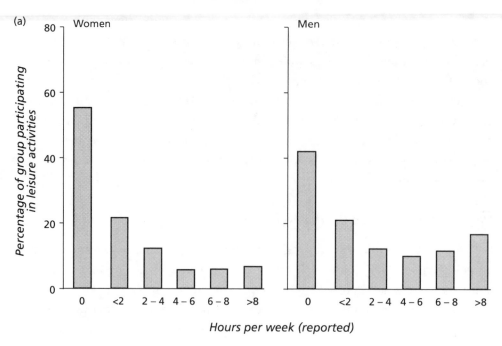

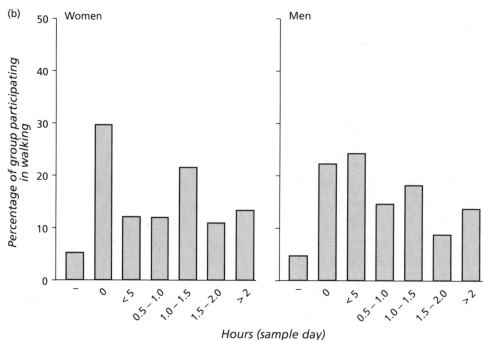

essential to ensure that exercise is a positive and enjoyable experience. This will require the co-ordinated action of government bodies, urban planners, leisure facility managers, health professionals, voluntary bodies and numerous others.

Summary

Despite a growing consensus of opinion that exercise plays a crucial role in the maintenance, and improvement of, functional ability and physical and mental health, a significant proportion of people in the third age do not take sufficient exercise. This should be of considerable concern to all those involved in providing for older people.

Gray (1987) suggests that, because of the growing public interest in leisure pursuits, future cohorts will have more positive attitudes towards exercise and health professionals will promote exercise more vigorously than to date. However, there is no room for complacency, steps must be taken to ensure that this happens, and to address the problems of the current cohorts.

This chapter has raised several research and practical issues that need to be considered. Research is required to clarify the amount and type of exercise required to promote fitness in the third age. A greater appreciation of why elderly people may not enjoy exercise, and research to define effective methods of stimulating large numbers of sedentary elderly people to exercise regularly is needed (Elward and Larson, 1992). Cheap, effective methods of identifying individuals at risk when exercising need to be tested rigorously.

Practical issues are wide ranging. Medical, nursing and paramedical professionals need to be educated about the effects of exercise, so that they are able to advise individuals appropriately, and identify those who need specialist attention. Clear guidelines should be available to 'front line' health workers such as general practitioners, health visitors and community nurses. The implications extend beyond the health professionals. Teachers responsible for physical education in the formative years of life should be encouraged to promote the benefits of exercise, and to make sport and leisure activities an enjoyable experience for all. Research is required to identify those leisure pursuits which are popular with older people. This could then form the basis for the development of facilities. Accessibility, transport, effective management and cost must also be considered.

The greatest challenges lies in changing the attitude and habits of the general public, and is one that can only be achieved by addressing the issues raised in this paper and by a concerted effort by a number of professions, government bodies, voluntary organisations and members of the general public. However, the potential benefits are great, not only in terms of the total sum of human happiness, but also on relieving some of the burden placed on health and social services by an ageing population.

References

Allman FM. Conditioning for sports. In Ryan AJ, Allman FM (eds), *Sports medicine*. Academic Press, New York, 1974.

American College of Sports Medicine. The recommended quantity and quality of exercise for developing and maintaining cardiorespiratory and muscular fitness in healthy adults. *Med Sci Sports Exercise*, 1990; 22(2): 265–272.

Aniansson A, Grimby G, Rundgren A, Svanborg A, Orlander J. Physical training in old men. *Age Ageing*, 1980; 9: 186–187.

Aniansson A, Sperling L, Rundgren A, Lehnberg E. Muscle function in 75 year old men and women. A longitudinal study. *Scand J Rehabil Med*, 1983; 9 (suppl.): 92–102.

Asmussen E. Aging and exercise. In Horvarth, Yousef (eds), *Environmental physiology: aging, heat and altitude*, pp. 419–429. Elsevier, North Holland, 1980.

Astrand PO. Comment on recommendations to follow for good physical fitness. *Acta Med Scand*, 1986; 711 (suppl.): 241–242.

Astrand PO, Rodahl K. *Textbook of work physiology: physiological basis of exercise*, International edn. McGraw-Hill, Singapore, 1987.

Badley E, Wagstaff S, Wood P. Measures of functional ability (disability) in arthritis in relation to impairment of range of joint movement. *Ann Rheum Dis*, 1984; 43: 563–569.

Barney JL, Neukom JE. Use of arthritis care by the elderly. *Gerontologist*, 1974; 19: 548–554.

Barry A, Daly J, Pruett E, Steinmetz J, Page H, Birkenhead N, Rodahl K. The effect of physical conditioning on older individuals. *J Gerontol*, 1966; 21: 181–191.

Bassey EJ. Age, inactivity and some physiological responses to exercise. *Gerontology*, 1978; 24: 66–77.

Bassey EJ, Bendall MJ, Pearson M. Muscle strength in the triceps surae and objectively measured customary walking activity in men and women over 65 years of age. *Clin Sci*, 1988; 74(1): 85–89.

Bassey EJ, Fiatarone M, O'Neil E, Kelly M, Evans W, Lipsitz LA. Leg extensor power and functional performance in very old men and women. *Clin Sci*, 1992; 82: 321–327.

Birren JE, Butler RN, Greenhouse SW, Sokoloff L, Yarrow MR. *Human aging*. US Government Printing Office, Washington DC, 1963.

Birren JE, Woods AM, Williams MV. Speed of behaviour as an indicator of age changes and the integrity of the nervous system. In Hoffmeister F, Miller C (eds), *Brain function in old age*, pp. 10–44. Springer-Verlag, New York, 1979.

Blair SN, Kohl HW, Paffenberger RS. Physical fitness and all cause mortality. *J Am Med Assoc*, 1989; 262: 2395.

Bland PK, Williams PT. Activity patterns of men attending for fitness assessment. *Br J Sports Med*, 1988; 22(3): 101–106.

Blumenthal JA, Williams RS. Duke University Centre for Research in Ageing and Human Development. *Adv Res*, 1982; 6: 3.

Brody H. Neuronal loss. In Schimke RT (ed.), *Biological mechanisms of aging*, p. 563. US Department of Health and Human Services, Washington DC, 1980.

Calkins E, Challa HR. Disorders of the joints and connective tissues. In Andres R, Bierman EL, Hazard WL (eds), *Textbook of geriatric medicine and gerontology*, 2nd edn, pp. 813–842. McGraw-Hill, New York, 1985.

Chapman EA, de Vries HA, Swezy R. Joint stiffness: effects of exercise on young and old men. *J Gerontol*, 1972; 27: 218–221.

Chung EB. Ageing in human joints I. Articular cartilage. *J Nat Med Assoc*, 1966a; 58(2): 87.

Chung EB. Ageing in human joints II. Joint capsule. *J Nat Med Assoc*, 1966b; 58(4): 254–260.

Dallosso HM, Morgan K, Bassey EJ, Ebrahim SBJ, Fentem PH, Arie THD. Levels of customary activity among the old and the very old living at home. *J. Epidemiol & Community Health*, 1988; 42: 121–127.

Dekoninck WJ. Viellissement des systèmes de contrôle: le système nerveux. In Bourlière F (ed.), *Gérontologie: biologie and clinique*, pp. 49–62. Flammarion, Paris, 1982.

Deshin DF. Motor activity and ageing. In *Muravov International Symposium on muscular activity and ageing, Kiev*, p. 369. Kiev, 1969.

de Vries HA. Exercise intensity threshold for improvement of cardiovascular respiratory function in older men. *Geriatrics*, 1971; 26: 94–101.

Elward K, Larson EB. Benefits of exercise for older adults. *Clin Geriat Med*, 1992; 8(1): 35–50.

Fenner NP. Leisure, exercise and work. In *The health and lifestyle survey*. Health Promotion Research Trust, London, 1987.

Firor WB, Faulkner RA. Sudden death during exercise: how real a hazard? *Can J Cardiol*, 1988; 6: 251–254.

Gore IY. Physical activity and ageing—a survey of the Soviet Literature III. *Gerontol Clin*, 1972; 14: 78–85.

Gray JAM. Practising prevention in old age. *Br Med J*, 1982; 285: 545–547.

Gray JAM. Education for health in old age. In Gray JAM (ed.), *Prevention of disease in the elderly*. Churchill Livingstone, London, 1987.

Gray JAM, Bassey EJ, Young A. The risks of inactivity. In Gray JAM (ed.), *Prevention of disease in the elderly*. Churchill Livingstone, London, 1987.

Green HJ. Characteristics of aging human skeletal muscles. In Sutton JR, Brock RM (eds), *Sports medicine for the mature athlete*, pp. 17–26. Benchmark Press, Indianapolis, 1986.

Grimby G, Saltin B. The ageing muscle. *Clin Physiol*, 1983; 3: 209–218.

Knudson RJ. Physiology of the aging lung. In Crystal RG, West JB *et al.* (eds), *The lung. Scientific foundations*. Raven Press, New York, 1991.

Lakatta EG. Aging of the cardiovascular system. In Williams TF (ed.), *Rehabilitation of the aging*. Raven Press, New York, 1984.

Lakatta EG. Heart and circulation. In Schneider EL, Rowe J (eds), *Handbook of the biology of aging*, 3rd edn, pp. 181–216. Academic Press, New York, 1990.

Lansing AI. Some physiological aspects of aging. *Physiol Rev*, 1951; 31: 274–284.

Larson L, Grimby G, Karlsonn J. Muscle strength and speed of movement in relation to age and muscle morphology. *J Appl Physiol*, 1979; 46: 451–456.

Lee P, Rooney PJ, Sturrock *et al.* The etiology and pathogenesis of osteoarthrosis: a review. *Sem Arthritis Rheumatol*, 1974; 3: 189–218.

Lexell J, Hendriksonn-Larson K, Sjostrom M. Distribution of different fibre types in human skeletal muscles. *Acta Physiol Scand*, 1983; 117: 115–122.

McHeath JA. *Activity, health and fitness in old age*. Croom Helm, London, 1983.

Munns K. Effects of exercise on the range of motion in elderly patients. In Smith BL, Serfass RC (eds), *Exercise and aging*, pp. 167–178. Enslow, 1981.

Rothman RH, Parke WW. The vascular anatomy of the rotator cuff. *Clin Orthopaedics*, 1965; 14: 176–186.

Rothman RH, Slogoff S. The effect of immobilisation on the vascular bed of the tendon. *Surg Gynecol Obstetr*, 1967; 122: 1064–1066.

Rousseau P. Exercise in the elderly. *Postgrad Med*, 1989; 85(6): 113–116.

Royal College of Physicians. Report, *Medical aspects of exercise*. Royal College of Physicians of London, London, 1991.

Saltin B, Blomquist JH, Mitchell RL, Johnson K, Wildenthal, Chapman CB. Responses to exercise after bed rest and after training. *Circulation*, 1968; 7 (suppl.): 1–78.

Sheldon JH. On the natural history of falls. *Br Med J*, 1960; 5214: 1685–1690.

Shephard RJ. Intensity, duration and frequency of exercise as determinants of the response to a training regime. *Int Z Angew Physiol*, 1968; 26: 272–278.

Shephard RJ. Can we identify those for whom exercise is hazardous? *Sports Med*, 1984; 1: 75–86.

Shephard RJ. *Fitness of a nation—the Canada fitness survey*. Karger, Basel, 1986.

Shephard RJ. *Physical activity and aging*, 2nd edn. Croom Helm, London, 1987.

Shook, NW, Norris AH. Neuromuscular coordination as a factor in age changes in muscular exercise. *Med Sport*, 1970; 4: 92–99.

Skelton DA, Greig CA, Davies JM, Young A. Muscle strength in healthy men aged 65–84. *Age Ageing*, 1992; 21 (suppl. 2): 8.

Stelmach GE, Diewart GL. Aging, information processing and fitness. In Borg G (ed.), *Physical work and effort*. Pergamon Press, Oxford, 1977.

Stephens T, Craig CL, Ferris BF. Adult physical fitness in Canada: findings from the Canadian fitness survey. *Can J Pub Health*, 1986; 77: 285–290.

Strandrell T. Circulatory studies on healthy old men. *Acta Med Scand*, 1964; 175 (suppl. 414): 1–44.

The Sports Council and Health Education Authority. The Allied Dunbar National Fitness Survey, 1992.

Vandervoort A, Hayes KC, Belanger AY. Strength and endurance of skeletal muscle in the elderly. *Physiotherapy Can*, 1986; 38(3): 167–173.

Vuori I, Suurnakki K, Suuranakki T. Risk of sudden cardiovascular death in exercise. *Med Sci Sports Exercise*, 1982; 14: 114–115.

Williams ME. A quantitative method of identifying older persons at risk for increasing long term care services. *J Chron Dis*, 1984; 37(9/10): 705–711.

Williams ME. Identifying the older person likely to require long term care services. *J Am Geriat Soc*, 1987; 35: 751–768.

Wright GR, Shephard RJ. Brake reaction time—effects of age, sex and carbon monoxide. *Arch Environ Health*, 1978; 33: 14–150.

Young A. The relative isometric strength of type I and type II muscle fibres in the human quadriceps. *Clin Physiol*, 1984; 4: 23–32.

Young A. Exercise physiology in geriatric practice. *Acta Med Scand*, 1986; 711 (suppl.): 227–232.

Young A. Muscle function in old age. *New Issues Neurosci*, 1989; 1: 141–156.

Visual and hearing abilities

Margaret Savory

Vision

Visual perception does not result from a single process, but from an integration of several aspects of both sensory and cognitive systems. Consequently, age-associated changes in vision result from a combination of processes that include disease, 'normal' age changes in the structure of the eye and sensory receptors and changes in the ability to process the information received from the eye. Therefore, 'people do not lose their sight in age chohorts marching lock step in obedience to some chronological imperative, rather as individuals each in her or his own way' (Sekuler, 1991).

Normal age changes

Structural changes in the eye   Many structural changes occur in the eye with advancing age and these include: (1) the decreased ability of ciliary muscles to control the thickness of the lens and therefore reducing focusing power; (2) the diminishing size of the pupil, therefore decreasing the amount of light that can enter the eye; (3) the thickening and yellowing of the lens, again reducing accommodative power and the amount of light entering the eye; (4) the loss of cells from the retina and optic pathway, thereby reducing acuity and appreciation of contrast (Weale, 1989; Verrillo and Verrillo, 1985).

Presbyopia   Accommodation is the ability of the eye to bring to focus objects at different distances. This ability declines with advancing age as a result of age-associated changes in the lens and ciliary muscles and gives presbyopia. This affects vision from age 15 years onwards, though corrective lenses are not usually required until the mid- to late-40s. There is a total loss of accommodative ability by the age of 60 (Verrillo and Verrillo, 1985).

Visual acuity   Cross-sectional and longitudinal studies confirm that individuals free from eye disease experience a decline in visual acuity, the ability to resolve fine spatial detail, beginning around 45 years of age (Davison and Irving, 1980; Fozard, 1990). In a longitudinal study documenting age-associated changes amongst 577 males measured over a 21-year period, Gittings and Fozard (1986) found that uncorrected distance acuity declined from age 30 to 80, whereas uncorrected near acuity showed most decline between the ages of 40 and 50 after which the decline lessened. Kline and Schieber (1985) argue that most of the changes in static visual acuity are due to changes in the eye structure, tending to decrease retinal illumination. Thus, increasing the luminance and contrast of materials can compensate for the deficit in visual acuity quite easily. This has been demonstrated experimentally.

Dynamic visual acuity, the acuity for moving objects, declines more rapidly than measures of static acuity (Kline and Schieber, 1985). Burg and Hulbert (1961) found that measures of static visual acuity were poor predictors of dynamic visual acuity, particularly when the speed of the moving target increased.

Visual field   The extent of the visual field, the total area over which sight is maintained when fixating forward, remains constant until the age of 35 years, declines slightly between the ages of 40 and 50 and thereafter declines at a progressively faster rate (Burg, 1968).

Light sensitivity   Under levels of low illumination, the visual system increases its sensitivity (maximally after about 30 minutes) through a process known as dark adaptation. Studies indicate a decrease in absolute threshold with advancing age, although the rate of adaptation does not appear to change (Fozard, 1990; Verrillo and Verrillo, 1985).

Colour vision   Studies have consistently shown that there is a progressive decrease in sensitivity to colours, starting around 20 years of age, becoming most marked at around the age of 70 (Verillo and Verillo, 1985).

Glare   Glare is the resultant reduction in visual effectiveness from excessively bright or inappropriately directed light. The relationship between glare and age has not been studied extensively, although studies have generally revealed an increased sensitivity with advancing age (Kline and Schieber, 1985). For example, older persons may show a protracted period of recovery from glare. Whereas times to recover from glare are 3.9 seconds in 20–24-year-olds, this rose to 5.57 seconds for 40–44-year-olds, and 6.83 seconds for those aged 75–79 (Burg, 1967).

Self-reported visual changes   There is still little known about visual performance in daily living, although self-report surveys have made a considerable contribution by indicating the everyday problems that older persons may have in coping with their visual environment. Surveys conducted amongst healthy adults show that more visual difficulties are usually reported with increased age (Kosnik *et al.*, 1988). Compared with younger counterparts, older adults reported more difficulty with visual processing speed, light sensitivity, dynamic vision, near vision and visual search.

Disease

Although it is clear that visual changes occur as part of a natural physiological ageing process, advanced age also leads to increased prevalence of various eye diseases, which can result in loss or impairment of vision. The four most serious threats are glaucoma, cataracts, diabetic retinopathy and macular degeneration.

The most comprehensive study of prevalence of these four diseases comes from the USA (Leibowitz *et al.*, 1980) though there has been a smaller recent British study of those over 65 (Wormald *et al.*, 1992). The USA findings for the four major diseases are shown in Table 16.1. This study also showed that these four diseases accounted

Table 16.1

Prevalence of the four main eye diseases in the Framingham Eye Study; percentage of individuals affected

Sex	Age	N	Cataract	Glaucoma	Diabetic retinopathy	Senile macular degeneration
M	52–64	601	3.5	1.5	2.2	0.8
M	65–74	346	11.3	3.5	2.9	4.3
M	75+	160	33.8	4.4	4.4	16.9
F	52–64	781	3.6	0.9	1.4	1.4
F	65–74	507	14.2	1.6	2.4	7.9
F	75+	236	46.6	3.0	5.9	21.6

Source: Leibowitz et al. *(1980).*

for 42% of poor vision (best eye 20/200 vision or worse) in those aged 52–64, 54% in those 65–74 and 86% over 75. Prevalence of poor vision of this degree was 2.7% aged 52–64, 5.5% aged 65–74 and 14.6% over 75. Prevention and treatment of these four diseases are thus of great importance.

Whilst prevention of cataract is not possible at present, there is effective treatment with particularly good results from lens replacement surgery. Glaucoma can be detected by screening before vision is affected; yields are small but effective treatment is possible. Diabetic retinopathy is a complication of insulin-dependent diabetes and is less likely where there is high quality control of the disease. Once retinopathy develops, some benefit may be gained from laser therapy. Senile macular degeneration cannot be prevented or treated effectively at the present time.

Hearing

As with impairments of vision, it is difficult to discern whether hearing loss reflects 'normal' ageing processes, or can be attributed to other causes, such as pathology or environmental influences (e.g. noise).

Prevalence of hearing impairment

Estimates of the prevalence of hearing impairment are based upon self-report of hearing difficulties or audiometric assessment. Audiometry generally consists of measuring the hearing threshold level at a range of frequencies (usually 0.5, 1, 2 and 4 kHz) and taking an average for each ear (results comparing either left/right or better/worse). This method preserves most of the important information and is generally a good guide to the ability of an individual to process speech (Davis, 1987). A hearing loss in the better ear of 25 dBHL (decibels hearing level) is generally accepted as the 'threshold of impairment', with 35 dBHL generally taken as the level of impairment sufficient to warrant clinical intervention. Although for the most part the 25 dBHL is considered to be subclinical, use of this level yields similar prevalence rates as self-report studies, people in the range 25–35 dBHL beginning to experience genuine communication problems (Haggard *et al.*, 1981).

According to the UK National Study of Hearing (NSH), approximately one-third of those aged 61–70 suffer from some form of hearing impairment (at least 25 dBHL in the better ear), rising to 60% of those between the ages of 71 and 80 (Davis, 1989) (Table 16.2). Other studies, though smaller in scale, have confirmed the high prevalence rates in the elderly. Herbst and Humphrey (1981) reported that 60% of their sample of 253 persons aged 70+ had a hearing impairment in the better ear of 35 dBHL or greater. Thus, there can be little doubt that hearing impairment is one of the commonest afflictions in later life. Indeed, OPCS (1988) estimates suggest that approximately 2 million people over the age of 60 suffer from some form of hearing impairment. This prevalence is second only to locomotor disabilities (approximately 3.3 million of those aged over 60).

Prevalence estimates from audiometric assessments tend to be greater than those obtained from self-report. For example, in one survey just 38% reported deafness, although 60% were defined as deaf by audiometry (Herbst and Humphrey, 1981). The difference can largely be accounted for by a substantial proportion of deaf people who either deny or do not realise the extent of their disability. This may be due to the stigma that continues to be attached to deafness, or to the diminishing expectations that people have of their sensory abilities as they age.

A longitudinal study (conducted in the UK and Denmark), confirms that the rate at which the auditory system deteriorates is highly dependent on age (rather than hearing level). For those aged over 55, the rate of change was 8.8 (left ear) and 8.5 (right ear) dB per decade, whereas those aged under 55 experienced deterioration at the rate of 2.6 (left ear) and 2.5 (right ear) dB per decade. Furthermore, it was suggested that at age 55 the incidence of new 25+ dBHL cases is about 1.8% per annum; at 35+ dBHL this is 0.8% per annum, representing 10 new cases per month in a typical British health district (Davis *et al.*, 1991).

Assuming constant prevalence rates, projections for England and Wales of the numbers of deaf in the future have also been made (Davis, 1991) (Table 16.3). The demographic changes will lead to large increases in the numbers of people with a

Table 16.2

The prevalence of hearing impairment and reported hearing impairment

Age group	Percentage self-report difficulty hearing in noise	Percentage with hearing loss at or above the threshold level (better ear)		
		≥25 dBHL	≥45 dBHL	≥65 dBHL
17–30	14.1	1.8	0.2	<0.1
31–40	20.0	2.8	1.1	0.7
41–50	26.5	8.2	1.7	0.3
51–60	31.2	18.9	4.0	0.9
61–70	35.2	36.8	7.4	2.3
71–80	43.9	60.2	17.6	4.0
81+	59.9			
Overall	26.0	16.1	3.9	1.1

Source: Davis (1989).

hearing impairment by the year 2016. Total numbers will be some 20% greater than 1988, predominantly affecting those aged over 60.

Provision and uptake of hearing aids

Hearing aids provide considerable benefit to those who suffer from a hearing impairment and generally improve quality of life (Davis *et al.*, 1992; Mulrow *et al.*, 1990). Yet surveys suggest that only around 20–30% of those considered to have a hearing impairment of sufficient severity to warrant (or benefit from) intervention actually have use of a hearing aid (Herbst *et al.*, 1991; Hickish, 1989; MacAdam *et al.*, 1981).

The current levels of provision for aural rehabilitation in Great Britain are considered to fall well below expectations, with service provisions for the older age groups being particularly inadequate (Davis, 1991; Davis *et al.*, 1992). Furthermore, with the projected future increase in the numbers of hearing-impaired, there will need to be a 1–2% per annum increase in resources (in real terms) just to maintain the current levels of (inadequate) provision, not improve them (Davis, 1991). By the year 2016, it is projected that there will be some 2.6 million people with hearing impairment greater than 45 dBHL (2.1 million over the age of 60), most of whom would experience considerable benefit from use of a hearing aid (Davis, 1991).

There are many reasons for the current low provision and uptake of hearing aids. Firstly, the negative public attitude towards the deaf is a major hindrance to people seeking help at early stages of hearing loss. Unlike spectacle wearing, there still remains a stigma attached to the possession of a hearing aid, which is hardly surprising, given that deafness has been described as 'social leprosy' (Brooks, 1976). Consequently, many people may be reluctant to admit to their deafness and may defer making a demand for assistance until it is too late. However, with advances in technology, making hearing aids less cumbersome and obtrusive (as well as more sensitive), it is likely that this will encourage the mildly impaired to wear a hearing aid—just as the mildly visually-impaired wear spectacles.

Table 16.3

Estimated future numbers (thousands) of hearing-impaired people in England and Wales

	Mild (25 dBHL +)			Moderate (45 dBHL +)			Severe (65 dBHL +)		
	18–60	*61–80*	*81+*	*18–60*	*61–80*	*81+*	*18–60*	*61–80*	*81+*
Female									
1991	812	1952	1224	162	552	612	43	152	161
2001	895	1875	1367	182	534	684	51	147	180
2011	926	1994	1413	186	548	706	51	154	186
2016	950	2114	1377	189	586	689	54	164	182
Male									
1991	1116	2089	374	263	466	206	80	114	55
2001	1276	2116	462	304	473	255	91	115	68
2011	1325	2359	538	305	524	297	83	129	79
2016	1389	2489	549	321	554	302	85	136	80

Source: Davis (1991).

A gradual hearing loss is also often seen as a part of the 'normal' ageing process for which there is little point in attempting rehabilitation, by both the individual concerned and, too often, the primary health care providers. Such lowered expectations lead to a hearing impairment not being perceived as such. To a certain extent this is already apparent from the discrepancy between self-report and audiometry (Herbst and Humphrey, 1981; Humphrey *et al.*, 1981). This may be compounded by ignorance of the rehabilitative services that are available. Humphrey *et al.* (1981) found that 33% of their hearing-impaired sample were unaware that the NHS provided a free hearing aid service. In addition, less than 20% were aware of other devices, such as amplified doorbells, telephones etc, all of which were available from Social Services. It is unclear whether ignorance remains at such a high level some 10 years on from the above survey.

Even when sufferers finally approach their general practitioner (GP) and the hearing disorder is recognised, there may be offputting delays before action can occur. This again may act as a deterrent for those seeking rehabilitative care, or may force them to pay for a hearing aid privately in order to speed up the process. Traditionally within the NHS the GP refers patients to ear, nose and throat (ENT) specialists who then refer on to a hearing aid clinic, if appropriate. The typical delay for an ENT appointment has been reported as around 16 weeks, although this average varies from five to 28 weeks, according to region (Johnson *et al.*, 1984). There are further subsequent delays for the appointment at the hearing aid clinic. The unacceptability of such lengthy delays and the unsatisfactory provision of hearing aids within the NHS were highlighted by the Royal National Institute for the Deaf (RNID) in their document 'Hearing aids—the case for change' (1988). The document advocated bringing hearing aid provision into the domain of primary health care by the creation of a new post, that of a hearing aid dispenser, who would operate in general practices, as well as the private sector. However, such an approach has been criticised, suggesting that specialist assessment is still desirable for patient safety in that certain important pathologies may be missed (Campbell and Nigam, 1991). Furthermore, some argue that the wait for specialist assessment is not the main causative factor of long delays; part of the cause is patients failing to seek help promptly (Watson and Crowther, 1989; Campbell *et al.*, 1989). The delays may also result from poor staffing levels.

The RNID proposals have not been implemented, although measures are being undertaken within the NHS to accelerate the rate of hearing aid provision. In particular, there is now a growing trend towards direct referral from GPs to a hearing aid clinic. This eliminates the need to see an ENT specialist (and the inevitable waiting period), provided there is no evidence of any pathology. A recent survey of the first wave of NHS 'opted-out' trust hospitals indicated that 14 out of 24 hearing departments surveyed (58%) were operating direct referral schemes (Bradley and Grover, 1991). Most departments restricted direct referral to those over 60 or 65. As yet, there is no published evaluative data on the direct referral system, although a Department of Health pilot study with this aim is being conducted at the Hester Adrian Research Unit of the University of Manchester. It is comparing both traditional and direct referral schemes on a number of measures, including staff and patient satisfaction and patient safety.

Use of hearing aids

Even when hearing aids are made available, they are not always used. Thomas and Herbst (1981) reported that 17% of respondents in their survey rarely or never used their NHS post-aural hearing aid. Only 38% said they always wore one. A later survey reported that for those with mild hearing loss (40 dB or less) only 14% used the aid more than eight hours a day. This rose to 40% for those with losses greater than 60 dB (Brooks, 1985). Low usage may occur for several reasons. Firstly, hearing problems still persist or are even introduced with an aid. Many wearers find that hearing aids are still unable to discriminate successfully between speech and background noise. However, advances in this direction rely as much on improvements in the understanding of the speech perception process as on gains at a technological level (Bootle, 1991). Secondly, some individuals may have difficulties with insertion of the ear piece (Brooks, 1985). Lastly, a person's attitude towards their deafness may be important in determining use and acceptance of an aid. Any disadvantages encountered may be compounded by users' unrealistic expectations, anticipating that an aid can restore hearing to the same level of perfection as, say, spectacles can for sight. Alternatively, there may be the (usually) unjustified belief that the hearing loss does not warrant the use of an aid (Brooks, 1985).

Screening for hearing loss

Current services rely on people seeking help for themselves, usually at a late stage, when their circumstances have become completely unacceptable to them. For example, Stephens et al. (1990) found an average age of 70 years at first presentation at a hearing aid clinic, with a preceding history of hearing problems for some 15 years. There is, therefore, a strong argument for a screening programme to identify those most likely to benefit from rehabilitative intervention. Given the dramatic increase in hearing impairment amongst those in the third age, this would be the most appropriate age for a programme of screening to be introduced. Pilot screening studies of 50–65-year-olds have already been conducted in Wales (Stephens et al., 1990; Davis et al., 1992). Efficacy has been demonstrated: levels of hearing aid uptake of those identified as impaired were raised from 3% to 9% as a result of one study (Davis et al., 1992), from 7% to 24% in another and from 8% to 22% in a third (Stephens et al., 1990). Successful screening does not need to be overly complex. Stephens et al. (1990) used postal questionnaires and found that two postings were sufficient to identify 96% of those who subsequently accepted hearing aids.

A screening programme at retirement age would have several benefits. Apart from improving the quality of life of the recipients, increased uptake would be likely to reduce the prevalence of those presenting at later ages with severe hearing losses. It would also introduce hearing aids to those that need them at an earlier age, when they are more likely to adapt and use the devices successfully (Brooks, 1985; Parving and Philip, 1991). For example, acquiring the skill of inserting an earmould may be made more difficult by diminishing dexterity in later old age. Finally, if there were a greater use of hearing aids by a relatively young age group, it may do more to reduce the stigma that is still associated with hearing impairment.

Secondary problems associated with hearing loss

Hearing loss can have negative secondary effects, particularly on psychological and social functioning, by depriving sufferers of the ability to communicate easily. This can contribute to a person passing from independence (and the third age) to isolation and dependence (the fourth).

Mental health and wellbeing

Apart from studies conducted in the early 1980s (Herbst and Humphrey, 1980, 1981; Thomas and Herbst, 1980), there appears to have been little subsequent research interest in the co-morbidity of psychiatric disturbance (in particular depression) and deafness. Yet the studies that have been conducted show that an acquired hearing impairment has a profound negative effect on social, emotional and behavioural function. In their study of community-dwelling Londoners aged over 70, Herbst and Humphrey (1980) reported that 69% of the 72 respondents who were depressed were also deaf. This relationship was statistically significant and remained so, even when controlling for age and socioeconomic status. A related finding has also been reported from a survey of hearing-impaired people of employment age, recruited by having received a hearing aid at clinics in the London area (Thomas and Herbst, 1980). Those with hearing impairment generally felt more lonely, demonstrating feelings of both social and emotional isolation.

Cognitive ability

It is fairly obvious that a hearing impairment may lead people to misunderstand what is required of them, posing difficulties in everyday life. However, Rabbitt (1968, 1991) has also demonstrated that even a mild hearing impairment may also interfere with cognitive capabilities by placing extra demand on the information processing capacity of the brain through having to extract sensory information under conditions of adversity. This leaves fewer resources available to rehearse and store the correctly extracted information in memory.

Rabbitt (1991) investigated how well subjects aged 50–82 years performed on recognition and recall of orally presented material. Subjects were recruited from those suffering a hearing loss of greater than 40 dB. They were compared against age-matched controls who were not deaf who were also matched for free recall scores of *visually* presented material. Subjects were presented with a list of 50 words and had to repeat back each word in turn. At the end of the presentation they were asked to recall as many words as possible.

Not surprisingly, age and hearing loss correlated with number of errors in the recognition part of the experiment, i.e. hearing loss makes recognising speech sounds more difficult. However, for analysis of the recall data, only those trials where the words were correctly repeated aloud were used, eliminating the possibility that any observed decrement in recall would be due to imperfect recognition. Yet the effects of age and hearing impairment still remained, with both increased age and greater hearing loss leading to more impaired recall accuracy. Deafness had the greatest effect in the older subjects. IQ measures were found to predict the extent to which either errors in shadowing or accurately recalling orally presented words increased with age and hearing loss. In essence, those with higher IQ scores could better compensate for the negative effects of hearing loss or age on performance.

It is highly probable, therefore, that in everyday life some of the cognitive deficits that begin to be noticed with advanced years (such as difficulties with remembering) may be misattributed to more organic central causes when they are in fact the sequelae of mild changes in the peripheral sensory organs—which with the appropriate intervention (hearing aid etc), are easily modifiable and rectifiable.

Summary

Visual abilities decline with advancing age. This can be attributed to either 'normal' age-associated changes in the structure of the eye or to the increased prevalence of disease. Structural changes include changes in the lens capabilities, changes in pupil sizes, as well as loss of retinal cells. These result in diminished accommodative powers and visual acuity. Other aspects of vision undergoing age-associated changes include the extent of the visual field, light and colour sensitivity and resistance to glare. Self-report methods have provided information about the visual difficulties older people encounter in everday life. A large proportion of these problems can be accounted for by underlying disease, the four most serious threats being glaucoma, diabetic retinopathy, cataracts and macular degeneration. Successful prevention or subsequent treatment of these diseases is therefore most important.

Hearing impairment is one of the most prevalent disabling conditions in older persons and the absolute numbers of hearing-impaired will continue to increase over the next two or three decades. Even at the mildest level, hearing impairment can interfere with a person's ability to communicate, causing social and emotional isolation, precipitating loss of satisfaction in life and ultimately depression. It may also be responsible for aspects of impaired cognitive performance, such as poorer recall, which are potentially easily reversible, if hearing is assisted. Use of a hearing aid provides considerable benefit to those with a hearing loss. Yet uptake remains low. This can be accounted for by attitudes of the consumer towards deafness, the fact that the available hearing aids are still not able to restore perfect hearing, as well as shortfalls in the method of provision in the NHS. Available evidence suggests that introduction of a screening programme aimed at those of retirement age (55–65) would prove most beneficial. It would prevent the mildly deaf from having to live through years of increased disability before seeking assistance. It may also maximise the chance of the success of rehabilitation through use of hearing aids before people are too old, and unwilling or unable to adapt to them. Finally, it may offer the greatest chance of eventually reducing the numbers of frail elderly, whose severe deafness is perhaps a contributory factor towards their dependence, but for whom rehabilitation comes too late. However, before a screening programme can be implemented, benefits and costs need to be properly evaluated.

References

Bootle C. Hearing aids of the future. *Soundbarrier*, July; 1991: 23.

Bradley J, Grover B. The effects of independent trust status on the provision of hearing aids through the NHS. A preliminary survey of the first wave trusts. Unpublished RNID Internal Report, 1991.

Brooks DN. The use of hearing aids by the hearing impaired. In Stephens SDG (ed.), *Disorders of auditory function II*, pp. 255–264. Academic Press, London, 1976.

Brooks DN. Factors relating to the under-use of postaural hearing aids. *Br J Audiol*, 1985; 19: 211–217.

Burg A. Light sensitivity as related to age and sex. *Percept Motor Skills*, 1967; 24: 1279–1288.

Burg A. Lateral field as related to age and sex. *J Appl Psychol*, 1968; 52: 10–15.

Burg A, Hulbert S. Dynamic visual acuity as related to age, sex and static acuity. *J Appl Psychol*, 1961; 45: 111–116.

Campbell JB *et al.* Provision of hearing aids: does specialist assessment cause delay? (Letter). *Br Med J*, 1989; 299: 855–856.

Campbell JB, Nigam A. Hearing aid prescribing: is the specialist opinion necessary. *Clin Otolaryngol*, 1991; 16: 124–127.

Davis AC. Epidemiology of hearing disorders. In Kerr AG (series ed.), *Scott Brown's otolaryngology*, 5th edn: Volume 2, Stephens D (ed.), *Adult audiology*, pp. 90–126. Butterworth, London, 1987.

Davis AC. The prevalence of hearing impairment and reported hearing disability among adults in Great Britain. *Int J Epidemiol*, 1989; 18: 911–917.

Davis AC. Epidemiological profile of hearing impairments: the scale and nature of the problem with special reference to the elderly. *Acta Otolaryngol*, 1991; 476 (suppl.): 23–31.

Davis AC, Ostri B, Parving A. Longitudinal study of hearing. *Acta Otolaryngol*, 1991; 476 (suppl.): 12–22.

Davis AC *et al.* Hearing impairments in middle age: the acceptability, benefit and cost of detection (ABCD). *Br J Audiol*, 1992; 26: 1–14.

Davison PA, Irving A. Research Report No. 945, *Survey of visual acuity of drivers*. Transport and Road Research Laboratories, Crowthorne, Berkshire, 1980.

Fozard JL. Vision and hearing in aging. In Birren JE, Schaie KW (eds), *Handbook of the psychology of aging*, 3rd edn, pp. 150–170. Academic Press, San Diego, 1990.

Gittings NS, Fozard JL. Age-related changes in visual acuity. *Exp Gerontol*, 1986; 21: 423–433.

Haggard M, Gatehouse S, Davis A. The high prevalence of hearing disorders and its implications for services in the UK. *Br J Audiol*, 1981; 15: 241–251.

Herbst KG, Humphrey C. Hearing impairment and mental status in the elderly living at home. *Br Med J*, 1980; 281: 903–905.

Herbst KG, Humphrey C. Prevalence of hearing impairment in the elderly living at home. *J Roy Coll Gen Pract*, 1981; 31: 155–160.

Herbst KG *et al.* Implications of hearing impairment for elderly people in London and in Wales. *Acta Otolaryngol*, 1991; 476 (suppl.): 209–214.

Hickish GW. Hearing problems of elderly people. *Br Med J*, 1989; 299: 1415–1416.

Humphrey C, Herbst KG, Faurqi S. Some characteristics of the hearing-impaired elderly who do not present themselves for rehabilitation. *Br J Audiol*, 1981; 15: 25–30.

Johnson JA, Grover BC, Martin MC. RNID Scientific and Technical Department Report, *A survey of national health service hearing aid services*. RNID, London, 1984.

Kline DW, Schieber F. Vision and aging. In Birren JE, Schaie KW (eds), *Handbook of the psychology of aging* 2nd edn, pp. 296–331. Van Nostrand Reinhold, New York, 1985.

Kosnik W *et al.* Visual changes in daily life throughout adulthood. *J Gerontol*, 1988; 43: 63–70.

Leibowitz HM, Krueger DE, Maunder LR *et al.* The Framingham eye study monograph. *Surv Ophthalmol*, 1980; 24 (suppl.): 335–610.

MacAdam D, Siegerstetter J, Smith M. Deafness in adults—screening in general practice. *J Roy Coll Gen Pract*, 1981; 31: 161–164.

Mulrow CD *et al.* Quality of life changes and hearing impairment: a randomized trial. *Ann Int Med*, 1990; 113: 188–194.

OPCS. OPCS surveys of disability in Great Britain, Report No. 1, OPCS, Social Survey Division, *The prevalence of disability among adults*. HMSO, London, 1988.

Parving A, Philip B. Use and benefit of hearing aids in the tenth decade and beyond. *Audiology*, 1991; 30: 61–69.

Rabbitt PMA. Channel-capacity, intelligibility and immediate memory. *Q J Exp Psychol*, 1968; 20: 241–248.

Rabbitt P. Mild hearing loss can cause apparent memory failures which increase with age and reduce with IQ. *Acta Otolaryngol*, 1991; 476 (suppl.): 167–176.

RNID. *Hearing aids—the case for change*. RNID, London, 1988.

Sekuler R. Why does vision change with age? *Geriatrics*, 1991; 46: 96–100.

Stephens SDG *et al.* Hearing disability in people aged 50–65: effectiveness and acceptability of rehabilitative intervention. *Br Med J*, 1990; 300: 508–511.

Thomas A, Herbst KG. Social and psychological implications of acquired deafness for adults of employment age. *Br J Audiol*, 1980; 14: 76–85.

Verrillo RT, Verrillo V. Sensory and perceptual performance. In Charness N (ed.), *Aging and human performance*, pp. 1–46. John Wiley, Chichester, 1985.

Watson C, Crowther JA. Provision of hearing aids: does specialist assessment cause delay? *Br Med J*, 1989; 299: 437–439.

Weale R. Eyes and age. In Warnes AM (ed.), *Human ageing and later life: multidisciplinary perspectives*, pp. 38–46. Edward Arnold, London, 1989.

Wormald RPL, Wright LA, Courtney P, Beaumont B, Haines AP. Visual problems in the elderly population and implications for services. *Br Med J*, 1992; 304: 1226–1229.

Psychological function and ageing: an overview of research findings

17

Margaret Savory

Introduction

Psychological processes are important in determining a person's ability to interact with and respond to the environment. General wellbeing and the pursuit of an active independent lifestyle depend as much on the maintenance of cognitive function, as on the maintenance of physical health. Therefore, research has been directed towards investigating whether changes in cognitive functioning are an unavoidable consequence of ageing. Consequently, there is now a vast and burgeoning literature covering every aspect of psychological functioning and ageing. It would be impossible to summarise and review them all in depth here. Rather, this section attempts to provide an overview of the salient research findings and highlight where controversy still remains.

Some methodological issues

Before discussing the research findings, it is worth commenting on the shortfalls of the methods used to investigate cognitive functioning. In a damning critique, Schaie (1988) points to the erroneous conclusions that are often drawn from the data, sometimes resulting in discrimination against older persons. In short, he identifies several areas of ageism in psychological research.

An important consideration is that age-associated differences observed either in real-life or in the laboratory may not be due entirely to the effects of age alone (see Figure 17.1). Cohort effects refer to differences that may occur to people born of different generations (also referred to as cohorts). Thus, for example, relative differences between persons aged 20 and those aged 60 may not result from the age gap alone, but instead reflect that the younger group were born in 1970 and benefited from improved nutrition, education and environment, whereas the older group were born in 1930 and did not.

Period effects refer to the influence of time of testing. Differences observed in an individual tested at age 20 and again at age 60 may reflect the changes and improvements in the environment that occurred in the intervening period, rather than the ageing process.

Other sources of artefactual age differences lie in the various sampling errors that can be made.

Cross-sectional studies

Cross-sectional studies are by far the most frequently used research design in psychological research. Information about *age differences* is obtained and com-

Figure 17.1
Possible influences
on observed age
differences.

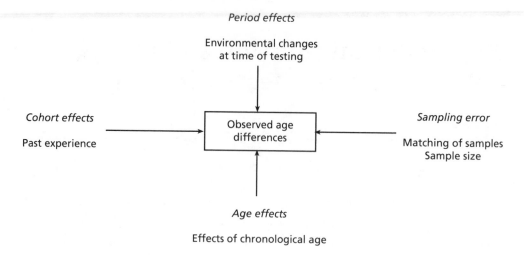

parisons are made between small samples of different ages at a single point in time. Age effects are, therefore, confounded by possible cohort effects. Although there are numerous discussions in the literature concerning the effects of cohort differences, little empirical attention is paid to them (Hoyer *et al.*, 1984).

In ageing research a fundamental assumption of a cross-sectional design is that the individuals in the study are equivalent in all aspects other than age. Many studies make this assumption, but fail to match sample subsets adequately in terms of educational status, health status, occupation and background (Botwinick, 1977). Both Rabbitt (1983) and Schaie (1988) argue the need for detailed descriptions of demographic variables in age-comparative studies. Otherwise, it is difficult to know whether any differences are true age effects, or reflect differences in other variables.

Comparison between studies is further hindered by lack of a precise definition of the term 'older person'. Schaie (1988) points out that 'any research findings that are based on a sample described as "over 60" would have as little validity as a study of child behavior that described its subjects as being "under 12" '. In their review Browning and Spilich (1981) found that those categorised as 'old subjects' ranged from as young as 35 years to as old as 100 years, 'middle-aged' subjects ranged in age from 40 to 70 years and 'young' subjects ranged from 18 to 49 years of age.

Finally, cross-sectional studies often report group means for a small number of subjects. Conclusions and generalisations, therefore, often ignore the differences between individuals. In addition to group means, distributions for the ages under comparison should be presented (Schaie, 1988).

Longitudinal studies

In a longitudinal design the scores for a sample of subjects born of the same cohort (or generation) are measured at different ages throughout their lifespan. This yields information about *age changes* that an individual may experience over time. However, as each measure is taken at a different point in time longitudinal studies may confound age effects with period effects. Moreover, they rely on subjects returning for assessment, which can lead to other biases. People generally improve their performance with repeated exposure to psychological tests (practice effects).

Or, alternatively, when subjects drop out of the study the results are biased in favour of the attributes possessed by those who remain. Often it is those of lower ability who drop out (Schaie and Strother, 1968).

UK data

Large UK data sets on psychological functioning and age are relatively scarce. Rabbitt and colleagues at the Age and Cognitive Performance Research Centre at the University of Manchester have established large-scale cross-sectional and longitudinal studies, involving hundreds rather than tens of subjects, and are some of the first to provide comprehensive demographic profiles of cognitive function in ageing, although the data are regionally biased. A recent survey of health and lifestyles conducted amongst a nationally representative sample (Huppert, 1987) introduced some psychological measures, although no repeat measures were taken. Most longitudinal data have been collected from studies conducted in the USA, notably the Duke Longitudinal Studies of Ageing (Busse and Maddox, 1985), or the Seattle Longitudinal Studies of Ageing (Schaie, 1990).

Intellectual abilities

Defining the pattern of intelligence in older persons has been one of the most investigated and controversial questions within the study of psychology and ageing. Most data have been derived from standardised psychometric tests which measure several different abilities (e.g. spatial orientation, verbal ability, numerical ability, problem-solving ability, vocabulary etc). The two most often used are the Wechsler Adult Intelligence Scale (WAIS) and Thurstone's Primary Mental Abilities Scale (PMA) (Doppelt and Wallace, 1955; Schaie, 1990).

Cross-sectional studies

Cross-sectional studies, comparing group mean performance on the above tests of samples of different ages, have generally pointed to a decline in intellectual function-ing after a peak attainment in young adulthood. However, such decline is not universal for all aspects of intelligence. A 'classic ageing pattern' has been demon-strated by many studies, and has been described as one of the best replicated results for a normal ageing population (Doppelt and Wallace, 1955; Botwinick, 1977). The cross-sectional pattern is one where tests of verbal ability (including vocabulary) remain stable over the lifespan, whereas non-verbal tasks show a steady decline. Horn (1982) formalised such a distinction by introducing the concepts of fluid and crystallised intelligence. The former refers to natural ability, relatively unbiased by education or cultural experience, and measured by tasks involving figural or semantic content. The latter, meanwhile, concerns abilities that depend on ex-perience, skills and knowledge gained through learning and is measured by tests of vocabulary, general information and arithmetic. Thus, fluid intelligence is thought to decrease over the lifespan whereas crystallised intelligence may remain stable or even increase over the years. In line with the above theory, Rabbitt (1991a) demonstrated an age-associated skewing of problem-solving (fluid), but not vocabulary (crystallised) scores in a large sample of British people aged 60 plus (Figures 17.2a, 17.2b).

Longitudinal studies

The description provided by cross-sectional data is by no means widely accepted. Results from longitudinal studies have done the most to challenge 'the myth of

Figure 17.2a
Distributions of scores on a vocabulary test (934 persons in sample).

Source: Rabbitt, 1991

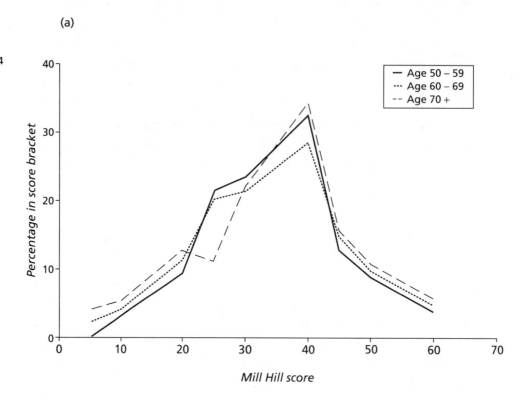

(a)

Figure 17.2b
Distributions of scores on a problem-solving test (934 persons in sample).

Source: Rabbitt, 1991

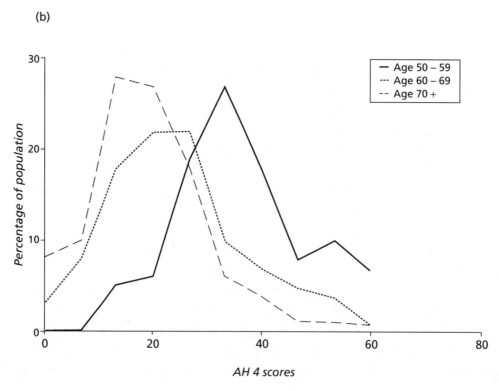

(b)

intellectual decline' (Schaie, 1974), revealing less decline than cross-sectional studies with any decrement starting later in life (Botwinick, 1977). Preservation of the specific intellectual functions shown in cross-sectional studies is also observed longitudinally.

Schaie and Strother (1968) compared cross-sectional and longitudinal data to provide estimated age gradients for the PMA tests. In most cases the longitudinal data presented a significantly more optimistic picture, with abilities on most tests holding up well over the years. A composite score of educational aptitude was also calculated, based on the subtest scores for verbal ability and reasoning ability (Figure 17.3). The longitudinal picture showed increments to age 55. Moreover, the estimated score at 75 was still above that at 25. The longitudinal design, however, may present an overly optimistic picture. The authors also advocated a cross-sequential strategy, consisting of repeated longitudinal and cross-sectional sampling from the same population, several birth cohorts being examined over the same chronological age period. The Seattle Longitudinal Study followed several hundreds of people over a 21-year period ranging in ages from 25 to 67 at the start of the study, measures being taken every seven years. Assessment of individual intellectual change from young adulthood onwards suggests that there are performance increments until the forties or fifties followed by stability until the mid-fifties or early sixties (Schaie, 1990). Significant decrements are not evident until the late sixties and are not apparent for everyone.

Individual patterns

Figure 17.4a demonstrates that, when assessed longitudinally, between 75% and 85% of subjects in the Seattle Longitudinal Study were able to maintain levels of performance on specific intellectual tests over a seven-year period at age 60 (Schaie, 1990). This proportion decreased with advancing age, though even at age 81 the proportion remained around 60%. Furthermore, few individuals showed a

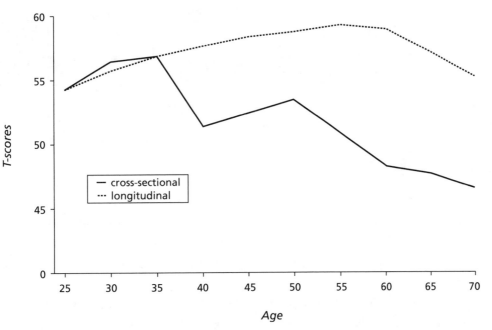

Figure 17.3
Comparison between longitudinal and cross-sectional scores on the Primary Mental Abilities Test showing Educational Aptitude.

Source: Schaie and Strother, 1965

Figure 17.4a
Proportion of individuals who maintain stable levels of performance over 7 years on 7 primary mental abilities.

Source: Schaie, 1990

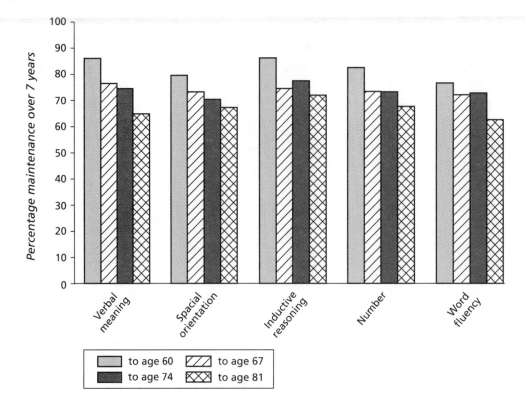

Figure 17.4b
Proportion of individuals who maintain stable levels of performance over 7 years on multiple abilities.

Source: Schaie, 1990

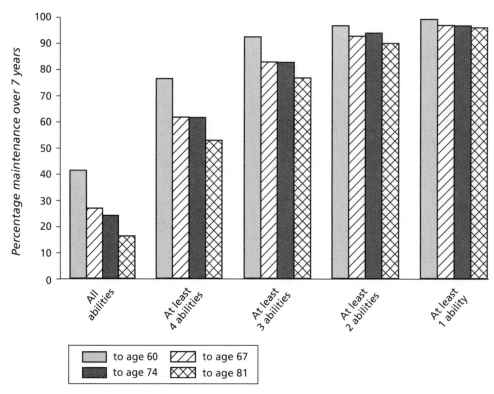

universal decline on all aspects of their mental abilities (Figure 17.4b). At age 60, approximately 90% of subjects maintained their level of performance over seven years on three or more abilities and at age 80 this remained true for 75% of the sample.

Thus, the evidence suggests that intellectual decline is not an inevitable consequence of ageing. For some individuals there may be a decrement of some (but not necessarily all) abilities in their sixties, but for others it will be even later, and in others not at all. Many people enter advanced old age still performing at the level of younger adults. Certainly in the period of the third age, most individuals will still be functioning at or near their peak levels.

Cohort effects

There is evidence to suggest that there have been generational shifts in the level of performance on standard intelligence tests. Flynn (1984, 1987) reported a trend towards increased IQ scores in 14 nations including the UK. Lynn and Hampson (1986) reviewed 11 British studies of children, aged between 11 and 14 years and reported that mean IQ scores have risen at the rate of 1.71 IQ points per decade since the 1930s. Schaie (1990) suggests that the IQ gains for later generations result from improved lifestyles and nutrition and the reduction of childhood diseases.

Such cohort effects may lead to false and overly pessimistic conclusions being drawn concerning intellectual abilities in later life. If, as is the case with IQ tests, later-born cohorts perform better than earlier-born cohorts at the same age, then this would have the effect of artefactually increasing age differences in a cross-sectional study comparing younger and older individuals.

Memory

Memory is generally perceived to decline with increased age. It is, however, a highly complex process and, as with measures of intellectual abilities, age-associated decrements vary according to the memory test implemented, the putative memory process in use and the individual concerned. Therefore, it is difficult to establish exactly which aspects of memory are affected by the ageing process. Certainly, any definitive statement about memory decline and 'normal' ageing would be an over-simplification.

Current memory research

Most studies of memory and ageing have been conducted within a framework that views memory as a multi-component system. Within this conceptualisation, research has attempted to describe age effects in terms of differential effects on the various modules of the memory system. There is a well-known theoretical distinction between immediate (or short-term) and secondary (or long-term) memory, which is usually used to describe the acquisition and retention of new information (Figure 17.5). Short-term or immediate memory is considered to be a limited capacity store, a temporary repository of information before it passes on to the unlimited, permanent long-term memory (Parkin, 1987).

Using such a structural distinction, several studies have found little or no age-associated loss in short-term memory (Craik, 1977). For example, tests which measure digit span, the number of randomly arranged digits that a person can repeat back in the correct order, and used as an indicator of short-term capacity, show only slight changes (if at all) with age. Larger age differences have been found with memory tasks that are thought to involve the acquisition and retrieval of new

Figure 17.5
Multistore model of
memory.

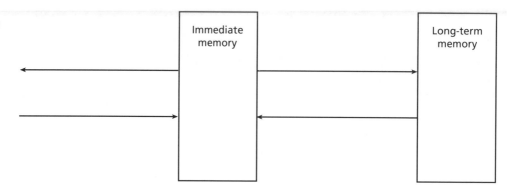

information from long-term memory, as exemplified by the free recall of word lists. However, this distinction is perhaps too simplistic, as age decrements are not consistently found for all stores and systems, depending on the task used (Craik, 1990). One possibility is that ageing may affect the ability to manipulate active processing, but may have a lesser effect on passive (storage) aspects of memory (Hultsch and Dixon, 1990). Thus, tasks which require passive recall of information (such as digit span) may show little effects of ageing, whereas others, which require a greater degree of manipulation, begin to show age effects. In a study comparing older with younger adults, no difference was apparent on a digit span task, but a significant age-associated decrement was observed for a task in which subjects were given short lists of words and then asked to say them back in the correct alphabetical order. Perhaps older adults are less able to execute and organise operations and are more dependent on the environment for support. Thus, older people encounter greatest difficulty when there is self-initiated activity in the task (as in the experiment above where subjects were required to recall in alphabetical order) (Craik, 1990). Such results have provided support for the concept of a working memory (rather than just a passive immediate memory). Again, this is conceptualised as a limited capacity system for the temporary storage of information, but also involving a central executive capable of attention, selection and manipulation. Tasks using working memory demand simultaneous storage of recently presented material as well as processing of additional information and it is possibly here that older persons are most disadvantaged.

Large-scale studies of memory functioning

Although most data on memory functioning have been derived from cross-sectional studies involving small numbers of subjects, there are a few large-scale studies where greater numbers of older persons are screened. The Health and Lifestyle Survey, gathering data from a nationally representative sample of *circa* 15,000 persons, found a strong association between memory and age using a free recall task—a task which involves retrieval from long-term memory (Huppert, 1987). Respondents were initially unaware that they were participating in a memory test. A list of foods was read out to them, on the pretext of examining knowledge of dietary fibre content. A few minutes later, they were asked to recall the words. Mean scores decreased with age, although there was overlap between the age groups. Men showed a greater decline than women (Figures 17.6a, 17.6b).

(a)

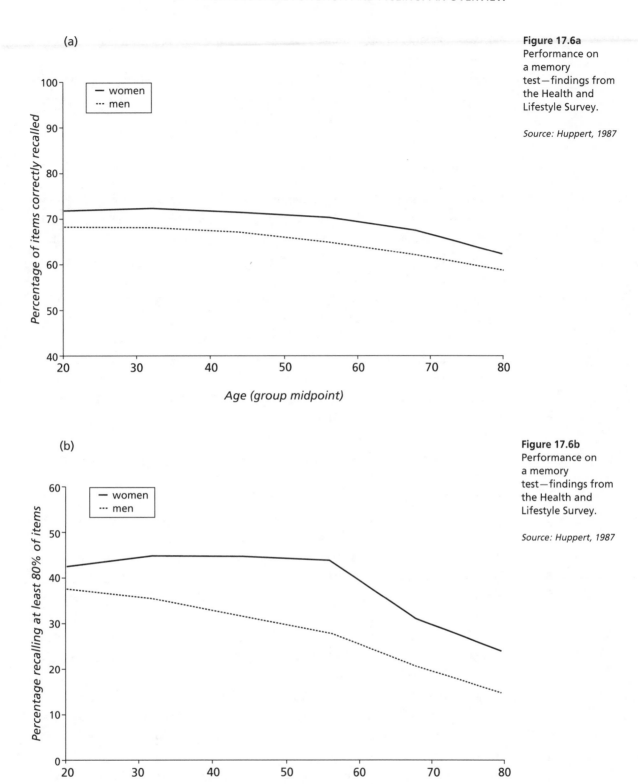

Figure 17.6a
Performance on
a memory
test—findings from
the Health and
Lifestyle Survey.

Source: Huppert, 1987

(b)

Figure 17.6b
Performance on
a memory
test—findings from
the Health and
Lifestyle Survey.

Source: Huppert, 1987

Rabbitt (1992) also provides data from a large UK sample. In studies following some 2,100 residents of Newcastle upon Tyne, aged 50+, it was found that with increasing age greater numbers were in the lower score categories for various memory tests. However, although there was an increased likelihood of lower scores, substantial numbers of older persons still retained their memory ability. Furthermore, in this large sample intellectual ability appeared to be a stronger predictor of memory performance than chronological age *per se*. When IQ score was taken into account, correlations between age and memory were greatly reduced. This does not mean that memory efficiency does not change with age, but instead that most changes can be identified from IQ tests (Rabbitt, 1992).

Reaction speed

There is considerable experimental evidence to show that reaction speed becomes slower with advanced age. Thus, a group of older adults will take longer, on average, to respond to stimuli than a group of younger adults. Again, changes suggested by cross-sectional studies tend to be larger than those from longitudinal studies (Schaie and Strother, 1968; Busse and Maddox, 1985).

Reaction times can be divided into a 'decision component', the time taken to process the information and decide what response to take, and a 'motor' component, the time taken to execute the appropriate response. These are also referred to as central and peripheral processes respectively. Some researchers argue for a slowing in the central processes, others peripheral. It is likely that both are affected with increased age, though it is thought that the central processes are of the greater magnitude (Krauss, 1987; Salthouse, 1985; Cerella, 1985).

Slowing of reactions has been demonstrated on a variety of tasks; from those that involve straightforward response to a presented stimulus, i.e. simple reaction time (Pierson and Montoye, 1958; Wilkinson and Allison, 1989), to those requiring more complex decisions. These include choice reaction time tasks, where different responses have to be made according to the stimulus presented (Waugh *et al.*, 1973), as well as scanning tasks, where targets have to be picked out of an array of non-targets, or mentally rotated before a response is made (Salthouse and Somberg, 1982b; Gaylord and Marsh, 1975).

Age-associated differences in reaction time increase with the complexity of the decisions that are to be made in completing the task. Hence, performance on a choice reaction time task will show greater absolute age differences than performance on a simple reaction time task. It is suggested there is a simple linear relationship between age and reaction time, with response speed of an older person (say aged 70) being approximately one and a half to twice as long as a younger person (age 20–30), irrespective of the task (Cerella, 1985; Salthouse, 1985). Nonetheless, in most cases the absolute difference between young and old in reaction time studies is generally under one second (Schaie, 1988).

As with other aspects of cognitive functioning, reliance on group means hides the large variation that occurs for individuals. Wilkinson and Allison (1989) analysed the performance of 5,325 subjects aged up to 70 years who participated in a simple reaction time task at a science exhibition. Although average reaction times increased significantly with age, fastest reaction time was less affected. Reaction time varied hugely within each age group and it was apparent that at each age group there were people who were faster than others in lower age groups. The authors concluded that 'the point at which people are on the distribution of their age group will exercise far more influence on their speed of simple reaction than will their age *per se*'.

The Health and Lifestyle Survey (Huppert, 1987) took measures of simple and choice reaction time and found similar results. Firstly, there was a decline with age in terms of mean reaction time, although for simple reaction time the response slowing was minimal until around age 50. Choice reaction time revealed greater age differences (Figure 17.7). In all cases the variability between the older individuals was greater than for the younger individuals.

So, there may be slowing of reaction speed with age, but is this important in the successful completion of everyday tasks? Schaie (1988) suggests not: 'I recently observed samples of these [truck scale enforcement] officers to determine whether the slowing of reaction time that would be expected from the sixth to the seventh decade of life would have a disabling impact on their occupational pursuits. In the case of the truck scale officers it became clear that speed of response was irrelevant to the ability to read the quite imprecise mechanical scales and that the magnitude of age change was trivial when compared to the time available to complete the necessary tasks. Similarly, in the job performance of game wardens it was virtually impossible to detect activities where increases in reaction time in fractions of seconds were at all relevant.'

Attention

Attention is defined as the limited capacity available to support cognitive processes and can be divided into selective attention, divided attention and sustained attention (or vigilance), although they are not necessarily independent (Plude and Hoyer, 1985; McDowd and Birren, 1990). Research, predominantly of cross-sectional design, has been directed towards ascertaining whether these resources are further reduced through the ageing process.

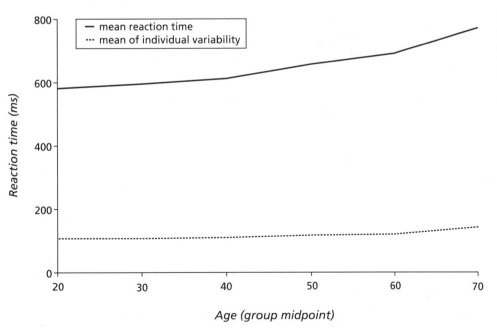

Figure 17.7
Choice reaction time and age—findings from the Health and Lifestyle Survey.

Source: Huppert, 1987

Selective attention

This is the selective allocation of attentional capacity and is considered a most basic function. For successful and efficient goal-directed behaviour, there must exist mechanisms to filter out the irrelevant and focus on the relevant information out of all that is available (McDowd and Birren, 1990). Rabbitt (1965) first suggested that there may be an age-associated decline in the ability to ignore irrelevant information. In this initial experiment, young and old subjects (aged 17–24 and 65–74 respectively, 11 persons in each group), were required to sort cards according to the presence or absence of certain target letters printed on the cards. Target letters were often printed alongside other irrelevant letters. In addition to being slower overall, older subjects were slowed disproportionately more when there were greater numbers of irrelevant stimuli on the cards (Figure 17.8).

Several studies have confirmed the above finding, but have introduced some qualifications. For example, difficulties may only be apparent when a search task is particularly effortful. Furthermore, the difficulties may lie in discrimination between relevant and irrelevant, rather than in ability to ignore the irrelevant (McDowd and Birren, 1990).

Divided attention

The ability to divide attentional resources is necessary when individuals are required to perform two tasks concurrently, but with equal success. Several studies have shown that older adults perform less well than younger adults under these conditions. Thus, it has generally been concluded that 'older subjects are more penalized when they must divide their attention' (Craik, 1977).

However, there are some caveats to this general conclusion. Much of the evidence was initially gathered using a single experimental paradigm—dichotic listening. This is one in which two different auditory messages are played simultaneously, one

Figure 17.8
Selective attention of younger and older adults.

Source: Rabbitt, 1965

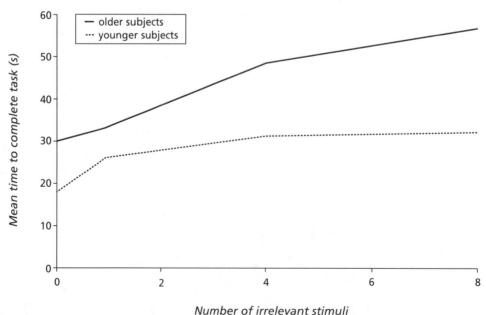

to each ear, and the subject is required to reproduce both messages as accurately as possible. Also, few divided attention experiments report on initial performance on the single task, where attention is undivided. Thus, age-associated differences could reflect difficulties with the task itself rather than difficulties in dividing attention (Somberg and Salthouse, 1982). Task complexity may also be an important influence. Somberg and Salthouse (1982) found no age differences for divided attention on a very simple visual search task, but McDowd and Craik (1988) and Salthouse *et al.* (1984) did, when examining a number of different tasks. Older subjects were at a greater disadvantage as the task complexity was increased.

Sustained attention

To maintain performance on a task over an extended period of time requires sustained attention, or vigilance. Tasks examining this aspect of attention usually last from between 30 and 60 minutes and require the subject to monitor a display and respond when an infrequent target is presented. Performance is measured in terms of reaction time to detect the target, detection accuracy and the false alarm rate. For all persons under such conditions there is a vigilance decrement: performance deteriorates over the course of task, with decreased likelihood of observing the target, but with increased response times (Davies and Parasuraman, 1982; Giambra, 1987). Evidence concerning the ability to sustain attention with increased age is somewhat mixed, appearing to depend on the type of task under study and the aspect of performance measured. Reviewing the results of 11 studies, Davies and Parasuraman (1982) reported that only half found a significant age effect on any measure of vigilance performance, showing the older groups to be disadvantaged. Poorer performance appeared to commence in those groups aged 60 or over, with older individuals showing a lower detection rate, and in some studies a higher false alarm rate.

There appears to be no evidence for the vigilance decrement experienced by older persons to be any greater than that of younger adults. However, absolute levels of performance in terms of accuracy or speed of target detection, may be lower for older persons. Davies and Parasuraman (1982) suggest that older people show less confidence and adopt more rigorous response criteria than younger people.

Slowing of cognitive processing

What can account for the many observed age-associated differences in cognitive functioning, such as impaired memory and IQ performance or increased time to react to stimuli? Salthouse (1985) proposed that an overall decrease in the speed at which the brain processes information may be responsible. Taking an example from memory, 'active' memory tasks, such as those involving working memory, might be expected to require greater levels of information processing. Thus, lower rates of information processing amongst older persons would lead to greater discrepancies between young and old on active tasks than between young and old on passive memory tasks, which is supported by empirical observation. Evidence for slowed information processing rates is also provided by the documented slowing of reaction speed, which is thought to have a 'central' as well as 'peripheral' component.

The underlying cause of the slowing is not yet known: whether it is due to one or several factors, and whether the origins are physiological or psychological. Speculations have included lowered arousal levels, or slowed neural conduction at the physiological level and decreased signal-to-noise ratio, lack of practice, or biases in response criteria towards accuracy at a psychological level. There is little empirical evidence for any of these.

Although there is considerable evidence for a theory of cognitive ageing incorporating the notion that the speed of mental operations slows with increased age, this may not be the dominant factor for all types of individual differences. As Salthouse (1985) comments 'in a sample homogeneous with respect to age, it is likely that other factors are probably responsible for more of the variance in cognitive performance than the rate of processing. However, as that rate slows with age, it may emerge as the principal factor responsible for differences in performance associated with increasing age'.

Health status and cognitive ability

Two alternative models of cognitive ageing have been proposed, 'continuous decline' and 'terminal drop' (Figure 17.9). The continuous decline model is demonstated by the numerous cross-sectional studies, where mean scores indicate a slow and gradual decline in cognitive performance from a peak in middle age. Alternatively, the terminal drop model suggests that any decline is associated with some underlying pathology, rather than as a result of age alone. Thus, a more optimistic picture is presented with the adult plateau continuing until later in life, eventually ending in decline, but as a result of health status rather than age (Rabbitt, 1983, 1991b, 1992).

Evidence for terminal drop has been provided by the several longitudinal studies which show that significant proportions of individuals are able to maintain cognitive abilities until later life, provided that physical health is maintained (Schaie, 1990;

Figure 17.9
Hypothetical functions for continuous decline and terminal drop models.

Source: Rabbitt, 1991b

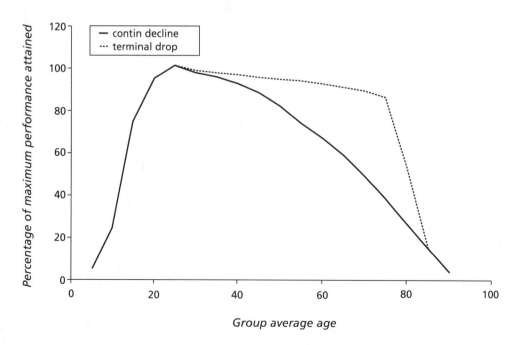

Busse and Maddox, 1985; Field *et al.*, 1988). Jarvik (1983) found that 'critical loss' in IQ scores predicted death for a significant proportion of ageing twins. In the Duke Longitudinal Study of ageing, a comparison was made between the test scores of those who completed all sessions and those who dropped out of the study because of death or illness. Those who remained, 'survivors', showed little or no intellectual decline over the 20-year period, until perhaps extreme old age, whereas those who subsequently dropped out of the study had begun to exhibit a decline before ceasing to participate (Siegler and Botwinick, 1979).

Which model is closer to the truth is still open to debate. Figure 17.10 demonstrates how cross-sectional data cannot distinguish between these two alternatives. Assuming individuals age at different rates, some individuals would reach their 'terminal drop' at earlier ages than others. As a consequence, groups of older individuals would include greater proportions of persons undergoing terminal drops, and a smaller proportion of individuals continuing to maintain their abilities. Thus, averages of a group (as are usually presented with cross-sectional data) would still yield an overall decline. Alternatively, the cross-sectional data may reflect the average of individuals' cognitive declines all commencing at different ages (Rabbitt, 1991b).

The only solution is to conduct longitudinal studies, which can compare individuals over time. However, these are time consuming (obviously) and difficult to run, and are not without methodological shortfalls (Rabbitt, 1983).

Compensatory effects of experience and skill

Experience and expertise appear to go a considerable way in counteracting potential adverse effects of age on performance in everyday activities. Salthouse (1990)

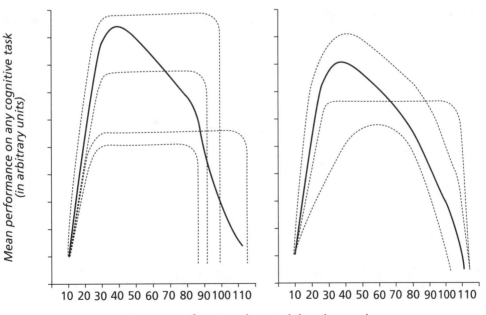

Figure 17.10
Hypothetical models for changes in group means.

Source: Rabbitt, 1991b

Mean performance on any cognitive task (in arbitrary units)

Mean age of separately tested decade-samples

— mean of all individual age-performance trajectories
--- possible individual age-performance
    trajectories contributing to group means

described this in terms of a difference between cognitive competence and cognitive ability. Cognitive ability refers to the individual's intellectual level, as measured by conventional tests of cognitive functioning, such as memory, intelligence etc. Cognitive competence, in contrast, is interpreted as the way in which a person can use abilities to adapt to the particular situation. Distinguishing between these two aspects provides a possible reason why results of many studies may not generalise out of the psychologist's laboratory. Laboratory tests investigate ability, whereas real-life tasks require competence.

In a study of typists (age range 19–72 years), Salthouse (1984) found that there was no correlation with age for typing skill. Although mean reaction time on standard laboratory psychomotor tests increased significantly with age, the speed of copy typing remained constant across age groups (Figure 17.11). Furthermore, maintained speed was not at the expense of accuracy, as older typists also made fewer errors. The older typists seemed to have larger eye–hand spans than did younger typists and could therefore preview more characters, possibly as a compensatory mechanism for their loss of psychomotor speed.

Further support for the compensatory effect of experience is provided by studies of chess players (Charness, 1981). Chess is regarded as a good model for problem solving in ageing as cohort differences are minimal: chess has been played consistently and the rules have not changed for hundreds of years. In a group of expert chess players aged 16–64 years, where age and skill were uncorrelated, it was found that critical aspects of performance were related to skill level and not to age. Despite a decline in efficiency on a separate chess-related memory task, older players were still able to solve chess problems as well as the younger players.

However, evidence has also been provided that expertise remains 'domain' specific. That is, skill or ability in one area does not necessarily lead to improved performance in other related areas. Rabbitt (1991a,b) reports a study by Winder (unpublished) in which 96 'expert' cross-word puzzle solvers (ages ranging from 45

Figure 17.11
Median interkey interval in milliseconds for normal typing and choice reaction time tasks. Each point represents a single typist; solid lines indicate the regression equations linking reaction time to age.

Source: Salthouse, 1984

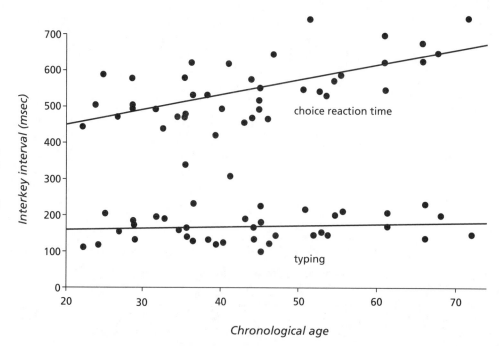

to 85 years) were matched to 'novice' controls of the same age, sex, intelligence level and occupational status. Performance at a cryptic cross-word puzzle was not affected by age for the experts, but novices did show an age-associated decline. Similarly, intelligence test scores did not predict cross-word scores for 'experts', but did so for the novices. However, intelligence scores decreased with age (obviously in a similar manner for both experts and novices as they had been matched for intelligence status). This suggests that given expertise in an area (in this case cross-word puzzle solving), level of ability remains stable with increasing age. However, such expertise is domain specific—there is no evidence that such expertise maintains other abilities, such as maintaining or enhancing scores in intelligence.

Capacity for learning and improvement

Effects of practice

Many experiments may not reflect the true capabilities of the older person as they involve minimal amounts of practice. Yet daily life requires skills that are generally well practised and refined. A 'disuse' hypothesis (e.g. Hultsch, 1974), proposes that many of the observed age differences on psychological tasks may result from lack of use of the appropriate cognitive skills by the older population and not a decline in cognitive capacity. Indeed, experimental reports consistently show that, given the opportunity to practise, older persons can considerably improve their performance in a variety of situations.

Salthouse and Somberg (1982a) examined the effects of extended practice (51 sessions over 2–3 months) for both eight young (ages 19–27 years) and eight older (ages 62–73 years) subjects on a series of single tasks, signal detection, memory scanning, and visual discrimination. In the initial sessions, older subjects performed significantly worse than their younger counterparts. Yet, over the period of extended practice, there was substantial improvement in mean performance on all tasks, for both age groups. Furthermore, for both the signal detection and the memory scanning tasks there was a greater improvement in absolute performance for the older rather than younger subjects. Improved levels of performance were also maintained over a period of one month after which subjects returned for a final session. However, in most cases extended practice did not fully remove the age differences: younger subjects still had a higher level of performance (Figure 17.12).

Several other studies have investigated the effects of practice on a variety of performance tasks for both young and old. These include psychomotor tasks (Anshel, 1978; Falduto and Baron, 1986; Wiegand and Ramella, 1983; Grant et al., 1978; Hoyer et al., 1978/79; Kerr and Teaffe, 1991), divided attention tasks (McDowd, 1986), memory tasks (LeBreck and Baron, 1987; Menich and Baron, 1990), problem solving (Charness and Campbell, 1988; Campbell and Charness, 1990) and visual perception (Ball and Sekuler, 1986). Measures have included those of speed (i.e. reaction time) and accuracy (i.e. percentage correct). Generally, the experimental results show a consistent pattern. On the one hand, younger and older persons are equally adept at acquiring and improving the task-related skills, which can remain for a considerable period after practice. But on the other, age differences are rarely

Figure 17.12
Choice reaction time and accuracy as a function of practice.

Source: Salthouse, 1985

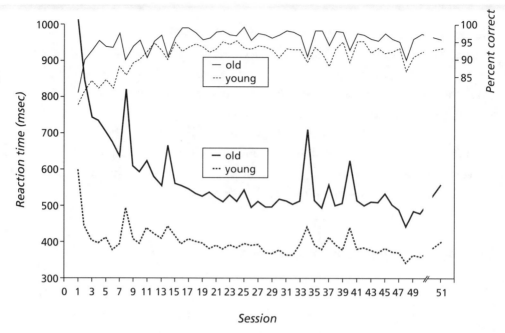

totally eliminated after extended practice. The young tend to retain their initial advantage. The latter point may be exaggerated in a cross-sectional design as there is an assumption that when the older subjects were young, they were capable of performing the tasks at the levels observed with the younger subjects.

There are just a few studies which show that older persons can attain the level of performance of younger individuals. In the most frequently quoted example, Murrell (1970) investigated choice and simple reaction time in three subjects, aged 17, 18 and 57 years. Although the older subject took longer to improve initially, performance differences were reduced and eliminated after some 12,000 trials, with the older subject reacting as quickly as the younger subjects. This study can only be interpreted with extreme caution because of the paucity of subjects. Nonetheless, it again reiterates how group means, often presented in cross-sectional studies, can conceal the range of abilities across individuals. Menich and Baron (1990) compared both group and individual performance levels. Twelve younger (19–26 years) and 12 older (64–74 years) subjects underwent 40–45 training sessions in a recognition memory task: some initial baseline sessions, followed by sessions where time limits were imposed. Group mean reaction times at the start and end of the study showed the consistent pattern of improvement for all subjects, but that the older subjects remained slower from start to finish. Analyses of individuals revealed that initially many of the older sample were within the range of performances of the younger ones and a few had extreme scores, sufficient to alter the older group's mean score. A major effect of practice, therefore, was to bring the lower scoring older members within the range of the younger subjects.

The effects of practice (or familiarity) have also been observed in longitudinal studies. Rabbitt (1991b) has demonstrated that even a single experience of a psychological test battery can improve subsequent performance on the test battery some three years later. Such improvements can completely counteract any age-associated differences.

Transferability

When examining the effects of practice, it is important to ask whether the positive effects of practice are limited to the tasks for which there is repeated exposure, or whether practice leads to a more general increase in performance level. Studies that have investigated this have led to unclear results. Hoyer *et al.* (1978/79) found that practice and improved performance on a reaction time task did not lead to improved performance on aspects of an intelligence task that involved speed of response. Menich and Baron (1990) on the other hand, found that in a recognition memory task, practice (and improved performance) using visual stimuli led to improvement on a similar version of the task with auditory stimuli.

Improving memory and intellectual functioning

If aspects of cognitive performance have begun to deteriorate the ability to learn means that there may still remain scope for the decline to be halted or reversed through skills training. Hill *et al.* (1990) compared the effect of memory skills training and incentives (against no training) on a subsequent free recall of a serial word list. Memory training consisted of a training manual and a subsequent class providing strategies to improve recall. Compared with a control group (who had received training in map-reading skills) or incentive group (received lottery tickets according to performance), those who had received memory skills training perfomed best (i.e. they recalled more in less time). Although incentives were superior to no training, there were no additional benefits to be gained by combining memory training with the incentives.

Other studies have also confirmed the benefits of cognitive skills training. Schaie and Willis (1986) recruited healthy, community-dwelling 64–95-year-olds from a longitudinal study where intellectual performance had been measured over an earlier 14-year period (1970–1984). The early measures represented a baseline, against which subsequent measures could be compared, as initially no subject had reached the age when cognitive decline begins to occur. Subjects were then classified into those who experienced a significant post-baseline decline in intellectual functioning and those who had not, according to certain IQ tests. Training procedures involved practising the IQ tests and developing strategies for their completion in five one-hour individual sessions. Training improved the performance of a substantial portion of 'decliners'. Indeed, some 40% of 'decliners' performed at (or better than) their earlier 1970 baseline level and approximately 60% were within one standard error of their 1970 measurement. Moreover, training also enhanced the performance of nearly 40% of those whose scores had remained stable over the 14-year period. The authors interpret the remediation of observed cognitive decline in large proportions of their subjects in terms of the disuse hypothesis. Training enabled skills and behaviours, already present, but inactive through disuse, to become reactivated (Schaie and Willis, 1986).

Learning new skills

For the older person the capacity to learn and improve should not be restricted to merely resurrecting or improving existing skills or capabilities. A programme of training conducted in Australia in the 1960s and 1970s amply demonstrated that 'old dogs can learn new tricks' (Naylor and Harwood, 1975). Eighty people, aged from 63 to 91 years volunteered for a course in learning to read German. None had previous knowledge of the language. Students were required to spend two hours per week in a laboratory teaching session, plus spend at least one hour daily on home study. After six months the students took an independently assessed exam. At the most conservative measure of success, 50% of the 'novices' reached or exceeded the standard expected of fourth year secondary school children.

It is evident, therefore, that capacity to learn new skills and improve on existing ones remains with people throughout their life and that age alone should not prevent people from undertaking new intellectual challenges.

Summary and conclusions

At the most pessimistic level, a review of the psychological literature presents considerable laboratory evidence for age-associated cognitive decline in most aspects of psychological functioning, including memory, intelligence and sensory abilities. This has been interpreted in terms of a general slowing in the speed with which information is processed in the brain. However, much of the evidence is based upon results from cross-sectional studies which may confound age with cohort effects. Studies already suggest that later-born generations are scoring more highly on IQ tests, which would artificially inflate differences between young and old. Additionally, cross-sectional studies often fail to match adequately, in terms of demographic backgrounds, the comparison groups of young and old subjects. By concentrating on differences between age groups it is likely that an overly negative picture of cognitive ability in later life has been presented.

In contrast, evidence from longitudinal studies suggests that cognitive decline is neither global nor inevitable. Many individuals can maintain function until late in life, and certainly beyond the third age. Results from longitudinal studies also indicate that a person's health status, rather than age, may be the greater predictor of cognitive functioning. People who maintain good physical health seem to continue to function successfully, whereas those who begin to suffer from disease may exhibit decline in cognitive functioning. However, as the prevalence of physical illness increases in an ageing population, it is difficult to distinguish between age or health effects.

There are other shortfalls in the laboratory data, which make predictions and generalisations about everyday life rather hazardous. For example, the effects of experience and expertise are frequently ignored. Laboratory tasks often measure straightforward ability rather than competence in dealing with everyday situations. In tasks undertaken in everyday life, any age-associated decrements may be compensated for by skill and experience, with the result that a high level of performance can be achieved and maintained across the lifespan.

Additionally, it can be argued that initial performance in laboratory cognitive tasks is not a totally valid indicator of what can be achieved. Most older individuals can improve performance and operate at a completely satisfactory level, if exposed to appropriate and supportive conditions. In studies where older individuals are provided with the chance to practise, there is considerable amelioration on the task. Older individuals have also benefited from training programmes specifically geared towards improving memory or cognitive functions. It is clear that older persons possess considerable reserve, which can be used to learn new information and improve performance throughout later life. This is evidenced, for example, by the success in academic study in institutions such as the Open University. In 1986, some 4.3% of undergraduate students at the Open University were aged 60 or over and achieved similar pass rates to younger undergraduates (Slater, 1988).

Finally, it is important to note that as age increases so does the variability between and within individuals. Thus, mere descriptions of 'average' performance grow less representative with the increasing age of the group under study. Many studies, unfortunately, still ignore individual differences and concentrate on group means. Where distributions are reported, there is often considerable overlap between the performance of young and older subjects. Indeed, differences within an age group can be as great as variation between age groups.

In the face of such overlap it is virtually impossible to make predictive statements as to if and when a particular task may become difficult or impossible. Some individuals will continue to perform better than others who are chronologically younger. Furthermore, successive generations can differ considerably from one another. Thus, predictions and expectations based upon data from the current elderly may not hold true for the elderly of twenty-five years hence.

Perhaps, therefore, the most important conclusion to be drawn is that functional capabilities, rather than age since birth, may be more meaningful in determining an individual's status (McFarland, 1973, see Figure 17.13). Given the evidence presented from psychological studies, it now seems certain that chronological age should not be the sole criterion by which a person is assessed.

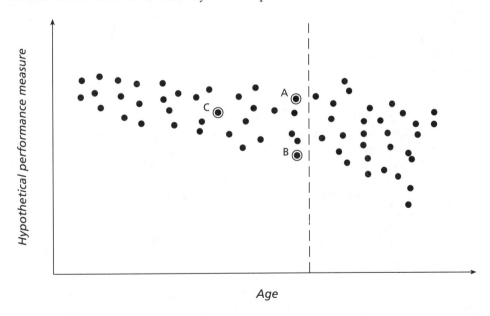

Figure 17.13
An illustration of the concept of functional age. Each point represents an individual's hypothetical score on a particular performance measure. A and B have the same chronological age, but different functional ages. C is chronologically younger than A but is functionally less able.

Source: Mcfarland, 1973

References

Anshel MH. Effect of aging on acquisition and short-term retention of a motor skill. *Percept Motor Skills*, 1978; 47: 993–994.

Ball K, Sekuler R. Improving visual perception in older observers. *J Gerontol*, 1986; 41: 176–182.

Botwinick J. Intellectual abilities. In Birren JE, Schaie KW (eds), *Handbook of the psychology of aging*, pp. 580–605. Van Nostrand Reinhold, New York, 1977.

Browning GB, Spilich GJ. Some important methodological issues in the study of aging and cognition. *Exp Aging Res*, 1981; 7: 175–187.

Busse EW, Maddox GL. *The Duke longitudinal studies of normal aging 1955–1980, overview of history, design and findings.* Springer, New York, 1985.

Campbell JID, Charness N. Age-related declines in working memory skills: evidence from a complex calculation task. *Develop Psychol*, 1990; 26: 879–888.

Cerella J. Information processing rates in the elderly. *Psychol Bull*, 1985; 98: 67–83.

Charness N. Aging and skilled problem solving. *J Exp Psychol: General*, 1981; 110: 21–38.

Charness N, Campbell JID. Acquiring skill at mental calculation in adulthood: a task decomposition. *J Exp Psychol*, 1988; 117: 115–129.

Craik FIM. Age differences in human memory. In Birren JE, Schaie KW (eds), *Handbook of the psychology of aging*, pp. 384–420. Van Nostrand Reinhold, New York, 1977.

Craik FIM. Change in memory with normal aging: a functional view. *Adv Neurol*, 1990; 51: 201–205.

Davies DR, Parasuraman R. *The psychology of vigilance.* Academic Press, London, 1982.

Doppelt JE, Wallace WL. Standardization of the Wechsler Adult Intelligence Scale for older persons. *J Abnormal Soc Psychol*, 1955; 51: 313–332.

Falduto LL, Baron A. Age related effects of practice and task complexity on card sorting. *J Gerontol*, 1986; 41: 659–661.

Field D *et al.* Continuity in intellectual functioning: the role of self-reported health. *Psychol Aging*, 1988; 3: 385–392.

Flynn JR. The mean IQ of Americans: massive gains 1932–1978. *Psychol Bull*, 1984; 95: 29–51.

Flynn JR. Massive IQ gains in 14 nations: what IQ tests really measure. *Psychol Bull*, 1987; 101: 171–191.

Gaylord SA, Marsh GR. Age differences in the speed of a spatial cognitive process. *J Gerontol*, 1975; 30: 674–678.

Giambra L. Vigilance. In Maddox GL *et al.* (eds), *The encyclopedia of aging*, p. 683. Springer, New York, 1987.

Grant EA, Storandt M, Botwinick J. Incentive and practice in the psychomotor performance of the elderly. *J Gerontol*, 1978; 33: 413–415.

Hill RD, Storandt M, Simeone C. The effects of memory skills training and incentives on free recall in older learners. *J Gerontol Psychol Sci*, 1990; 45: 227–232.

Horn JL. The theory of fluid and crystallized intelligence in relation to concepts of cognitive psychology and aging in adulthood. In Craik FIM, Trehub S (eds), *Aging and cognitive processes*, pp. 237–278. Plenum Press, New York, 1982.

Hoyer FW *et al.* Training response speed in young and elderly women. *Int J Aging Human Develop*, 1978/79; 9: 247–253.

Hoyer WJ *et al.* Research practices in the psychology of aging: a survey of research published in the *Journal of Gerontology*, 1975–1982. *J Geront*, 1984; 39: 44–48.

Hultsch DF. Learning to learn in adulthood. *J Gerontol*, 1974; 29: 302–308.

Hultsch DF, Dixon RA. Learning and memory in aging. In Birren JE, Schaie KW (eds), *Handbook of the psychology of aging*, 3rd edn, pp. 258–274. Academic Press, San Diego, 1990.

Huppert FA. Cognitive function. In Cox B *et al.* (eds), *The health and lifestyle survey*, pp. 43–50. Health Promotion Research Trust, London, 1987.

Jarvik LF. Age is in—is the wit out? In Samuel D *et al.* (eds) *Aging of the brain*, pp. 1–8. Raven Press, New York, 1983.

Kerr R, Teaffe MS. Aging and the response to changes in task difficulty. *Can J Aging*, 1991; 10: 18–28.

Krauss IK. Reaction time. In Maddox GL (ed.), *The encyclopedia of aging*, pp. 557–558. Spinger, New York, 1987.

LeBreck DB, Baron A. Age and practice effects in continuous recognition memory. *J Gerontol*, 1987; 42: 89–91.

Lynn R, Hampson S. The rise of national intelligence: evidence from Britain, Japan and the USA. *Personal Individ Diff*, 1986; 7: 23–32.

McDowd JM. The effects of age and extended practice on divided attention performance. *J Gerontol*, 1986; 41: 764–769.

McDowd JM, Birren JE. Aging and attentional processes. In Birren JE, Schaie KW (eds), *Handbook of the psychology of aging*, 3rd edn, pp. 222–233. Academic Press, San Diego, 1990.

McDowd JM, Craik FIM. Effects of aging and task difficulty on divided attention performance. *J Exp Psychol: Human Percept Perform*, 1988; 14: 267–280.

McFarland R. The need for functional age measurements in industrial gerontology. *Indust Gerontol*, 1973; 19: 1–19.

Menich SR, Baron A. Age-related effects of reinforced practice on recognition memory: consistent versus varied stimulus response relations. *J Gerontol*, 1990; 45: 88–93.

Murrell FH. The effect of extensive practice on age differences in reaction time. *J Gerontol*, 1970; 25: 268–274.

Naylor G, Harwood E. Old dogs, new tricks—age and ability. *Psychol Today*, 1975; 1: 29–33.

Olsho LW et al. Aging and the auditory system. In Birren JE, Schaie KW (eds), *Handbook of the psychology of aging*, 2nd edn, pp. 332–377. Van Nostrand Reinhold, New York, 1985.

Parkin A. *Memory and amnesia.* Basil Blackwell, Oxford, 1987.

Pierson WR, Montoye HJ. Movement time, reaction time and age. *J Gerontol*, 1958; 13: 418–421.

Plude DJ, Hoyer WJ. Attention and performance: identifying and localising age differences. In Charness N (ed.), *Aging and human performance*, pp. 47–95. John Wiley & Sons, Chichester, 1985.

Rabbitt P. An age decrement in the ability to ignore irrelevant information. *J Gerontol*, 1965; 20: 233–238.

Rabbitt P. How can we tell whether human performance is related to chronological age? In Samuel D et al. (eds), *Aging of the brain*, pp. 9–18. Raven Press, New York, 1983.

Rabbitt P. Management of the working population. *Ergonomics*, 1991a; 34: 775–790.

Rabbitt P. Factors promoting accidents involving elderly pedestrians and drivers. In Grayson GB, Lester JF (eds), *Behavioural research in road safety: proceedings of a seminar held at Nottingham University*, pp. 167–183. Transport and Road Research Laboratory, Crowthorne, Berkshire, 1991b.

Rabbitt P. Memory. In Grimley Evans J, Williams TF (eds), *Oxford textbook of geriatric medicine*, pp. 463–479. Oxford University Press, Oxford, 1992.

Salthouse TA. Effects of age and skill in typing. *J Exp Psychol: General*, 1984; 113: 345–371.

Salthouse TA. *A theory of cognitive aging.* Elsevier, North Holland, Amsterdam, 1985.

Salthouse TA. Cognitive competence and expertise in aging. In Birren JE, Schaie KW (eds), *Handbook of the psychology of aging*, 3rd edn, pp. 310–319. Academic Press, San Diego, 1990.

Salthouse TA, Somberg BL. Skilled performance: effects of adult age and experience on elementary processes. *J Exp Psychol: General*, 1982a; 111: 176–204.

Salthouse TA, Somberg BL. Isolating the age deficit in speeded performance. *J Gerontol*, 1982b; 37: 59–63.

Salthouse TA et al. Division of attention: age differences on a visually presented memory task. *Memory Cognition*, 1984; 21: 613–620.

Schaie KW. Transitions in gerontology—from lab to life: intellectual functioning. *Am Psychol*, 1974; 29: 802–807.

Schaie KW. Ageism in psychological research. *Am Psychol*, 1988; 41: 179–183.

Schaie KW. Intellectual development in adulthood. In Birren JE, Schaie KW (eds), *Handbook of the psychology of aging*, 3rd edn, pp. 291–309. Academic Press, San Diego, CA, 1990.

Schaie KW, Strother CR. A cross-sequential study of age changes in cognitive behavior. *Psychol Bull*, 1968; 70: 671–680.

Schaie KW, Willis SL. Can decline in adult intellectual functioning be reversed? *Develop Psychol*, 1986; 22: 223–232.

Siegler IC, Botwinick J. A long-term longitudinal study of intellectual ability of older adults: the matter of selective subject attrition. *J Gerontol*, 1979; 34(2): 242–245.

Slater R. Memory in later life: an introduction to the basics of theory and practice. In Gearing B, Johnson M, Heller T (eds), *Mental health problems in old age*. John Wiley, Chichester, 1988.

Somberg BL, Salthouse TA. Divided attention abilities in young and old adults. *J Exp Psychol: Human Percept Perform*, 1982; 8: 651–663.

Waugh NC et al. Effects of age and stimulus repetition on two-choice reaction time. *J Gerontol*, 1973; 28: 466–470.

Wiegand RL, Ramella R. The effect of practice and temporal location of knowledge of results on the motor performance of older adults. *J Gerontol*, 1983; 38: 701–706.

Wilkinson RT, Allison S. Age and simple reaction time: decade differences for 5,323 subjects. *J Gerontol*, 1989; 4: 29–35.

Psychological function and ageing: practical aspects and implications

18

Margaret Savory

Introduction

The practical implications of any age-associated changes in psychological functioning are perhaps at their greatest for those individuals in the third age. They represent a considerable proportion of the workforce and still take an active role in community life.

This paper first investigates the abilities and competence of older workers in terms of their performance and their capacity for retraining. In particular the specific requirements to assist them in the training process are considered. Second, the abilities and difficulties of older drivers are also considered.

Work and employment

Work performance

The stereotype of the older worker who is less competent and less productive still persists. Yet, the empirical evidence to support a hypothesis that job performance declines with age is at best 'mixed'. In a review of 25 empirical studies conducted over the last 30 years, Rhodes (1983) concluded that any observed age–performance relationship depends on the performance measure used, the demands and nature of the job and the individual experience of those being measured, such as training, or length of service. Indeed, in the studies she examined, performance was shown to increase, decrease or remain the same with advancing years!

In their review Davies and Sparrow (1985) concluded that performance generally improved until the mid-forties, but then declined. However, in most cases the performance of the oldest groups was still superior to the youngest groups and the decreases in performance were relatively small in magnitude. This is exemplified by an early study by Clay (1956) who investigated age differences in productivity at two British printing works. Production records were obtained for three 13-week periods spread over three years. Productivity of workers declined in their fifties, but only by between 2% and 16% from their previous peak level, according to the type of job performed (Figure 18.1).

Other studies, however, have found either little difference or even improvements with increasing age. Giniger et al. (1983) examined the productivity of garment industry workers. Significant positive correlations between age and productivity were observed. This was true for jobs defined either as using 'speed' or 'skill', with older workers earning the greatest amount (and hence greatest productivity because of their piece rate of pay) (Figure 18.2). Experience and expertise were as important as age in predicting performance: when age was taken into account there remained significant positive correlations between productivity and length of service.

Figure 18.1
An example of the inverted-U relationship between age and performance.

Source: Clay (1956).

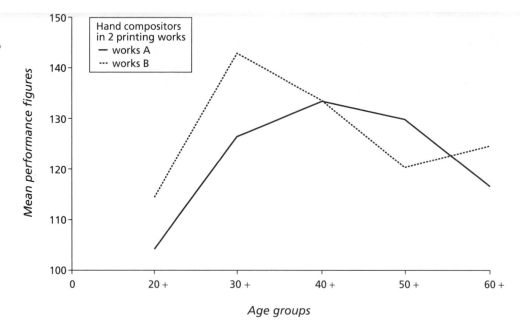

Figure 18.2
Productivity of garment workers.

Source: Giniger et al. (1983)

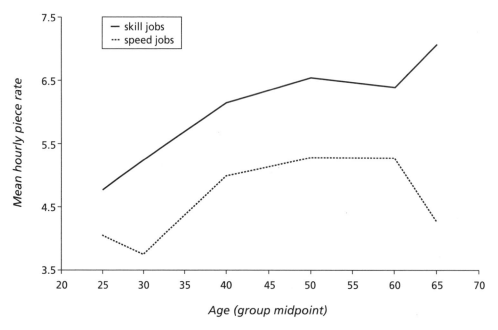

Many studies restrict themselves to reporting averages for a particular age group. This may hide the fact that many older workers continue to outperform younger individuals. This was illustrated in studies conducted by the Bureau of Labor Statistics (see Greenberg, 1961). Taking a relative index of 100 for the average performance of workers in the age range 35–44, it was found that over 30% of factory workers aged 55–64 scored higher than 100. For office workers, 44% of those aged 55–64 outperformed the average for the 35–44 age group. However, mean average scores for the factory workers declined with increasing age, although this was not large until the age of 65 (Table 18.1).

Many of the discrepancies in the data are accounted for by the methodological problems incurred in studies of performance in the occupational setting. Firstly,

Table 18.1

Distribution of indices of output per man hour of US office workers (100 = mean output for 35–44 age group)

Age	All		Those with at least 9 months experience	
	Mean index	Percentage greater than 100	Mean index	Percentage greater than 100
<25	92.4	25	98.7	43
25–34	99.4	48	101.9	52
35–44	100	50	100.8	51
45–54	100.1	46	100.8	48
55–64	98.6	44	99.5	45
65+	101.2	45	101.1	44

Source: Greenberg (1961).

there are no consistent means of assessing performance. In the work setting it is usually measured through an analysis of productivity records (normally for skilled and semi-skilled workers) or through supervisory or peer ratings (for managerial and professional jobs). Neither ratings nor productivity measures are without possible biases. Ratings are susceptible to personal biases on the part of the peers or supervisors, whereas productivity measures may favour the older worker due to 'survival of the fittest'. Davies and Sparrow (1985) argued that if productivity in the occupational setting showed a steady decline, there may be a voluntary or involuntary transfer to other work, or perhaps even dismissal. Selective retention, in contrast, operates in the opposite direction (McEvoy and Cascio, 1989). Workers who work successfully on beyond the retirement age may not be 'average' workers. They are, perhaps, the ones who were above average for the cohort. Alternatively, as Rhodes (1983) suggested, the older worker group in an organisation may also contain individuals whose performance has declined, but who have been retained until retirement. Comparisons of job performance may, therefore, only provide useful information when turnover rates, or internal transfer rates are low (Sparrow and Davies, 1988).

Another major problem is the difficulty in obtaining sufficient numbers of workers in the oldest age range. McEvoy and Cascio (1989), reviewing the results from 96 studies where age and work performance were examined, found that only seven studies had samples containing workers over the age of 60. Moreover, all 96 studies were cross-sectional in design. None examined the performance of the same workers at different ages. There is, therefore, a clear need for studies that specifically look at the experiences of the 50–70-year-old cohort. Data are currently lacking on the occupational performance of the third age group and many conclusions drawn about the 'older worker' are speculations and extrapolations based upon a trend observed at an earlier age.

The conclusion to be drawn is best summarised by Davies *et al.* (1991): 'Overall, however, no clear evidence emerges of a universal age deficit in job performance, although older workers may be disadvantaged in particular kinds of jobs, for example those requiring physical strength, speeded reactions, or close attention to visual detail. The range of performance variation is considerable, probably more so among older than among younger workers, and in many cases older workers seem able to perform at least as well as, and sometimes better than, younger colleagues.'

Training

Instead of passively facing inexorable decline with advancing years, individuals are able to learn new tasks and improve performance with practice. Older workers are, therefore, equally likely to benefit from training (and in turn benefit the employer). Yet it must also be acknowledged that their requirements may be different from those of young workers. Older workers are liable to be disadvantaged in training and retraining if the methods used to train younger workers are applied without modification. Training programmes need to recognise these specific demands in order to help (rather than hinder) people in achieving their full capacity.

The results from several studies have suggested a number of features that should be incorporated into training programmes in order to benefit older persons:

1. Self-pacing   Several studies indicate that a fast pace, for either presentation or recall, handicaps the older learner. Or alternatively, if older persons are allowed to work at their own chosen, but usually slower, pace or speed, their performance can equal that of younger individuals.

Shooter *et al.* (1956) examined the success rates across ages of tram drivers retraining as bus drivers and found that whereas 97% of the 30–35-year-olds passed the test after three weeks, this figure fell to 71% for those aged 51–55 and 44% for those aged 56–60. However, most of those who failed initially passed after six or seven weeks. Eventually, 90% of 51–55-year-olds were successful (Table 18.2).

In a study where older (58–84 years) and younger (20–39 years) subjects were trained to use a software package, Zandri and Charness (1989) found that the older adults took twice as long as young adults to learn a software package, but achieved nearly equal performance levels. Similarly, in a word processing training programme, older subjects took significantly longer to master the basics, although all subjects, irrespective of age did so satisfactorily (Elias *et al.*, 1987).

Table 18.2

Results of retraining tramdrivers as bus drivers

			Percentage passing course		
Age	n	In 3 weeks	In 4 weeks	In 7 weeks	Total
26–30	104	96	3	1	100
31–35	106	97	2	1	100
36–40	146	90	9	0	99
41–45	92	83	12	2	97
46–50	63	65	23	5	93
51–55	62	71	8	11	90
56–60	61	44	25	24	93
61–67	60	32	10	21	63

Source: Shooter et al. *(1956).*

Welford (1988) also argues for control over the pace of instruction, suggesting that written instructions may be of greater value than lectures. Similarly, a video may be preferable to a demonstration, because it can be repeated or run slowly.

2. Instructions should be comprehensive and comprehensible   Some of the difficulties encountered by older people when undertaking experimental tasks may be due to misunderstanding of the instructions provided by an experimenter (Welford, 1958). Noticeable age-associated increases in the proportions of subjects who do not understand what is required of them have been reported for situations where the trainer checks understanding before proceeding with the task.

3. Training on the task rather than memorising instructions   As older adults tend to be less successful at recall than younger adults, training that avoids unnecessary memorisation may be advantageous. Belbin (1958) demonstrated that older subjects improved their performance if they learned a task through activity rather than memorisation. The task involved posting numbered cards into a box with different coloured slots, whilst maintaining the relationship between the colour of the slot and number (e.g. numbers in the 20s went into the pink slot etc). Subjects had to learn the task so that they could conduct it as quickly as possible with the minimum number of errors. Both memorisation and activity groups were allowed unlimited time and were instructed to continue until satisfied that the task was learnt. Activity training led to better levels of performance amongst the older age groups than did memory training, both in terms of speed of response and accuracy.

4. Errors early in training should be prevented   Kay (1951) noted that in a serial learning task subjects in their fifties and sixties were both slower and less accurate. After learning an initial task, subjects were required learn a similar task, but with serial positions changed. Older subjects persisted with errors made in earlier trials. Older subjects' subsequent learning involved unlearning of the earlier errors, which they were less able to do. The persistence of errors may also result from patterns of responses being more difficult to modify in older persons than to be formed in the first place (Welford, 1958).

5. Attitudes and motivation   Performance efficacy in older persons, depends not only upon their capabilities, but on factors such as their attitudes or motivation (Welford, 1976). This is not just a matter of an unwillingness to perform one's best: older people can be more hesitant to committing themselves to action, or more cautious, gathering more information before making decisions. Other factors to hinder performance may be fear of failure, or having to 'compete' against younger trainees, perhaps with higher educational attainments. In order to maintain a person's confidence, it is important that positive feedback is provided.

The discovery method of training (Belbin, 1969; Welford, 1988) is a synthesis of many of the above points and has often been found superior to conventional methods of training for both young and older workers. In this method, those undergoing training are given a minimum of instruction and then allowed to discover for themselves how the task is to be completed, in controlled circumstances, where they are required to make active decisions and any errors are immediately corrected. Such methods may require higher levels of input by the trainers, but the obvious reward is the greater success for the older trainee.

Driving

The ability to drive is often an important contribution to a person's active and independent life at any age, but its usefulness in maintaining such a lifestyle is, perhaps, more pronounced as one becomes older. In a survey of 1,000 drivers over the age of 55 years, more than three-quarters of respondents felt that in overall terms, having a car was essential or very important to their way of life (AA Foundation, 1988).

As driving is a complex task which relies heavily on both visual information processing and speed of reaction, it is often assumed that driving performance deteriorates with age, given the large body of evidence pointing to declines in psychological function. However, as Rabbitt (1991) points out, 'although all these, and many other, pessimistic conclusions from laboratory experiments must be taken seriously, they all derive from very small-scale studies and so allow us to make only very limited generalisations about the abilities of the entire elderly population. They must therefore be taken only as useful indicators of possible trends of age-related competence in the real world, and as stimuli for devising help and remediation, rather than as excuses for Procrustean legislation to curtail the rights of elderly road users.'

Accident data

One possible indicator of driving performance is to examine whether older drivers are more or less liable to accidents. Most recent statistics indicate that actual driver casualties per head of population decrease with age (Road Accidents of Great Britain, 1990; Table 18.3). However, this information is of limited value in determining

Table 18.3

Casualty rates per 100,000 population

				Age			
	17–19	*20–29*	*30–39*	*40–49*	*50–59*	*60–69*	*70+*
Car drivers							
Killed	6.9	5.1	2.8	2.3	2.2	2.1	2.7
KSI[a]	97	67	40	30	25	19	17
All[b]	610	449	287	210	161	100	72
Car passengers							
Killed	6.7	2.8	0.8	1.0	0.8	1.2	2.2
KSI	88	34	15	12	12	13	14
All	505	223	101	82	83	78	70

Source: Road Accidents of Great Britain (1990).
[a]KSI, killed and serious injuries.
[b]All, all severities.

driving performance in that the likelihood of being injured may increase with age. Moreover, travel survey data indicate that the oldest and youngest drivers travel less than the 'average' driver (Planek and Fowler, 1971; Evans, 1988).

When distance travelled is taken into account for accident involvement, the pattern becomes one where accident and casualty rates are relatively high among young drivers, then start to fall with age, and then rise again. UK statistics available for 1986 show that this rise starts to occur between 60–65 years of age, with slight differences for males and females (Broughton, 1987; Table 18.4). However, it is only in the age range of 75+ that highest rates are observed. For both men and women the data indicate that accident involvement rates between the ages of 69 and 73 are still lower than for drivers up to the early thirties. Furthermore, the observed upturn in accident rates for older drivers may be an exaggeration because of a non-linear relationship between mileage and accidents (Janke, 1991). People who have lower mileage tend to accumulate this in a higher risk environment, usually urban, whereas high-mileage drivers gain most miles on motorways, where the driving task is less complex and the accident rate per distance travelled is lower. Some of the upturn may, therefore, be accounted for in terms of a higher proportion of 'more difficult' miles being driven by certain age groups.

Thus, although the increase in accident rates amongst older drivers are a cause for concern, they should not be used as a reason for discrimination. Indeed, if accident rates were the sole criterion for deciding which age group were safe to drive, then, perhaps, it would be the younger driver who would be excluded!

Analysis of accident data, however, has proved useful in indicating that older and younger drivers differ in the accidents to which they are prone. Whereas young drivers are more frequently involved in accidents caused by speeding, older drivers are more liable to make intersection-related driving errors, such as turning and yielding to right of way. These situations are usually more complex, but occur at lower speeds (McFarland *et al.*, 1964; Planek and Fowler, 1971). For example, Cooper

Table 18.4

Accident rates: car drivers by sex and age, Great Britain 1986

| | Accident involvement rate per 100 million vehicle kms | |
Age	Males	Females
17–20	440	240
21–24	180	180
25–28	140	140
29–33	104	135
34–38	83	105
39–43	80	104
44–48	70	84
49–53	64	91
54–58	61	76
59–63	68	100
64–68	83	110
69–73	96	130
74+	170	360

Source: Broughton (1987).

(1990) examined accident records for British Columbia and found whereas 66.5% of 36–50-year-old drivers' crashes took place at intersections, this value increased to 69.2% for those aged 55–64, 70.7% for those aged 65–74 and 76.0% for those over 75. In the UK the involvement of older drivers in accidents at junctions increases with age and is greater in rural areas (Broughton, 1988).

Many studies lack a comparison group of younger and middle-aged drivers, so it is difficult to draw detailed conclusions across the whole age range within the same population. Nonetheless, the trend has been confirmed on the few occasions when data are available for both older and younger drivers. Panek and Rearden (1987) surveyed police reports for a one-year period for accidents amongst rural drivers and categorised accidents by type, and the individuals deemed at fault by age and gender. Accidents involving laterally moving vehicles or attentional deficits (disobeying traffic signals etc) tended to increase with age. Conversely, following and skidding accidents appeared to decrease with age, probably related to the decreasing inclination to drive at high speed.

Self-reported driving experiences

Questionnaire-based surveys have attempted to identify subjective views on the problems associated with increasing age that are of relevance to driving (Cooper, 1990; Planek and Fowler, 1971). From these it appears that older drivers recognise some areas of difficulty and modify their behaviour accordingly, usually by avoiding that situation. Holland and Rabbitt (1992) found that once previously unaware individuals, who had been made aware of visual or hearing losses, also reported making subsequent changes in their driving behaviour to compensate for these sensory changes. Furthermore, Rabbitt (1991) found that accident rates proved to be lower amongst those who had altered their driving behaviour because of noticing a change in their sensory abilities.

In particular, older drivers appear to be concerned by visual problems and tend to avoid night-time driving when visual deficits become most pronounced. In a survey comparing the views of drivers 55+, the proportion of drivers avoiding night-time excursions rose from approximately 25% between the ages of 55 and 65 to over 50% at age 75 (Cooper, 1990). Visual problems may also be one of the main causes of the decision to cease driving, a survey revealing that the most visual problems were reported by those elderly subjects who had recently given up driving (Kosnik et al., 1990).

Specific problems apart, many older drivers perceive that they have altered their approach to driving. In the AA survey, when asked what changes had been made since they were aged 50, only 19% reported no changes overall. In particular, drivers asserted that they left more distance from the vehicle in front and were more cautious. These views were more apparent in the 65–74 and 75+ age groups than the 55–64 age group. However, there are also indications that older persons are not aware of all the particular extra risks and areas of difficulty to which they may be prone. This may indicate a greater need for re-education and feedback to encourage awareness of problem areas. For example, in the AA survey junctions were not highlighted by respondents as causing problems—only 12% of the total sample tried to avoid busy junctions, and only 7% felt they were now less quick at decisions, such as when to turn out from junctions compared with when they were 50 years old. Yet the accident data indicate that junctions represent a greater risk for older drivers.

Visual abilities

Vision plays a crucial role in driving processes. Although there is now considerable information about the age-associated changes in visual functions, there appears little in the literature which integrates these changes into the effects on everyday performance. Sekuler (1983) states that 'we cannot even specify with any precision the visual requirements for daily tasks such as driving or walking'. The situation appears to have changed little since. Fozard (1990) writes 'nor have there been significant improvements in the assessment of visual problems in driving and related tasks that are most salient to older persons'.

The nature of the relationship between visual abilities and driving performance remains unclear. Vision is just one of many other factors affecting driving. Further-more, most visual tests are not geared specifically to driving and their direct relevance may be questioned. An analysis of the data on 14,000 Californian drivers failed to find any correlation between poor visual performance and high accident rates for drivers under the mid-fifties. For those older than mid-fifties, a weak relationship between dynamic and static visual acuity and accident rates was found (Hills and Burg, 1977), but it was unclear at what age this relationship developed as everyone was grouped into the same 'over 54 years' age category. A similar association between accident history and visual acuity in older drivers was found in a survey of 1,000 British drivers, although, as in the previous study, all drivers over the age of 55 years were placed into one category (Davison, 1985).

For all age groups, visual acuity decreases in conditions of low illumination, although older people are particularly disadvantaged (Sturgis and Osgood, 1982). It has been suggested that 65 years is the critical age after which visual acuity becomes significantly poorer under conditions of degraded illumination (Sturr and Taub, 1990). Few studies have attempted to investigate the practical implications of decreased visual acuity under lower illumination. Sivak et al. (1981) investigated night-time legibility of road signs. Twelve young (18–24 years) and twelve older (62–74 years) subjects sat in a moving car and were required to indicate as soon as they could correctly identify the orientation of a test road sign. For the older subjects, the mean distance at which the sign became legible was from 23% to 35% shorter than those for younger subjects, despite the two groups being selected for similar mean high luminance visual acuity. Therefore, improvements in road lighting may be of particular benefit to the older driver.

Peripheral visual field loss is another important consequence of ageing, and this may, in part, account for the problems experienced by older drivers at junctions. In a study of some 10,000 Californian drivers, Keltner and Johnson (1987) reported that the prevalence of visual field loss was 3.0–3.5% for individuals aged between 16 and 60 years, but this figure rose to 7% for those aged 60–65 and 13% for those over 65. Drivers with visual field loss in both eyes had twice as high accident and conviction rates than an age- and sex-matched control group with normal visual fields. However, those with visual field loss in one eye were not at greater risk than controls. There is some evidence that functional field loss occurring in some older people is reversible by training (Sekuler and Ball, 1986).

Attention

Problems in dividing attention may contribute to older drivers' difficulties at junctions. Ponds *et al.* (1988) have shown that older (61–80 years) subjects are disadvantaged compared with middle-aged (40–58 years) or younger (21–37 years) subjects, when required to divide attention between a simulated driving task and a choice reaction time task. There are few other studies to provide any evidence.

Reaction speed

As already indicated, considerable experimental evidence suggests that with increasing age, the speed of response becomes slower, with greatest apparence in complex tasks. Older subjects may be less sensitive to velocity changes than younger subjects and this may be relevant to driving where decisions about relative velocity of other vehicles are of paramount importance (Brown and Bowman, 1987). However, speed of reaction has not been directly related to driving performance, so many of the pessimistic conclusions concerning a driver's ability to react quickly in traffic do not have any direct empirical support. In fact, the few field studies that have been carried out indicate that reaction speed *per se*, does not affect speed of response in the driving situation (Olson and Sivak, 1986; Korteling, 1990). For example, a field study was conducted on older and younger subjects who had already completed a laboratory-based choice reaction time task. In the laboratory task, older subjects were significantly slower than younger subjects. Yet when driving, where the time interval for drivers to brake in response to the brake lights of a leading car was measured, there was no significant difference between older drivers and the younger controls.

Again these examples suggest that for everyday activities, such as driving, the effects of practice and experience go a considerable way in counteracting difficulties caused by diminished abilities. Indeed, in a comparison of healthy young and older drivers on a standardised road test, the older group were found to have superior driving skills and made fewer errors (Carr *et al.*, 1992).

Summary and conclusions

Despite the findings from laboratory-based comparisons which generally show older persons to be disadvantaged, the evidence from real-life comparisons suggests that the older worker or older driver is generally able to maintain a good level of performance.

Investigations in the workplace have failed to find consistent relationships between age and performance. The increased experience that comes with advancing age appears to be important.

Older workers may be at a disadvantage in novel situations, where there is little or no experience to call upon, but they are adaptable and amenable to training. Older learners may have greater difficulties than younger counterparts, but if training is provided which maximises their potential (by providing sufficient time, ensuring the instructions are understood, providing a motivating and supportive environment), then they would probably be as successful as younger trainees.

Although older drivers begin to experience problems (particularly with vision), the accident data suggest that drivers aged between mid-fifties and seventies are relatively safe, with lower accident rates than those in their twenties. It is only beyond the mid-seventies that accident rates are disproportionately high. Increased prevalence of accidents at junctions are a cause of concern, and may indicate slowing of reaction speed and difficulties of attention. However, there are few studies which attempt to integrate the effects of a psychological deficit (e.g. vision or reaction speed) in terms of practical issues such as driving. In fact, studies which have specifically looked at speed of response in the driving situation have failed to show that older drivers are disadvantaged.

Questionnaire studies have yielded particularly encouraging findings. Older persons start to self-regulate and modify their behaviour if they become aware of problems. This is evidenced by the avoidance of night-time driving (when visual difficulties are most apparent). Furthermore, there is evidence that when given feedback about their sensory abilities, older persons will adjust their driving behaviour accordingly. Perhaps there is a role for greater driver education and feedback, rather than legislation.

Finally, it appears that some of the greatest barriers to an active and independent life in the third age are not a person's cognitive abilities, but the negative stereotypes that are held and sweeping generalisations that are often made. Like younger individuals, older individuals are a heterogeneous group and should be so considered.

References

AA Foundation for Road Safety Research. *Motoring and the older driver*. Automobile Association, Basingstoke, Hants, 1988.

Belbin E. Methods of training older workers. *Ergonomics*, 1958; 1: 207–221.

Belbin RM. *The discovery method: an international experiment in retraining*. OECD, Paris, 1969.

Broughton J. Casualty rates by age and sex. In *Road accidents of Great Britain 1987: the casualty report*, pp. 60–64. HMSO, London, 1987.

Broughton J. *Variation for car drivers' accident risk with age*, RR135. Transport and Road Research Laboratory, Crowthorne, Berkshire, 1988.

Brown B, Bowman K. Sensitivity to changes in size and velocity in young and elderly observers. *Perception*, 1987; 16: 41–47.

Carr D et al. The effect of age on driving skills. *J Am Geriat Soc*, 1992; 40: 567–573.

Clay HM. A study of performance in relation to age at two printing works. *J Gerontol*, 1956; 11: 417–424.

Cooper PJ. Elderly drivers' views of self and driving in relation to the evidence of accident data. *J Safety Res*, 1990; 21: 103–113.

Davies DR, Sparrow PR. Age and work behaviour. In Charness N (ed.), *Aging and human performance*, pp. 293–232. John Wiley, Chichester, 1985.

Davies DR, Matthews D, Wong SK. Ageing and work. In Cooper CI, Robertson IT (eds), *International review of industrial and organizational psychology*, Volume 6, pp. 149–211. John Wiley, Chichester, 1991.

Davison PA. Interrelationships between British drivers' visual abilities, age and road accident histories. *Ophthal Physiol Opt*, 1985; 5: 195–204.

Elias PK *et al.* Acquisition of word-processing skills by younger, middle-age and older adults. *Psychology Aging,* 1987; 2: 340–348.

Evans L. Older driver involvement in fatal and severe traffic crashes. *J Gerontol,* 1988; 43: S186–S193.

Fozard JL. Vision and hearing in aging. In Birren JE, Schaie KW (eds), *Handbook of the psychology of aging,* 3rd edn, pp. 150–170. Van Nostrand Reinhold, 1990.

Giniger S *et al.* Age, experience and performance on speed and skill jobs in an applied setting. *J Appl Psychol,* 1983; 68: 469–475.

Greenberg L. Productivity of older workers. *Gerontologist,* 1961; 1: 38–41.

Hills BL, Burg A. *A reanalysis of Californian driver vision data: general findings,* LR768. Transport and Road Research Laboratory, Crowthorne, Berkshire, 1977.

Holland CA, Rabbitt PMA. People's awareness of their age-related sensory and cognitive deficits and the implications for road safety. *Appl Cogn Psychol* (in press).

Janke MK. Accidents, mileage and the exaggeration of risk. *Accident Anal Prev,* 1991; 23: 183–188.

Kay H. Learning of a serial task by different age groups. *Q J Exp Psychol,* 1951, 3: 166–183.

Keltner JL, Johnson CA. Visual function, driving safety and the elderly. *Ophthalmology,* 1987; 94: 1180–1188.

Korteling JE. Perception-response speed and driving capabilities of brain-damaged and older drivers. *Human Factors,* 1990; 32: 95–108.

Kosnik W *et al.* Self-reported visual problems of older drivers. *Human Factors,* 1990; 32: 597–608.

McEvoy GM, Cascio WF. Cumulative evidence of the relationship between employee age and job performance. *J Appl Psychol,* 1989; 74: 11–17.

McFarland RA *et al.* On the driving of automobiles by older people. *J Gerontol,* 1964; 19: 190–197.

Olson PL, Sivak M. Perception-response time to unexpected roadway hazards. *Human Factors,* 1986; 28: 91–96.

Panek PE, Rearden JJ. Age and gender effects on accident types for rural drivers. *J Appl Gerontol,* 1987; 6: 332–346.

Planek TN, Fowler RC. Traffic accident violations and exposure characteristics of the aging driver. *J Gerontol,* 1971; 26: 224–230.

Ponds *et al.* Age differences in divided attention in a simulated driving task. *J Gerontol,* 1988; 43: P151–P156.

Rabbitt P. Factors promoting accidents involving elderly pedestrians and drivers. In Grayson GB, Lester JF (eds), *Behavioural research in road safety: proceedings of a seminar held at Nottingham University,* pp. 167–183. Transport and Road Research Laboratory, Crowthorne, Berkshire, 1991.

Rhodes SR. Age-related differences in work attitudes and behavior: a review and conceptual analysis. *Psychol Bull,* 1983; 93: 328–367.

Road Accidents of Great Britain. *The casualty report.* HMSO, London, 1990.

Sekuler R. Some research needs in aging and visual perception. *Vision Res,* 1983; 23: 213–216.

Sekuler R, Ball K. Visual localization: age and practice. *J Opt Soc Am,* 1986; A3: 864–867.

Shooter AMN *et al.* Some field data on the training of older people. *Occup Psychol,* 1956; 30: 204–215.

Sivak M *et al.* Effect of driver's age on nighttime legibility of highway signs. *Human Factors,* 1981; 23: 59–64.

Sparrow PR, Davies DR. Effects of age, tenure, training and job complexity on technical performance. *Psychology Aging,* 1988; 3: 307–314.

Sturgis SP, Osgood DJ. Effects of glare and background luminance on visual acuity and contrast sensitivity: implications for driver night vision testing. *Human Factors,* 1982; 24: 347–360.

Sturr JF, Taub HA. Performance of young and older drivers on a static acuity test under photopic and mesopic luminance conditions. *Human Factors,* 1990; 32: 1–8.

Welford AT. *Ageing and human skill.* Oxford University Press, Oxford, 1958.

Welford AT. Thirty years of psychological research on age and work. *J Occup Psychol,* 1976; 49: 129–138.

Welford AT. Preventing adverse changes of work with age. *Int J Aging Human Develop,* 1988; 27: 283–291.

Zandri E, Charness N. Training older and younger adults to use software. *Educ Gerontol,* 1989; 15: 615–631.

Summary

J. Grimley Evans

Our review suggests that the health of people in the third age is likely to improve if present trends continue. A few factors can be identified which might interrupt these trends. One is the failure of cigarette smoking in young women to diminish and its implications for vascular disease and osteoporosis in middle age and beyond. The second possibility that has to be borne in mind is that of a major epidemic of AIDS, although this seems an unlikely catastrophe for the third age in the short to medium term. The increasing numbers of people from ethnic minorities in the third age may also modify the overall optimistic picture in view of the higher rates of hypertensive and cardiovascular disease recorded in Afro-Caribbean and Asian groups. We also have to recognise the deleterious impact on health of poverty and unemployment, which may be an increasing influence in the next decades. If European Community legislation removes the current high tax on alcohol, and reduces the real cost of cigarettes, it is likely that the British population will suffer an increased burden of alcohol- and smoking-related diseases.

Climatic and environmental change may bring some deleterious effects, for example in an increase in skin cancer due to increased ultraviolet radiation passing through a disrupted ozone layer. These are unlikely to be major effects, at least in the short term, and there are more important reasons for concern over the environment. We also have to recognise that there may be unpredictable environmental hazards or cultural changes in lifestyle that might slow down or reverse the present encouraging trends in third age health.

The data also suggest an increased consumption of health resources, probably reflecting increased expectation rather than increased morbidity but perhaps also an increased public awareness of what health interventions are available. We anticipate that improvements in health technology, notably less traumatic interventions such as angioplasty compared with open surgery and laparoscopic abdominal surgery compared with laparotomy, will increase the applicability of health interventions in later age groups. Interventions will become increasingly worthwhile at increasingly older ages. We would therefore not expect, at least in the medium term, for the improved health of the third age population to be reflected in any diminution in health resource consumption. Indeed the use of health resources by older age groups may have been kept inappropriately low through covert age discrimination that should be abolished.

There are some dangers for older people in the new arrangements in the National Health Service. Age discrimination could arise if purchasing authorities negotiate contracts separately for different age groups. There is already evidence of age discrimination in terms of access of older people to coronary care and thrombolysis. The designation of some old people as 'geriatric' is one way in which age discrimination can become institutionalised and we regard it as crucial that access of older people to the best of specialist medical care should be on the basis of physiological assessment, rather than age. Covert age discrimination may arise if Hospital Trusts, being paid a flat rate for particular interventions, designate older people whose lengths of stay may be longer than average as 'medically' unsuitable for intervention when the true determinant is their poorer profit margin. Fundholding general practitioners may be tempted to inhibit the access of their older patients to expensive but beneficial specialist care. Explicit efforts will be needed to prevent fiscal pressures leading to such age discrimination. One approach will be through rigorous case-mix specifications monitored by specific audit. All professionals who act as gatekeepers in the various parts of the health and social service systems should recognise that older people should not be offered prosthetic care until all possibilities for therapeutic interventions have been explored. This is a message which particularly needs to be built into the training of social workers whose traditional orientation has been towards 'care' rather than 'cure'.

It is not easy to predict the economic consequences of these trends of increasing health and increasing health resource consumption. It is facile to assume that increased longevity will inevitably lead to increased numbers of people reaching ages at which average health costs rise. The data suggest that the longer one delays the onset of disabling disease the shorter the average period of survival in a disabled state. Total costs per life year may therefore not correlate directly with average life expectancy. The framework within which economic analyses of this kind have to be made needs to be defined ideologically. Most citizens, we believe, would regard prevention of disabling diseases and prolongation of healthy life as good things and, from society's point of view, a good investment.

At present, estimates of active live expectancy in later life do not appear to reflect objective changes in health, probably because they are dominated by increases in expectation and aspirations. It is highly desirable that some form of standard and objective means to monitor healthy active life expectancy in the population past middle age be developed at a national level. This would provide a valuable measure of the effectiveness of health and social services and would also give early warning of problems arising through the advent of unpredicted problems.

The single most important way in which the health and wellbeing of people in the third age could be improved is undoubtedly through the control of cigarette smoking. Smoking should be forbidden in all communal areas, tobacco advertising banned and every effort made to increase the real costs of tobacco products. The evidence for the efficacy of these methods of control is now totally persuasive.

Throughout both private and public sectors, thought should be given to increasing incentives for healthy behaviour. A number of possibilities present for consideration. Insurance incentives for non-smokers and moderate drinkers might be enhanced and taxation used to control cigarette and alcohol consumption and encourage non-motorised transport. Retailers might give thought to distributing their profit margins on foods so as to favour purchase of healthy as opposed to unhealthy foods, particularly by those unemployed or on low incomes.

The importance of physical exercise in promoting health in the third age needs to be reflected in public policy. Exercise could be facilitated by discouraging or preventing cars from entering urban areas, the provision of more pedestrian precincts and facilitating safer bicycle transport. Some local authorities already make efforts to encourage older people to use public facilities for exercise and this is to be commended.

The media should be enjoined to do more to inculcate healthy lifestyles, particularly among those in the lower educational classes who could most benefit. We do not accept that the task of the media is merely to 'reflect real life' rather than to offer beneficial social messages and role models. Social power should be linked to social responsibility. The contrast between the middle and working class cultures often presented in British television for example compares dispiritingly with American television in which the poor and the rich are assumed to share the same aspirations. By presenting health information and education in forms mainly watched by the middle classes but 'real life' programmes for the lower classes in which, for example, tobacco addiction and excessive drinking are presented as acceptable or amusing, the media may be contributing to social class disparities in health.

Formal health education efforts might best be concentrated on those parts of the UK with highest mortality and morbidity rates. However, it is difficult to assess the effectiveness of the various health education initiatives. Some data suggest that health education is improving knowledge without affecting behaviour. Clearly much work needs to be done on the evaluation of these programmes since they would be a poor investment if they satisfied the conscience of government and society without achieving their intended ends.

An encouraging trend is the involvement of general practitioners and other members of primary care teams in preventive health care, notably effective in modifying cigarette smoking and alcohol consumption. We would hope to see an increasing orientation towards preventive medicine in both primary and secondary care. There seems enormous scope for an enhanced role for nurses in this regard. Prevention appears to have focused mainly on younger adults but we see the need for training and incentives to bring health care professionals to recognise and implement the potential for preventive action in later life.

Older age groups are still the victims of many negative stereotypes. Our data show that far more positive views should be adopted, for example with regard to the older worker or driver, and that older age groups are well able to benefit from training, though style of training should be appropriate. Exercise can delay or reverse physical declines whilst psychological deterioration with age is not inevitable and is often more than adequately compensated for by knowledge and experience. These positive views need to be actively propagated. The USA has led the way in recognising, at least in principle, that compulsory retirement is an infringement of civil rights. It might be unrealistic in the present economic and political situation in the UK to hope for increased opportunities for remunerated occupation for older workers. Greater scope for voluntary work and for education will help maintain mental function and prevent the corrosive effects of social alienation. The identification of third age people as a valuable social resource with responsibilities as well as privileges might make for a healthier society as well as happier individuals.

Our report points to many requirements for further research. We are concerned that research is often under-regarded and perhaps feared by the public. Research is essential to further improvements in health and wellbeing at all ages and it vitally depends on members of the public volunteering to take part in studies. There is undoubtedly a gap in understanding between the scientific community and the general public over research, and particularly over the nature of and need for randomised controlled trials. It is not at all clear how this gap, which probably reflects a more general failure of scientific education in the UK, could be overcome. It is perhaps conceivable that local ethical committees, linking their responsibilities to the public to their knowledge of scientific principles, could take on an educational role in this regard. It might be reassuring also to the scientific community if the thought processes of ethical committees were made more public.

Ultimately it must be the responsibility of older people themselves to help in the creation of an environment that subserves their needs and aspirations. In particular they must learn to use their voting power to its best effect. The success of retired people in the USA in achieving massive improvements in social provision for older age groups is a testimony to the power of tactical voting. In a democracy the world we vote for is the world we deserve.

Finally, in the intense interactions between health and lifestyle it is important to recognise the impact of social policy working throughout life in the impact of work, education and activity on health. The concept of what constitutes the 'health budget' needs to be widened to include housing, education and fiscal policy. The provisions of the recent white paper on the health of the nation, much of which is directly or indirectly concerned with problems affecting the third age, seem to offer scope for this conceptual regrouping of social resources in the service of health and wellbeing. We will all hope to see this reflected in a programme of policies coherent between departments and between central and local governments.